With anxiety now ubiquitous because of the pandemic, Dr. Gregory Jantz's new book *The Anxiety Reset* is needed at this critical time. The book is loaded with useful tools to help people lower anxiety and overcome fear and worry. I highly recommend it.

> **DANIEL G. AMEN, MD,** psychiatrist, founder of Amen Clinics,
> and author of the national bestseller *The End of Mental Illness*

A practical and useful read for anyone who struggles with anxiety or knows someone who does. *The Anxiety Reset* offers a fresh and timely perspective on this rapidly growing medical issue—and offers some of the best hope, help, and encouragement I have found for overcoming it.

> **DR. TIM CLINTON,** president of the American Association
> of Christian Counselors

*The Anxiety Rese*t is a clearly written, comprehensive, and helpful guide to overcoming different types of anxiety. It describes many up-to-date strategies for managing anxiety in a whole-person approach that includes mind, body, and soul. Highly recommended!

> **SIANG-YANG TAN, PhD,** professor of clinical psychology at Fuller Theological
> Seminary and author of *Counseling and Psychotherapy: A Christian Perspective* and
> *Shepherding God's People: A Guide to Faithful and Fruitful Pastoral Ministry*

the
Anxiety
Reset

A Life-Changing Approach to Overcoming
Fear, Stress, Worry, Panic Attacks, OCD, and More

Gregory L. Jantz, PhD

WITH KEITH WALL

TYNDALE
MOMENTUM®

The Tyndale nonfiction imprint

Visit Tyndale online at tyndale.com.

Visit Tyndale Momentum online at tyndalemomentum.com.

TYNDALE, Tyndale's quill logo, *Tyndale Momentum*, and the Tyndale Momentum logo are registered trademarks of Tyndale House Ministries. Tyndale Momentum is the nonfiction imprint of Tyndale House Publishers, Carol Stream, Illinois.

The Anxiety Reset: A Life-Changing Approach to Overcoming Fear, Stress, Worry, Panic Attacks, OCD, and More

Designed by Libby Dykstra

Edited by Jonathan Schindler

Published in association with The Bindery Agency, www.TheBinderyAgency.com.

For information about special discounts for bulk purchases, please contact Tyndale House Publishers at csresponse@tyndale.com, or call 1-855-277-9400.

ISBN 978-1-4964-4112-6 (HC)
ISBN 978-1-4964-4113-3 (SC)

Printed in the United States of America

27 26 25 24 23 22 21
7   6   5   4   3   2   1

*This book is dedicated to all the people who have
suffered with anxiety—and found the courage
to pursue healing and live with freedom.
There is a path of peace.*

Contents

Foreword

If you are one of the tens of millions who battle anxiety, you will appreciate this book from its very first word. If you are not one of us, you almost certainly know someone who is—not just "out in the world" but right near you, in your family or in your close orbit. Everyone is afraid of something, of someone, of some situation, of some role, of some period of life. We are an anxious species, and we know it, and that can often just increase our anxiety.

In some ways, our natural anxiety is a good thing. The anxious person lives in constant potential, especially potential for reframing anxiety from paralyzing fear into courageous action. If we are anxious, we have the opportunity to be inspired by bravery, as Dr. Gregory Jantz tells us in *The Anxiety Reset*. Bravery and courage are not just for heroes and saints but for all of us. They are our equal psychological inheritance. But they are not a given. In fact, quite often, we let our anxiety be more of a given than our courage. This can be changed.

Sitting down to write this foreword, I felt fear blooming in me. I felt it in my gut, a situational anxiety because Dr. Jantz is not only a colleague but a friend, and I want to do my job of foreword writer well for him. Not only does anxiety inspire courage, but it also reminds us of the fact that we are living lives in which something is at stake. That is a good thing. As I got started on my task, some of my anxiety abated. Actually doing the work quieted me, as every small courageous action can do.

The anxiety Dr. Jantz writes about in this book is not often as simple as mine was in this case. Today's difficult world has millions of people living on the anxiety spectrum, more of us than know it. Some forty million Americans fit on the anxiety spectrum, and with around forty million Americans struggling with sleep issues (sleep disorders use some of the same chromosome markers as anxiety), we have an overlap that probably exceeds the forty million number.

If you spend a lot of time ruminating on your faults, on the negatives that could happen in your life, on the harm that has been done to you or the harm you may be doing, or on how inadequate you feel to face the world, you are likely anxious. Without realizing it perhaps, you accept personal debilitation inside the core human fear of inadequacy. *I am not adequate,* your mind is saying, *and I don't know how to be adequate.* This fear of inadequacy grounds anxiety in the brain via rumination loops.

There is constant rumination synaptic connectivity between the amygdala's fear centers and other areas of the brain that focus your brain's attention on the fear itself, the inadequacy, the debilitation. The anxious person's brain stays there unless they get help to change. Once help comes, the first step of courage can occur, the shot of dopamine and adrenaline that says to the system, *I am going to do something new to make gold of this fear, to push through it, to reframe, to reset, to be adequate.*

Dr. Jantz's *Anxiety Reset* gives you that shot of dopamine and the template for courage and thus helps direct you toward an empowered future. I cannot remember the poet who said this, but I've never forgotten the line: "Experience shreds us into bits as it forms its wholes." That is a mind bender, I know, but I think the poet is saying that as you live life, you will be shredded somewhat by what happens to you, but even as you fragment and feel afraid, you are forming a person of meaning. You can become *whole.*

The holistic approach of *The Anxiety Reset* echoes this poetic quote. There is no single thread in this book that promises perfect living. Instead, help from various fields and disciplines—neurology, psychology, and nutrition, to name a few—congregates in this book, matched with actual case studies from decades of Dr. Jantz's clinical practice. This meeting of science and human life is, on its own, compelling reading, and it's all the more powerful to those of us who feel anxiety.

My hope for you now is that you will set aside the time to read the first thirty pages of this book uninterrupted. Do it as an act of courage, in one sitting. If you do this, I believe you will then see what Dr. Jantz is doing here, the gift he is giving. You may feel that anxiety is not just *a* path toward wholeness, but *your* path. For whatever reason—spiritual, psychological, genetic, developmental—you are on this path of anxiety. Now you have in your hands a guide not only to holistic healing but also to other, larger life themes: courage, bravery, adequacy, and living a life of meaning.

Dr. Michael Gurian
Executive director of the Gurian Institute
and New York Times *bestselling author*
of Saving Our Sons *and* The Minds of Girls

PART 1

Where You Are, How You Got Here

Surveying the Landscape of Your Anxiety

CHAPTER 1

Living in the Age of Anxiety

*Anxiety may have dominated your life until now—
but you can overcome it!*

You've come to this book looking for answers to your anxiety. Perhaps you come with a sense of distress or even desperation. Maybe you feel aggravation or even agony.

Here's what I can offer you: hope and help, each in plentiful portions.

Here's what I can't offer you: a quick fix or magic formulas.

I believe this rings true for you, because it's likely you have been struggling with anxiety for a long time—months, years, or decades—and you've tried different remedies that haven't brought lasting relief. You know that to experience true healing and wellness, you need expert guidance with compassion and clear direction.

What's more, you know you need to invest yourself in the process, devoting yourself to following the proven, whole-person approach that is detailed in the pages ahead.

So if you have opened this book hoping to discover "secret" ways to eradicate anxiety from your life, I'm afraid you'll be disappointed.

William Shakespeare summed up the reason why in *Much Ado about*

Nothing. The character Leonato is engulfed in grief after learning of the untimely passing of his gentle young daughter Hero, and he believes the girl was "done to death" by false accusations. His brother, Antonio, calls his emotional response childish and counsels patience.

Leonato will have none of that. "I will be flesh and blood!" he says. "For there was never yet philosopher that could endure the toothache patiently."

The valuable truth contained in the scene is this: we are *all* flesh and blood. We feel what we feel, and no person alive can claim to have never felt crippling fear or suffered sleepless nights in worry over some unwelcome and unexpected event. Periodic anxiety and fear—even to the point of panic—are universal human emotions. They are instinctive responses to life's frightening challenges, as automatic as breathing.

As strange as it may seem to say so, this is actually *good* news. It means that, if you have picked up this book because you are at your wit's end in your own struggle with runaway anxiety, you are not the only one. You are in the company of many others who know precisely what you're going through and who are also determined to find healing solutions that work.

Figures compiled by the Anxiety and Depression Association of America confirm this:

- Anxiety disorders are the most common mental illness in the United States.
- More than forty million American adults—nearly one in five—are afflicted by anxiety disorders.
- Anxiety disorders affect 25.1 percent of children between thirteen and eighteen years old.[1]

Furthermore, these numbers have steadily increased in recent decades. It's not hard to see why. Urban, technological society—by its demanding and fast-paced nature—seems destined to ramp up the stress and the reasons for anxiety each of us lives with every day.[2] We face a much larger and more varied number of "threats" than did our distant ancestors—perhaps not to life and limb, but what did they know of the pressures of financial insecurity or social status? Or fragile professional standing? Or vague and complex political uncertainties? How about perceived danger to children from drugs, pornography, social media, bullying, or health hazards beyond our control?

These days many people add the looming prospect of global environmental catastrophe to the bundle of burdens they carry. The list of reasons for feeling stressed and anxious in the course of "ordinary" life could go on and on.

My point is not to reinforce those fears—far from it! It is to invite you to fully embrace a fact that is highly valuable as you embark on your journey to manage your anxiety and reclaim your life: *You are not alone!*

- You are not alone, because millions of others are walking the same path as you.
- You are not alone, because you are surrounded by people willing to help.
- You are not alone, because you have access to experts who are specially trained to equip you for success.

You are also not alone, because God stands ready with mercy and healing grace whenever you ask. As we'll see throughout this book, faith can be a powerful ally in your healing journey.

Here are other things we can say you are *not*: You are not weak, broken, fragile, or "making it all up." You are not simply stubborn or using your fear as an excuse to be the center of attention—or any of a hundred other such things you have heard from others, or told yourself, over the years.

You are human—nothing more, nothing less.

And you can have a better life than you currently enjoy. Let that sink in for a moment. In my experience, this simple truth is something people who struggle with mental health issues tragically stop believing somewhere along the way. First they lose hope, then they lose the belief they even have a *right* to hope.

My purpose in writing this book is to convince you that line of thinking is wrong. *Very* wrong. You *can* reset your anxiety to a manageable, even productive, level. You *can* heal for good!

Tested by Experience

In the pages ahead I'll present all I've learned in more than three decades of working with clients at The Center: A Place of Hope. I've been privileged to help thousands of courageous people who were determined to heal and regain control of their lives. I've listened to their stories and grown professionally by witnessing their setbacks and sharing their ultimate triumphs.

But my most valuable insights and experiences have been gained in the trenches of dealing with intense anxiety in my own life. Those lessons are also found on every page and have provided me with hard-won confidence that the solutions presented here are not just theoretical but proven—in some of my own toughest moments of fear.

In 2013, my wife, LaFon, was diagnosed with a fast-growing breast cancer. The instant a routine mammogram revealed suspicious spots, our lives were turned upside down. Frightening uncertainties immediately multiplied in my mind, threatening to overwhelm my ability to function in my busy, demanding life. Those uncertainties ran the gamut from how the illness would impact our family and our thriving business to the ultimate fear—would I lose the person I love?

A detailed chronicle of her five-year journey to recovery—through surgery, aggressive chemotherapy, and comprehensive naturopathic care—would require a book of its own. In it, you would see my own "flesh and blood" battles with paralyzing fear, fretful doctor appointments, sleepless nights, and the temptation to despair. But you would also read how God's grace saw LaFon and our family through the dark night and how, with many ups and downs along the way, I was made stronger by my own journey through anxiety and fear. Every gut-wrenching lesson—about what works and what doesn't, what's healthy and what isn't—has made me a better person, husband, and father.

The experience has also boosted my ability to say to you: Yes, you *can* heal. You *can* overcome with the right mix of desire, determination, and willingness to ask for help and face what lies between you and wellness. As we travel together through these pages, I'll share all I've learned—professionally and personally—to show you how.

I am profoundly grateful to say that LaFon has been cancer free for six years. She celebrated her six-year milestone by leading our family on a climb up Mount Rainier. In many ways, it was a metaphor for the long, arduous journey we had traveled together. And we made it.

I can say to you with utmost confidence that whatever anxiety-producing mountain you are currently facing, you can climb it and conquer it with a sense of victory!

Keep Reading If You Want Relief

As I alluded to earlier, there isn't a single cure for anxiety disorders, because there also isn't a single cause. A wide range of factors contribute to a person's inability to regulate their fear and maintain natural emotional resilience. These include genetic and biochemical predisposition, but also lifestyle conditions such as an unhealthy diet, lack of exercise, chaotic sleep habits, substance use or abuse, excessive time spent online or watching television, and any number of behavioral addictions. Unchecked toxic emotions like anger, guilt, and bitterness also play a huge role in escalating anxiety.

Addressing one underlying cause while leaving the others untouched is like changing only one tire on your car when all four are bare. It's unlikely to solve your problem and can even leave you more frustrated than when you first began. That's why, in the first part of this book, we will dive deeply into the many causes of anxiety and different forms of anxiety. When you fully understand your own anxiety, you will be better equipped to implement the many effective treatment solutions in the second part of the book.

This book is intended for anyone who is ready to undertake a full-spectrum inventory of their lives and do the work of real change across the board:

- *People looking for tools to better cope with ordinary life stress.* Not all anxiety rises to the level of a mental health disorder. Many people live under the cloud of low-level fear and could use a little help regaining the upper hand.
- *People for whom the daily experience of anxiety is no longer "ordinary."* It's one thing to feel general discomfort and unease around strangers, for example. But it's quite another to refuse to leave the house for long stretches of time to avoid the possibility. The pages ahead are full of strategies for taming those responses and reclaiming a fulfilling life.
- *People for whom medication has proven to be not enough.* As you'll see in coming chapters, anti-anxiety drugs continue to be the go-to remedy for patients and doctors alike. While these medications certainly have a role to play in responsible treatment, they will never take the place of broad attention to the whole person.

- *People who have gained control over crippling symptoms but can't seem to move on to lasting wellness.* If your best efforts have left you feeling stuck, chances are there is some factor at work in your life that you have not yet examined. I'm confident you'll discover it here.
- *People hoping to better understand a loved one who struggles with anxiety and to offer informed help.* Recovery from mental health issues is a team effort. The more you know about what your family member or friend is dealing with, the better able you are to be part of the solution.

Some level of anxiety is normal, and fear can even be an ally at times when some course correction or protective action is needed. But none of us should live as a slave to anxiety and fear. If you feel that describes your life to any degree, then it's time for an anxiety reset.

Lasting healing, freedom, and peace can be yours!

Your Personal Reset Plan

You stand at the threshold of a fruitful journey toward healing and restoration. Far from being alone on the road, you travel in the company of many others like you—but don't take my word for it. As you set out, prove it to yourself beyond a doubt. Here's how:

1. **Accept fear as a universal part of life.** When you believe your fear makes you different from everyone else, you've created a false wall around yourself. Tear down that wall by acknowledging that your fear doesn't *separate* you from everyone else; it *connects* you. Fear is universal to the human experience. Finish this sentence in as many ways as you can think of: "We *all* feel afraid when . . ."

2. **Be your own best travel companion.** There is wisdom in the common saying, "Wherever you go, there you are." How sad, then, that so many of us go through life with a harsh and unforgiving attitude toward the person we're closest to—ourselves! The road ahead is long. How about lightening the load by easing up on yourself?

   For one day, carry a pad and pen with you and pay attention

to your inner dialogue. What things are you saying to yourself throughout the day that could be adding to your anxiety? Examples of negative self-talk that increases anxiety include mind reading (*She didn't say hello when I walked in, so she must be upset with me for something*), labeling (*I'm a loser*), and overgeneralization (*I'll* never *get it right; this* always *happens to me*).

Would you plant these kinds of self-defeating thoughts in the mind of your best friend? Of course not. Be a better friend to yourself.

And while you're carrying around that pad of paper, make a list of thirty of your best qualities. Every day for the next thirty days, pick one quality every morning and, while looking in the mirror, compliment yourself on that quality. Out loud.

3. **Join a support group.** In every community, people just like you gather on a regular basis to move just a little further down the road to freedom from anxiety in their own lives—and to help others do the same. Find them. Join them.

   Spend twenty minutes today doing a little research on ways to connect. How do you find a support group in your community? Ask friends for their recommendations. Look online. Make a few phone calls. And then make plans to visit several to find the right fit.

4. **Look for opportunities to become involved—or more involved— in church.** As you'll see in the pages ahead, spirituality is perhaps your most valuable asset in your quest for wellness. Modern life seems determined to undermine faith in God at every step. That's why we gather: to remind ourselves we are not isolated—not from each other and not from God.

   If you are attending a local church, take ten minutes and visit your church's website for information about small groups or opportunities to join a team that is serving in some way, whether that means providing childcare, manning the coffee shop, or greeting people as they walk in the door.

   And if you are not attending church and are open to doing so, take ten minutes and google churches in your neck of the woods. Check out a website or two to see when services are held. If you don't see something that piques your interest, call at least one friend and ask where he or she attends. Then choose a church to visit this week or next.

Finding a spiritual community can play a vital role in your growth and healing.

5. **Seek out a mentor.** As you settle in to your new group relationships, keep your eyes open for someone among them who is ahead of you on the path and who seems to have gained the perspective and wisdom you seek. Invite them to coffee or lunch and ask them to share what they've learned.

Mentoring doesn't have to be a formal arrangement with weekly meetings. Look for positive, encouraging people who seem interested in your growth, tell them you'd like to learn from them, and see where things go from there.

CHAPTER 2

Causes & Catalysts

*Understand the roots of your anxiety
so you can address it.*

Conventional wisdom holds that it's not the dangers you know about that will get you. It's those you aren't aware of and can't see coming that pose the biggest threat.

Most people cope by assuming they'll be able to handle the unknown when it arrives and by generally expecting positive outcomes. But someone who struggles with anxiety often sees the potential for full-blown disaster behind every door and around every corner. To them, a chart of the unknown in their lives would resemble maps made by early cartographers and explorers—illustrated with unearthly sea monsters and precipitous falls into the abyss.

It is ironic, then, that anxiety itself can be a source of more anxiety because its causes are so often unexplored and unknown to those living in its grip. *Where do panic attacks come from? What is the source of persistent, paralyzing dread?* Most damaging of all: *Is there something hopelessly wrong with me?* How frightening it is to go stumbling around in the dark looking for answers to questions like these. Left to the imagination, our personal monsters have a way of proliferating and becoming invincible.

Luckily, we are not stuck there. With every passing year, researchers understand the varied causes and catalysts of destructive anxiety better and better. And as any determined explorer knows, the best way to shrink rumored monsters down to size is to sail out and have a look for yourself. With that in mind, here is a list of the known origins of anxiety, many of which will be discussed in greater detail in subsequent chapters. Though it is rare for any one of these factors alone to account for the presence of anxiety in your life, it's helpful to examine them one at a time and see them as they really are, not as you fear them to be.

Physical Roots

Underlying Medical Conditions

Doctors have learned through experience and research that anxiety and other mood disorders often accompany related physical ailments and that anxiety is sometimes the first symptom to appear, warning that something is amiss with a person's health.[1] Examples include

- degenerative neurological conditions, such as multiple sclerosis, Parkinson's disease, Alzheimer's disease, and Huntington's disease;
- diabetes;
- stroke;
- heart disease;
- some nutritional deficiencies, such as a lack of vitamin B12;
- thyroid disorders that cause glands to produce too little or too much of particular hormones;
- cancer (or pending diagnosis);
- asthma; and
- estrogen or progesterone imbalance.

For this reason, many health care professionals begin with a thorough physical exam when treating someone with overt symptoms of anxiety. If these are caused by related medical conditions, they may disappear once the underlying conditions are treated.

Genetic Predisposition

Researchers have confirmed that a person's genetic makeup has a role to play in their susceptibility to anxiety. Heritability estimates, drawn from numerous clinical studies, range from 30 to 67 percent. In general, the variants believed to be responsible for heightened anxiety risk are found in genes involved with regulating stress hormones in the body. Even if you don't undergo a thorough genetic screening, if you have one or more family members with a history of anxiety-related disorders, this could be a reasonable indicator of personal risk.

As Emory University professors Dr. Jessica Maples-Keller and Dr. Vasiliki Michopoulos state, "While both nature and nurture can be at play with family history, if several people have anxiety disorders, genetic vulnerability to anxiety likely exists in that family." However, the writers also point out that genetic research may hold out hope for future treatment breakthroughs, since "genetic factors can also bestow resilience to anxiety disorders."[2]

Gender and Hormones

In the same report, Maples-Keller and Michopoulos acknowledge that "women are twice as likely as men to suffer from anxiety. Overall symptom severity has also been shown to be more severe in women compared to men, and women with anxiety disorders typically report a lower quality of life than men."[3]

Though researchers have a long way to go before fully understanding why this is so, some studies suggest that ovarian hormones—estrogen and progesterone—are the likely culprits. Cyclical changes in hormone levels over time have been linked to fluctuations in the severity of anxiety symptoms. However, the writers admit, "it still remains unclear how these hormones and their fluctuations increase women's vulnerability to anxiety."[4]

Oxidative Stress

"Free radicals" are naturally occurring compounds in the body. Unfortunately, they are unstable compounds that can damage other cells in your body through a process called oxidation. Oxidation itself is part of our body's normal functioning, and free radicals help to fight off pathogens, which can cause infections. But oxidative stress can occur if free radical activity and antioxidant activity experience imbalance.

Free radicals are created in the course of normal metabolism and sometimes by exposure to external chemicals found in cigarette smoke, fried foods, pesticides, alcohol, and air pollutants. When antioxidants can no longer balance out free radicals in the body, the free radicals can cause damage. For example, free radicals can harm fatty tissue, DNA, and proteins, which can lead to disease over time.

Ordinarily the body employs antioxidants that "donate" electrons and neutralize potentially harmful free radicals. When those defenses become compromised, the result is oxidative stress, which has been linked to a wide range of illnesses, including mental health challenges such as depression and anxiety.

Brain Chemistry

For many years, a popular theory among medical professionals held that disorders like depression and anxiety were the result of chemical imbalances in the brain—that is, too much or too little of certain neurotransmitters like serotonin or dopamine. Correct the imbalance with medication, it was thought, and the problem would be solved.

These days, that idea has become controversial, even to the point of being largely discredited. Researchers have found that the truth is much more complex.

An article published by the Harvard Medical School states, "To be sure, chemicals are involved in this process, but it is not a simple matter of one chemical being too low and another too high. Rather, many chemicals are involved, working both inside and outside nerve cells. There are millions, even billions, of chemical reactions that make up the dynamic system that is responsible for your mood, perceptions, and how you experience life."[5]

Nevertheless, researchers continue to try to understand that complexity better and identify ways to influence how the brain functions to help people who suffer from anxiety and other disorders. (Chapter 6 will address this subject in more detail.)

Psychological Roots

Past Trauma or Significant Loss

It should come as no surprise that dramatic, repeated, or long-term exposure to danger or abuse can trigger symptoms of anxiety. Personal safety—physical and psychological—is a basic and nonnegotiable human need. The lack of it can take a toll on a person's ability to manage even ordinary life stress.

What may be less obvious is the range of life events and conditions that qualify as traumatic, leading to an increased risk of anxiety later on. In some cases, the conditions responsible for the trauma are long gone, perhaps even forgotten. Sometimes the source of trouble is (or was) chronic, occurring over long periods of time. Other incidents—like involvement in a serious accident, being the victim of a robbery or assault, or witnessing an instance of mass violence—happened only once but continue to be a source of increased fearfulness and anxiety long after the fact. Even surviving a natural disaster, such as a hurricane or earthquake, can leave a person with lasting feelings of powerlessness and insecurity.

These traumatic events can sometimes lead to the development of post-traumatic stress disorder (PTSD) or other related disorders. According to information published by the Anxiety and Depression Association of America, "Symptoms [of PTSD] may include flashbacks and nightmares; emotional numbness and avoidance; difficulty sleeping and concentrating, feeling jumpy, and being easily irritated. Most people recover from their experiences, but people who have PTSD continue to be severely depressed and anxious for months—or even years—following the event."[6]

Researchers suspect that chronic childhood trauma, abuse, or neglect could be especially damaging, as traumatic experiences often alter brain chemistry. These events can include the loss of a parent, physical or sexual abuse, illness, divorce, and repeated exposure to danger or lack. Recent studies suggest that persistent insecurity may interfere with healthy brain development, particularly in circuits needed for balanced regulation of fear.[7] Those changes can follow a person into adulthood and increase the risk of anxiety.

Temperament

It's a serious overstatement to say that a person suffering from anxiety was simply "wired to worry" at birth. Too many other diverse factors converge and contribute to a person's state of mental health.

Nevertheless, some research that has followed a group of otherwise healthy children over two decades or more suggests that some indeed are born with a "lower threshold" for activating the parts of the brain responsible for producing the stress hormone cortisol. In essence, a hyperactive amygdala is a recipe for "high-reactive" personality types.

Reporting on one such longitudinal study for the *New York Times Magazine*, journalist Robin Marantz Henig writes,

> The tenuousness of modern life can make anyone feel overwrought. And in societal moments like the one we are in—thousands losing jobs and homes, our futures threatened by everything from diminishing retirement funds to global warming—it often feels as if ours is the Age of Anxiety. But some people, no matter how robust their stock portfolios or how healthy their children, are always mentally preparing for doom. They are just born worriers, their brains forever anticipating the dropping of some dreaded other shoe.[8]

These people tend to be society's inhibited and introverted perfectionists and pessimists, researchers say. Still, temperament only indicates a predilection toward anxiety, not specific outcomes. Marantz Henig concludes that a high-reactive person can grow up to be "anxious and suicidal, or simply a poet. Temperament is important, but life intervenes."[9]

Unresolved Emotional Conflict

At The Center, we've helped thousands of people over the past thirty years to recover from crippling depression and anxiety. True, every person comes from a different background and unique circumstances, but as we listen to so many stories, it's impossible to miss elements that nearly all of them have in common. One of those is the presence of what I call the three toxic emotions: anger, guilt, and fear.

Perhaps these stem from failed or troubled relationships, from actions of your own that you regret, or from old offenses you have never forgiven. Often these emotions reinforce each other in a vicious circle. For example, irritability and aggression (anger) are common symptoms of anxiety, which can lead to feelings of guilt over how you are treating someone you care about and then to the fear that you may lose them as a result, reinforcing and adding to anxiety, which is where the cycle began. Left untended, this can become a negative feedback loop that spirals out of control.

Many people want to believe their struggles with anxiety have nothing to do with things like forgiveness, letting go, or working to heal broken relationships. But experience has taught us that unresolved negative emotion has a direct role to play in mental health.

Lifestyle Roots

Cumulative or Chronic Stress

Modern life can be full of inherently stressful things—traffic jams, car repairs, demanding bosses, family conflicts, bills to pay, ladders to climb, people to please. Most of the time there is an ebb and flow to such stressors that allows us to meet their challenges and keep our balance.

Sometimes, however, a storm surge of life seems to bring them ashore all at once, overwhelming our defenses. Add to that one or more extraordinary events—a death in the family, the loss of a job, unforeseen financial misfortune, divorce, kids in trouble—and you've got a recipe for real anxiety, especially for someone already influenced by other factors listed above. Even the demands of seemingly positive events like a wedding or vacation can tip the scales.

Excessive Busyness or Perfectionism

Many stress-inducing events and obligations are unavoidable. Bills have to be paid, and illness generally arrives uninvited. But not all. Some of the anxiety we experience is self-inflicted and self-perpetuating.

Henry David Thoreau once wrote, "It is not enough to be industrious; so are the ants. What are you industrious about?" That is an excellent question we all should ask ourselves, especially in our hectic and harried modern culture. Some people seem genuinely afraid of spare time and rush to fill it whenever it threatens to appear in their lives. Already frazzled, they volunteer to organize the company Christmas party, serve as president of the neighborhood homeowner's association, or lead the overnight camping trip for twenty Girl Scouts. They schedule their children for a different sport, lesson, or playdate for every day of the week. These well-meaning people say yes to everything but themselves, and real anxiety is often the price they pay.

That's because no matter how fervently we claim to be good at multitasking, research has demonstrated again and again it is not true. Try to do five things at once, and all of them will be perpetually on the verge of falling through the cracks—and none of them will be done well. Living like this means we routinely have to add failure to our list of things to be anxious about.

When searching for the origins of anxiety, it can't hurt to start by looking at your daily calendar.

Substance Abuse and Other Addictive Behaviors

Mental health professionals have long ago settled the question, Do addiction and anxiety disorders go hand in hand? The answer is a definitive yes. *Psychiatry Times* reports,

> Anxiety and substance use disorders are among the most frequent psychiatric problems in the United States, with lifetime rates of 28.8% and 14.6%, respectively. The presence of an anxiety or substance use disorder is also a risk factor for the presence of the other disorder, as shown in both epidemiological and clinical samples.[10]

That means it's impossible to look for the causes of anxiety—and choose effective treatments—without also addressing harmful substance use habits and addictions. The two are intertwined and mutually reinforce one another. For example, chances are that people who suffer from elevated anxiety choose to self-medicate with substances. Then, the stress of hiding illegal drug use or excessive alcohol use from friends, family, employers, and authorities can become yet another source of worry and anxiety.

Furthermore, severe anxiety is a well-documented physical component of withdrawal from drugs and alcohol.

However, substance use isn't the only impulse-control disorder that can lead to increased risk of crippling anxiety. "Process" addictions include things like pornography, gambling, shopping, overeating, shoplifting, video gaming, internet surfing, and social media connection. Mental health professionals define an addiction, in part, as participation in an activity a person can't control, in spite of obvious negative effects on their life. Once again, those negative consequences can add fuel to the fire for anyone prone to anxiety.

Information Overload

A huge percentage of people in our society tend to overconsume news and information, and much of this is low-value information, meaning it is data, details, and discussions that we really don't need in our everyday lives. Are you one of the overconsumers?

Consider how much information the average person processes in a single day: emails, phone calls, voice mails, text messages, social media posts, traffic reports, appointment alerts, news updates, advertisements, online entertainment, and shopping. That's before you consider the demands of the workplace and actual conversation with friends and family. It's enough to wear anyone's nerves thin.

Beyond the sheer volume of information we must handle, much of what we see prods us to be afraid, vigilant, worried about what we're missing out on, or aware of things that could go wrong if we don't give them our full attention. In other words, to someone already predisposed to anxiety, it's positively toxic.

As I said at the beginning of the chapter, a person's struggle with anxiety can never be traced to a single source. This list makes clear that many inter-dependent factors are at play—some physical, some psychological, and some a matter of lifestyle choices. The good news is, no matter the source, with patience and determination healing is *always* possible.

In the coming chapters, we'll explore these different sources of anxiety because understanding the cause is a powerful first step to recovery. It sheds light on the unknown, shrinks monsters down to size, and arms you with the knowledge you need to slay them.

Your Personal Reset Plan

You may never have a definitive answer to the question, *Why do I struggle with anxiety?* There are simply too many factors, interwoven in ways that are too complex for such clarity. But that doesn't mean there aren't clues to what those factors may be. Investigating them can not only calm your uncertainty but also lead you to unexpected solutions.

Here are five ways to get started:

1. **Affirm that you are not flawed beyond recovery.** Early in this chapter we acknowledged one of the questions that vexes a person with an anxiety disorder: *Is there something seriously wrong with me?* I and others can reassure you the answer is no, but that will be of little help if you don't believe it yourself.

   In a journal, start a page that's strictly for affirmations:

   - I am not broken. I have challenges to meet.
   - My condition is a riddle I am capable of solving.
   - I have everything I need to be well—if I choose to act on it.

   Be kind to yourself with new entries each day. Shower yourself with positive words. Then, when in need of a boost, read through the list—and believe it.

2. **Take inventory.** Complete the following checklist of possible root causes of anxiety. Resist going on a witch hunt, where you see enemies behind every tree. Be realistic, however, about potential causes that have evidence to back them up. Note that several of the possible

causes of anxiety on this checklist are voluntary and therefore fully under your control.

- I have underlying medical conditions.
- Genetic disposition/heredity may be a factor.
- My gender and hormones may be playing a role.
- Lifestyle choices (smoking, drinking, eating fried foods) may be increasing the impact of free radicals in my body.
- I have experienced past trauma or significant loss.
- I struggle with anger, guilt, or fear.
- I experience chronic stress in my life.
- I'm too busy.
- I'm a perfectionist.
- I am addicted to something.
- I am on information overload.

3. **Enlist the help of a trusted adviser.** Self-assessment like I just described is often difficult without the benefit of an outside perspective. As you begin to discover the possible roots of your anxiety, ask someone close to you to help you see which items are most plausible. This person can also point out which things you may have left off because you are too close to your circumstances or perhaps too reluctant to be honest with yourself about them.

    Identify someone you trust and with whom you can discuss the checklist above. Write the name of that person here: _____ _____ . When you have contacted them to arrange or have this conversation, check this box: ▪

4. **In your journal, describe a time when you did not feel afraid.** This exercise has two goals. First, to remind you that you are not your fear. However far back you must go to find it, there was a time before anxiety took over your life. Second, as you take stock of that time, notice what circumstances and conditions are *not* there but which are a part of your present life. In this way you may see more clearly the relationship between an illness and your anxiety, or lifestyle choices that have developed over time into problem areas. Make a detailed list of those things, and use it in your further investigations.

5. **Go on selective "fasts" to identify sources of stress.** A person being treated for severe allergies is often asked to eliminate certain foods or chemicals from their diet to test the body's response to their absence. Consider doing that with the voluntary items on the lists you've made. Go a week without watching the news, for example. Or eat only healthy foods. Turn off your phone for meaningful periods of time and commit to ignoring social media. In your journal, write about how these things make you feel at first, and then over time. Log the outcomes in your journal.

CHAPTER 3

The Three-Headed Monster: Worry, Anxiety & Stress

How these emotions combine forces to make you miserable.

No one is immune to the havoc and hardship caused by unrelenting anxiety—and that includes people we consider to be successful, accomplished, and highly regarded. Anxiety does not just affect people struggling with unemployment, financial troubles, serious illness, or legal problems.

Anxiety is an equal-opportunity troublemaker, laying siege to people all across the economic, professional, religious, and age spectrums.

Diane is living proof of that truth. But she is also proof that addressing anxiety and adopting healthy practices can indeed bring well-being and peace.

It was on a crisp fall morning that Diane arrived at The Center after several years of assuming that her increasingly oppressive anxiety would eventually just go away if she could power through and press on. She worked at a large and well-known Seattle-area software development company, where she was senior vice president of legal affairs. Her job brought her admiration among her peers, an enviable income, and all the perks of a prestigious position.

When she had filled out the intake forms online prior to her arrival, she mentioned her ongoing struggle with stress and anxiety, also saying that friends had urged her to consult with a professional counselor. So on her first day at our clinic, I met with her to talk through a treatment plan.

As she settled into one of the comfortable chairs in my office, Diane exhaled audibly and offered a nervous smile. After some get-acquainted time, I asked how my team and I could best assist her. I couldn't help noticing how Diane clutched one of the decorative pillows in front of her.

"I constantly feel overwhelmed—totally stressed out," she ventured. She sighed deeply and shook her head as her eyes studied the floor between us. "Life just feels out of control. In fact, three of my closest friends staged an intervention of sorts. They could see how my life was starting to unravel—me, the one who's always on-task and in control."

We took a while to probe what, specifically, seemed to be causing her stress. Diane recited a litany of stressors that had gathered into a perfect storm in her life: never-ending pressures at her demanding job, conflict with a teenager at home, coordinating daily transportation and schedules for two younger children, her husband's heavy travel schedule, an elderly mother recently diagnosed with Alzheimer's disease, and serving on busy community and church committees.

"That's a lot to deal with," I said. "Is it all keeping you awake at night?"

"Sometimes."

"How often?"

She thought for a moment. "Three or four nights a week, I can't fall asleep till after one or two o'clock. Or I wake up at three or four with my mind racing."

"What are you worrying about in the middle of the night?"

"Something that happened the previous day," Diane said. "Or something I'm facing the next day. Sometimes I just have this overall restless feeling, and I'm not sure what's causing it."

I thought about her words and then asked, "What goes on inside you during the day? What does it feel like?"

"Tightness in my gut," Diane said. "Sometimes I have trouble concentrating." For the first time since we had sat down, she made sustained eye contact with me.

"So during those times, would you say you feel nervous?"

"Yep, much of the time," she acknowledged. "I've almost forgotten what 'peaceful' feels like."

As we talked further, it became apparent to me that Diane suffered from generalized anxiety disorder (GAD), in which stress, worry, and anxiety all coalesced into a vicious cycle to make her daily life feel at best uncomfortable and often practically intolerable. I was so glad that Diane had the courage to seek help and address her anxiety. That's because being weighed down by worry every day and every night undermines the joyful, contented life that everyone can—and should—experience.

A life weighed down by worry certainly is not what God intended. As Jesus said, "Come to me, all you who are weary and burdened, and I will give you rest. Take my yoke upon you and learn from me, for I am gentle and humble in heart, and you will find rest for your souls. For my yoke is easy and my burden is light."[1] Diane would indeed describe her life as *weary* and *burdened* . . . and not *easy* and *light*. At least not yet. But hope is always available!

Of course, Diane was not alone. As we've seen, anxiety negatively affects millions of otherwise-healthy individuals, sapping not only their health and energy but also their perspective and enjoyment of life.

The Difference Makes a Difference

As in war, we must, as the wise saying goes, "Know the enemy." So our focus here is to get to know the culprits called worry, anxiety, and stress and how they conspire to rob you of power for living. Knowing the enemy will prepare you for the help you're going to find in this book—and give you a solid foundation for victory.

First, we need to realize the differences between worry, anxiety, and stress. Indeed, they do differ from one another, yet they frequently form a devastating combination that can suck the soul and strength from the sufferer. I refer to these forces as a three-headed monster, which can sound quite threatening and daunting. But the good news is that this monster is menacing but manageable. In fact, you can learn to keep this monster on a tight leash so it doesn't control your life. Taking control begins by understanding the difference between worry, anxiety, and stress.

Worried about Worry

While we sometimes use the words *worry* and *anxiety* as if they mean the same thing, there is a distinct difference between the two. They represent different psychological and emotional conditions.[2]

Worry can be seen as a component of anxiety but is not anxiety in itself. Often it is a precursor to anxiety and stress, and it can also be a result of stress. Knowing the difference will be helpful in your journey to wholeness and peace.

Worry tends to be more specific, while anxiety is more generalized. We may worry about a certain upcoming medical procedure (a specific threat), but we feel anxious about visiting doctors (a nebulous concern).

Worry is often a temporary state (though it can be chronic), while anxiety can linger beyond the threat. Worry declines and disappears after the specific threat is behind us, while anxiety can linger as general unease after the immediate threat is resolved.

Worry is cognitive, centered in our brains, while anxiety is felt throughout our bodies. In other words, worry is a mental process, while anxiety results in physical symptoms. Since worry is specific and temporary, it is centered in our thoughts. Anxiety, which is less specific and long-term, is pervasive—we feel it throughout our bodies. Worry may keep the mind racing, while anxiety can manifest in headaches, muscle aches, tension in the stomach, intensified heartbeat, increased blood pressure, inability to concentrate, and even physical illness.

Worry, a learned emotion, is controllable, while anxiety can be more challenging and requires different strategies to control. Worry can move us to troubleshoot and resolve what's causing us concern. If you're worried about paying off debt, you can problem-solve by sticking to your budget and taking on a side gig to earn extra cash. If you're worried about your child's attention deficit disorder, you can problem-solve by reading books on this condition and pursuing treatment options. But anxiety is often less controllable and less prone to result in problem-solving action. You may experience a general unease about your financial issues or your child's condition, but it's difficult to convince yourself that all is well.

**THE THREE-HEADED MONSTER:
WORRY, ANXIETY, STRESS**

Worry
  * centers on a specific trigger
  * is usually cognitive
  * goes away when situation/trigger is over

Anxiety
  * is generalized and unspecific
  * can be felt throughout the body
  * exists on a spectrum

Stress
  * results from an unfavorable, difficult, or exhausting situation
  * can be positive (eustress) or negative (distress), depending on how you respond
  * can be harmful to your body over the long term

Anxious over Anxiety

Let's take this discussion a step further by examining the characteristics of anxiety more closely.[3] Dr. Luana Marques, professor of psychology at Harvard Medical School, represents a good number of mental health professionals who consider anxiety to be the main culprit and worry just one component of anxiety. "Anxiety is your body's natural threat response system," she says, while "anxiety has three main components: emotional, physiological, and cognitive."

The *cognitive* component of anxiety involves negative thoughts about what has happened in the recent past ("I can't believe I said that!") or what may happen in the near future ("I'm going to panic if the boss calls on me at the meeting!"). But distressing thoughts coursing through your mind are just one part of the equation.

Closely related are fear and dread, both feelings that exemplify the *emotional* component. And "you may also notice bodily sensations, such as heart palpitations, sweating, or a tightness in your stomach, which represent the *physiological* component," says Dr. Marques. "So, while worry is an important part of anxiety, it is only one of the three main building blocks."

27

According to this line of thought, not all anxiety is necessarily bad. This view says that "normal levels of anxiety lie on one end of a spectrum and may present as low levels of fear or apprehension, mild sensations of muscle tightness and sweating, or doubts about your ability to complete a task. Importantly, symptoms of normal anxiety do not negatively interfere with daily functioning," Dr. Marques explains. "They may actually improve your attention and problem-solving, motivate you to work harder toward a goal, or warn you about a potential threat."

However, moving toward the opposite end of the spectrum, anxiety levels can rise enough to markedly decrease performance and functionality and impair well-being. This is considered "clinical anxiety," a full-on anxiety disorder that, according to Dr. Marques, entails "severe, persistent worry that is excessive for the situation, and extreme avoidance of anxiety-provoking situations. These symptoms cause distress, impair daily functioning, and occur for a significant period."

On the anxiety spectrum ranging from normal to clinical, another category might be called "mid-scale." This doesn't mean it does not greatly affect a person's life—it certainly does. People struggling with mid-scale or mid-range anxiety have levels of stress, weariness, and worry that put them beyond the somewhat benign, normal level. But this degree of anxiety may not be perilous enough for the condition to be considered a critical, clinical anxiety disorder. Some experts call this a state of being "almost anxious."

I readily admit that the term "almost anxious" is a misnomer, because anyone experiencing this gray, in-between level of anxiety is indeed anxious and still struggling for focus and confidence while fighting negative thoughts or unpleasant bodily sensations. Indeed, all three components of anxiety—emotional, physiological, and cognitive—chisel away at the soul and psyche of anyone who lives in this gray area, just not as ruthlessly or relentlessly as at the more dangerous clinical level.

Stressed about Stress

Our third culprit is stress. If you're like nearly everyone living on planet Earth, it's difficult to get through one week without feeling stressed about something. In fact, the modern-day perspective is often that if you are not

THE PHYSICAL DANGERS OF STRESS

Stress leaches health out of your body, and if not adequately mitigated, this stress can eventually lead to anxiety. Stress and anxiety not only negatively affect your emotional and mental health; they also wreak havoc on your body. Here are some of the most common physical symptoms of stress:

Your heart. Stress causes your heart to speed up. Often when blood pressure increases, your heart seems like it might burst out of your chest. This increased demand on the heart can produce an irregular heartbeat called an arrhythmia.

Your lungs. People suffering from high stress tend to breathe heavily and rapidly, putting heavy strain on their lungs. Sometimes this can result in a panic attack, which often includes gasping for air or hyperventilating. This rapid intake of air provides more oxygen than your body needs and results in a corresponding drop in carbon dioxide in your blood, forcing your heart to work even harder.

Your stomach. Stress puts your gastrointestinal system through the wringer. The longer your stomach stays in a state of agitation, the greater the possibility of ulcers and irritable bowel syndrome. You can experience all the symptoms of a digestive system imbalance: indigestion, acid reflux, constipation, nausea, and diarrhea.

Your muscles. Many people manifest their stress in a specific region of the body, such as the back, face, or neck. The constant contraction of these muscles leads to tension and pain. The longer the tension lasts, the harder it is to release the resulting knots and experience true relaxation. Even during sleep, some people clench their jaw muscles and grind their teeth.

Your immune system. Stress is like the story of the boy who cried wolf when there was no wolf. People stopped trusting the boy, even when a real wolf arrived. Similarly, when you are constantly under stress, you are crying wolf to your immune system. Eventually, your immune system wears down and can no longer respond appropriately to real danger.

Your weight. Your body has a variety of stress hormones. One is cortisol, which increases blood sugar levels while suppressing the immune system. Its job during stress is to get you physically pumped up with energy and systemically less reactive. While this is good if you need to race across an airport to catch your plane, it's not especially helpful in everyday life. Cortisol causes people to put on excess weight, leading to hypertension and cardiovascular problems.

Your head. Stress is painful, especially when it is manifested in chronic headaches and migraines. Women are almost twice as susceptible to tension headaches as men.

stressed, you're not working hard enough. In today's workplace, to our detriment, we wear stress almost as a badge of honor.

Stress is generally the tension or strain we feel when placed in unfavorable, difficult, or exhausting situations. We may say, "He's under a lot of stress," meaning that someone is bearing very challenging mental or emotional burdens. A contemporary euphemism for stress is feeling overwhelmed, meaning that the volume and severity of someone's task list and life problems may dominate that person's waking moments and even hinder sleep.

It's interesting (and telling) that the original meaning of *stress* was much more neutral and benign than our present-day definition. Dr. Hans Selye, one of the world's foremost pioneers in stress research and author of the classic book *Stress without Distress* and cofounder of the Canadian Institute of Stress, said that the original meaning of stress was "the non-specific response of the body to any demand for change."[4] That doesn't sound particularly harmful, does it? Yet the contemporary perception most of us live by is that all stress is unhealthy and can lead to anxiety, high blood pressure and stroke, and cardiovascular disease.

In its purest form, stress is simply a conditioned response to a real or perceived stressor. In that respect, stress is neutral and can go either way. A negative response can lead to pain, panic, or paralysis. But a positive response helps heighten our senses and improve our performance. In extreme, fight-or-flight situations, stress can even save our lives.

The Good News about Stress

The key to handling stress is to determine the difference between helpful and harmful stress. Selye provided an invaluable perspective in this regard. He said there are two different types of stress: *eustress* (helpful, productive stress) and *distress* (harmful, unproductive stress).

Research subsequent to Selye's has confirmed that *eustress* typically

- has a short duration,
- energizes and motivates,
- seems manageable,
- feels exciting and uplifting, and
- enhances focus and performance.

Distress, on the other hand, typically

- lasts long-term;
- triggers concern, worry, or anxiety;
- surpasses your perceived ability to cope (overwhelms);
- contributes to mental, emotional, and physical problems; and
- hinders focus and performance.[5]

So while stress is a reaction to a real or perceived stressor, it is how you relate to the stressor that determines whether you will experience eustress or distress. How you choose to process and regard the situation internally will determine whether the stressor will be helpful or harmful.

Consider this example: you're at your desk and your workload is piled high, but your boss calls you into her office and assigns a new, more urgent task that has to be done in time for a meeting tomorrow.

Momentarily stunned, you have a choice.

The boss's challenge is a stressor. But is it eustress or distress?

You could regard the challenge with internal dismay: *Are you joking? I'm so buried already. When will I find time? Why didn't you think of this earlier? No way can I do this. With so little time, you're setting me up to fail.*

Or you could respond by asking yourself healthy questions: *What's good about this situation? How can I respond to this challenge in a positive way?* And by regarding the stressor with composure: *My supervisor believes I can meet this demand and do a good job. It's a chance to demonstrate a can-do spirit. I can consult her on what tasks can wait while I direct attention to this task. I will come through with something helpful and important to contribute to the upcoming meeting.*

How will you choose to regard and process the challenge? Asking yourself, *What's good about this?* will shift your mindset from panic to power. The choice you make—your perspective on the stressor—will determine whether the stressor will be one of distress or eustress for you. Which will be more productive? Which will give you better focus, help you think more clearly, and help you do your best work?

The key is to be aware of the two types of stress and to choose the empowerment of good stress over the enslavement of bad stress. Instead of feeling out of control, you will feel in control because you're exercising the power of choice. You're choosing eustress, whic: tel.   xiety to take a hike—and empowers you to focus on the task with posi. 'e enthusiasm and a sound mind.

Your Personal Reset Plan

Knowing how the related concepts of worry, anxiety, and stress work together in your life will help you better navigate your path toward healing. Try these ideas this week as you examine your own worry, anxiety, and stress.

1. **Identify recent events in which you felt worried or anxious.** Think back on any worry or anxiety you've experienced during the past couple of weeks. Spend twenty minutes with your journal or on the computer and identify any events in the past two weeks that you can recall. Write answers to the following questions about each event:

    • Can you identify something specific that prompted the event?
    • How long did it last?
    • What symptoms did you experience?
    • How did you find relief from the experience?

2. **Determine what is worry and what is anxiety.** Reread the "Worried about Worry" section of this chapter. Using that information, evaluate your answers from the last reset plan item. Determine whether each of your listed events is a matter of *worry* or *anxiety*. Write a few sentences explaining why you think an event is one or the other.

3. **Identify resolving actions.** Particularly when it comes to worry, taking an action that addresses the concern can often bring resolution and relief. These actions might involve resolving a conflict with someone, tackling a problem you've been avoiding, or completing a task that has been languishing. Doing so will lighten your burden—and your worry—as you move forward with confidence.

    Next to each event that you've identified as worry, write one action you might have taken (and perhaps can still take!) to eliminate or reduce that particular concern.

Learning how to distinguish worry from anxiety and how to identify actions we can take that will alleviate the source of that worry is a powerful skill that can keep us from feeling powerless.

4. **Recognize the difference between eustress and distress.** It's easy to identify and remember distress. But we tend to forget that stress is also part of rising to a challenge and experiencing growth or success as a result.

Take a moment and identify three to five accomplishments of which you are proud. Did you complete a degree? Accomplish something big at work? Implement a significant life change? Achieve a difficult personal goal? Kick a bad habit to the curb? Reinvent your health or weight? Write them down.

As you think about each accomplishment, can you recall moments of stress? Maybe even panic? Can you remember how you managed to turn those stressful moments into eustress, helpful stress that motivated you toward positive change?

5. **Ask yourself a key question.** Recognizing the positive power of stress today can help you embrace a more empowering perspective when you face stressors in your future.

Today or tomorrow, as you contemplate a stressor that you're dealing with, remember that it's how you relate to the stressor that determines whether you will experience eustress or distress.

Take a three-by-five card, write down the following three questions, and post the card on a bathroom mirror or kitchen window—somewhere you'll see it every day. The next time you feel stressed, answer the questions:

- Would better planning or self-care have prevented these feelings of stress?
- What is this stress motivating me to do or to achieve?
- What's an action I can take today?

CHAPTER 4

What Is Your Anxiety Type?

Knowing the facts can help you prevail.

One of the most intriguing and illuminating aspects of my work as a mental health professional is hearing the stories my clients share in the course of our time together. Many people tell me the issues they are dealing with and the struggles they are trying to work through. Often I hear snippets of conversation from everyday life that have brought individuals unexpected insight or awareness. I heard one such story recently.

"Do you realize you are always worried about *something*?" Rosie's husband posed the question with both love and frustration in his voice. "And even when something you're worried about gets resolved, you start worrying about something else."

Rosie, fifty-two, blinked. *Do I really do that?* she wondered.

The next day, she thought about recent events in their lives.

When her daughter and son-in-law had made an offer on a house in Rosie's neighborhood, worry had eclipsed her excitement for days. Would their offer be accepted? Rosie's anxiety wasn't off the charts, but it was nonstop until she learned the seller had agreed to the price.

With the offer accepted, Rosie had shifted her worry to her daughter's future neighbors. They had barking dogs and a perpetually overgrown yard. Would her daughter regret buying the house? Rosie had worried about *that* for weeks.

As that concern subsided, she'd found something else to worry about. And something else after that.

With a start, she realized that Frank, her loving husband of four years, had pinpointed something she had never realized about herself.

That evening as she and Frank grilled burgers together, she winced and admitted, "I've been thinking about what you said yesterday—about moving from worry to worry—and I think you're right. I do that. I had no idea!"

Rosie knew she struggled with anxiety. In fact, for years she had struggled to shake the ominous feeling that bad news lurked just around the corner. She'd often wondered if living for fourteen years in an emotionally abusive marriage with her first husband had trained her brain to anticipate disaster at every turn. Being married to Frank had brought stability, peace, and healing to Rosie's heart. She had hoped that eventually her anxious brain would heal too.

But Frank's observation had opened her eyes.

When Rosie came to The Center for help, she shared her story with tears in her eyes. Low-volume, constant anxiety played a bigger role in her life than she'd ever imagined.

The Many Faces of Anxiety

Rosie's struggle is much different from that of Todd, a client I visited with last week.

When Todd was seventeen, he witnessed a shooting at a movie theater in his community. In fact, Todd was standing less than twenty feet from the gunman as he killed several of the victims. The mass shooting made national news.

Eight years later, Todd still has nightmares about what he experienced and witnessed. He is unable to frequent public places or even pursue a career. He is haunted by survivor guilt, convinced he should have stopped the shooter somehow. He feels overwhelmed with grief and sadness. His eyes well up with tears as he admits he doesn't socialize with friends because he is overcome every day by feelings of sadness and fear.

Todd's post-traumatic stress disorder (PTSD) has different causes and symptoms from the generalized anxiety disorder (GAD) that plagues Rosie.

But Rosie and Todd have one thing in common: their symptoms impact the quality of their lives.

TYPES OF ANXIETY DISORDERS

Generalized Anxiety Disorder (GAD)

GAD is characterized by persistent anxiety and worry that is not traceable to a specific trigger. Environmental stress, genetics, and brain chemistry can all contribute to GAD. Symptoms often include physical ailments like headaches, rapid heartbeat, difficulty swallowing, feeling edgy or restless, and feeling light-headed or out of breath.

Post-Traumatic Stress Disorder (PTSD)

PTSD can follow a traumatic experience and isn't always associated with wartime events. A key symptom is avoidance of something connected with a traumatic event. Military veterans, first responders, victims of assault, and those who have experienced the sudden death of a loved one are most at risk.

Social Anxiety Disorder (SAD)

SAD is one of the most common forms of anxiety and is characterized by extreme discomfort in social settings. Symptoms include avoiding social situations, feeling physical discomfort when in social situations, and feeling anxiety in anticipation of a future social event.

Panic Disorders

Nearly 3 percent of US adults experience panic attacks. Panic attacks are characterized by the sudden onset of panic resulting in sweating, shaking, racing heart, difficulty breathing, chest pain, dizziness, nausea, or fear of losing control or of dying.

Phobias

Phobias are an irrational response to a specific trigger and are pinpointed to certain things (like a fear of spiders, heights, or enclosed spaces). Exposure to a trigger can result in severe anxiety or a panic attack.

Obsessive-Compulsive Disorder (OCD)

OCD is characterized by relentless, obsessive thoughts around something dreaded (e.g., the death of a loved one or visualizing something repulsive). These obsessive thoughts are paired with a compulsive activity meant to drive the obsession away (e.g., washing hands or organizing in a precise way).

The truth is that anxiety has many sources, can accompany many disorders (such as PTSD), and can wear many faces. In this chapter, we'll look at some of the different ways that anxiety can present itself in your life. The descriptions below are offered in the spirit of "knowledge is power." That is, the more you know about your type of anxiety and its specific symptoms, the better equipped you will be to explore further about the source of your struggles and share the information with your physician or mental health specialist.

In part 2 of this book, we will explore numerous treatment avenues for you to pursue; here, I want to provide a foundation of understanding so you will be prepared to effectively apply particular remedies.

Generalized Anxiety Disorder (GAD)

Rosie's suspicion that an abusive first marriage may have contributed to her anxiety is not off base. Environmental stress—including relationship and family stress—is one of the factors that can contribute to general anxiety disorder. Genetics and brain chemistry are also factors. And one study from the Stanford University School of Medicine has linked GAD with muddled communication being sent by distinct regions of the amygdala, the almond-shaped structure in each hemisphere of the brain that processes emotion, fear, and memory. According to Dr. Amit Etkin, a Stanford University professor and lead researcher on the study, people who experience GAD may engage in excessive worry to distract themselves from their emotions, which can feel overwhelming. Amygdala connectivity issues can also contribute to the inability to truly discern between serious problems and everyday annoyances.[1]

GAD is sometimes diagnosed by looking at physical ailments brought on by its constant stress. It is often linked to gastroesophageal reflux disease (GERD), thyroid issues, and heart disease. Doctors also examine a client's family history when diagnosing GAD, since the condition tends to run in families.

Rosie does, indeed, suffer from GERD and an underactive thyroid. She exhibits other telltale signs as well, such as difficulty sleeping, trouble concentrating, and fatigue.

Other common GAD symptoms include headaches, rapid heartbeat, difficulty swallowing, feeling "edgy" and restless, and feeling light-headed and out of breath.

Post-Traumatic Stress Disorder (PTSD)

We often hear about this next disorder in the context of service men and women experiencing PTSD in the wake of traumatic wartime events. But any traumatic event—such as the one Todd experienced—can trigger PTSD. And even non-life-threatening events can lead to PTSD.

One of the criteria for diagnosing PTSD is the existence of an avoidance symptom, for example, avoiding places, events, or things associated with the traumatic event. In fact, one client of mine chooses her doctors based on whether the physician's office is located on the first floor. After experiencing a panic attack when a parking garage elevator opened between floors and she was confronted with a brick wall, Nina is unable to ride in elevators, even though her initial scare happened many years ago.

More than eight million Americans have been diagnosed with PTSD, with women up to three times more likely than men to be diagnosed in their lifetime. Military veterans, first responders such as firefighters and police officers,

PTSD SYMPTOMS TO WATCH FOR

- feeling upset by new experiences that remind you of past, painful experiences
- experiencing nightmares, vivid memories, or flashbacks of the traumatic event, causing you to feel like it is happening all over again
- feeling emotionally isolated and cut off from others
- difficulty sleeping—chronic insomnia or frequent wakefulness
- feeling numb, detached, and uninterested in things you used to care about
- loss of interest in life and daily activities
- constantly feeling guarded, vigilant, and alert to danger or threats
- easily irritated, annoyed, or angered
- trouble focusing and concentrating
- easily startled and frequently feeling "jumpy"
- experiencing physical reactions to reminders of trauma (shaking, nausea, sweating, or a pounding heart)
- avoiding activities, places, thoughts, and feelings that remind you of painful events
- a sense of not leading a normal life and having a persistently negative outlook on life

victims of rape and assault, and people who have experienced the sudden death of a loved one are among those most likely to experience PTSD.[2]

Not everyone who experiences trauma develops PTSD. Among those who do, however, nearly half also experience moderate to severe depression.[3]

Social Anxiety Disorder (SAD)

Social anxiety disorder (SAD) is one of the most common forms of anxiety and is characterized by extreme discomfort in social settings, especially when meeting new people.

People with SAD aren't just shy. They can experience debilitating fear, worry, anxiety, panic attacks, and going "blank" and not knowing what to say. SAD can also trigger physical symptoms like a racing heart, sweating, nausea, and abdominal pain.

For someone with social anxiety disorder, even making eye contact can feel excruciating.

Like other types of anxiety, SAD impacts multiple areas of life, including work, school, and dating.

SOCIAL ANXIETY DISORDER SYMPTOMS TO WATCH FOR

The Mayo Clinic offers this list:

- excessive self-consciousness in everyday social situations
- fear of situations in which you might be judged
- worry about embarrassing or humiliating yourself
- intense fear of interacting with or talking to strangers
- fear that others will notice that you look anxious
- physical discomfort, including upset stomach, nausea, trembling, racing heart, sweating, or feeling lightheaded
- avoiding doing things or speaking to people out of fear of embarrassment
- avoiding situations where you might be the center of attention
- having anxiety in anticipation of a feared activity or event
- enduring a social situation with intense fear or anxiety
- analyzing your performance and identifying flaws in your interactions
- expecting the worst possible outcome from a social situation[*]

[*]"Social Anxiety Disorder (Social Phobia)," Mayo Clinic, August 29, 2017, https://www.mayoclinic.org/diseases-conditions/social-anxiety-disorder/symptoms-causes/syc-20353561.

Panic Disorders

Brian texted his roommate at 11:20 p.m.

"I'm in the ER."

His roommate, Danny, didn't text back but immediately called. "What happened?" he asked when Brian picked up. "Are you okay?"

"I had a panic attack. I couldn't breathe. I was shaking and sweating, and my heart was racing. I thought I was going to die."

"Dang it, Brian!" Danny sounded upset. "You know you're not going to die. This happens all the time. You know what this is. You know it passes. Now you're going to have another huge bill. . . ." The words hung unsaid: *And have a hard time making rent again.*

Brian agreed with most of what Danny was saying, except that when the panic attacks hit, he was never *certain* he wasn't going to die. The sudden onslaught of panic—with no warning and no apparent cause—was always terrifying, no matter how often it happened.

Panic attacks are unpredictable and include both emotional and physical symptoms. Six million adults in the United States—nearly 3 percent of the overall population—experience panic attacks, with women more likely to experience them than men.[4]

Panic attacks don't last a long time—they usually begin to wane after about ten minutes and dissipate within half an hour—but it can feel as if they are going to last forever. During a panic attack, common symptoms and experiences include sweating, shaking, a racing heart, difficulty breathing, chest pain, dizziness, nausea, numbness, fear of losing control, or fear of dying.

Someone can be diagnosed with panic disorder when they experience frequent panic attacks and live in fear of having the next panic attack.

In fact, living in fear of that next attack can actually lead to yet another form of anxiety called agoraphobia, which we'll look at in the next section.

Specific Phobias

While GAD is often a vague but pervasive condition, characterized by extraordinary worry over ordinary things, another anxiety category concerns issues that are very specific and focused. A phobia is an anxiety disorder that causes an irrational reaction to a certain trigger, setting off disproportionate anxiety and fear in typically innocuous settings. Phobias combine the elements of ordinary things and extraordinary terror.

If you do an online search, you will find more than a hundred phobias listed, some relatively common, others quite obscure. One of the most common phobias is agoraphobia, which is a fear of crowds, open areas, or public spaces. It's no surprise that living in fear of having a panic attack can lead to anxiety over, well, having a panic attack, especially in a public setting. In fact, a third of those who suffer from a panic disorder develop agoraphobia, which is the fear of finding yourself in situations where you can't get help or escape.

Another fairly common phobia is claustrophobia, which is the fear of being closed or trapped in a confined space. It is a situational phobia triggered by an irrational and intense fear of tight, crowded, or chaotic spaces. It can be triggered by things like being locked in a closet, getting stuck in an elevator, or having a crowd of people press in on you.

Here is a list of some other common phobias:

- acrophobia, fear of heights
- aerophobia, fear of flying
- arachnophobia, fear of spiders
- astraphobia, fear of thunder and lightning
- autophobia, fear of being alone
- cynophobia, fear of dogs
- hemophobia, fear of blood
- hydrophobia, fear of water
- mysophobia, fear of germs
- necrophobia, fear of death
- nomophobia, fear of being detached from device connectivity
- ophidiophobia, fear of snakes
- trypanophobia, fear of injections and needles
- xenophobia, fear of strangers
- zoophobia, fear of animals

Some phobias may seem strange to an outside observer, but they are extremely serious for those who suffer from them. Exposure to the object of a specific phobia can trigger a severe anxiety reaction or even a panic attack.

Obsessive-Compulsive Disorder (OCD)

Obsessive-compulsive disorder is a harsh taskmaster. People who suffer from it live with an endless bombardment of obsessive thoughts. These thoughts are not positive or uplifting; they are filled with dread, and sometimes are truly dreadful—imagining the death of a loved one or visualizing an act that is violent or sexual and always personally repulsive.

The International OCD Foundation defines the condition this way:

> Obsessive compulsive disorder (OCD) is a mental health disorder that affects people of all ages and walks of life, and occurs when a person gets caught in a cycle of obsessions and compulsions. Obsessions are unwanted, intrusive thoughts, images, or urges that trigger intensely distressing feelings. Compulsions are behaviors an individual engages in to attempt to get rid of the obsessions and/or decrease his or her distress.[5]

OCD is an individual's thought life under siege. To cope with despised, intruding thoughts, those who suffer from OCD use specific actions to mitigate, manage, or control them. It's almost as if the actions are offered as a sacrifice to appease the thought tyrant. The actions become imperative.

OCD is all about keeping obsessive thoughts at bay with compulsive rituals. These thoughts can be composed of unwanted images or impulses, often personally or religiously upsetting or repugnant. Because they are so upsetting and repulsive, great desperation is involved in trying to control them.

The National Institute of Mental Health offers specific examples:

> Obsessions are repeated thoughts, urges, or mental images that cause anxiety. Common symptoms include:
>
> - Fear of germs or contamination
> - Unwanted forbidden or taboo thoughts involving sex, religion, or harm
> - Aggressive thoughts towards others or self
> - Having things symmetrical or in a perfect order

Compulsions are repetitive behaviors that a person with OCD feels the urge to do in response to an obsessive thought. Common compulsions include:

- Excessive cleaning and/or handwashing
- Ordering and arranging things in a particular, precise way
- Repeatedly checking on things, such as repeatedly checking to see if the door is locked or that the oven is off
- Compulsive counting[6]

The rituals used often have to do with checking things over and over again, counting, or physically touching items in a particular sequence. It is not just what the ritual entails that is important but the ritual itself. The preoccupation with the ritual helps to mask the obsessive thought as well as to act as an appeasement so the dreaded thought or image will not return.

Reading about a type of anxiety that corresponds with your own symptoms can be anxiety producing in its own right, but I hope this exercise has the opposite effect. I hope that seeing, in print, struggles that are common to so many people gives you optimism and courage. After all, understanding the various types of anxiety can empower you to effectively address the particular anxiety disorder that is wreaking havoc in your life.

Take courage from the fact that you are not alone in this struggle. As you talk to people in your life whom you know and trust, you may be surprised to discover who in your community of family and friends has similar struggles. Because of the various types of anxiety, their triggers may be different from yours, but the commonality will be the anxiety that results.

Your Personal Reset Plan

I hope that by seeing some of the different types of anxiety disorders, you have a better understanding of your own anxiety. Here are some things that will help you as you further examine your own situation.

1. **Review the anxiety types discussed in this chapter.** You will find a self-assessment tool in appendix 1. Which of these types fits your particular anxiety? Journal for fifteen minutes, identifying your type of anxiety in your own words. Describe the specific ways your anxiety type is lived out in your daily life and how it affects you.

2. **Identify possible sources of your anxiety.** Do you always feel on edge, as if you are waiting for something horrible to happen? Or are there specific things that trigger feelings of anxiety or panic? Identify several experiences you've had with anxiety, noting what brought on the event.

3. **When you feel particularly anxious, what helps?** Do the feelings go away on their own after a period of time? Does removing yourself from your current setting help, or perhaps calling someone and hearing a reassuring voice on the other end of the phone? Identify and write down actions you've taken in the past that have contributed to the reduction of anxiety.

4. **Identify any harmful labels you may have attached to your experience with anxiety.** While it's helpful to identify your specific type of anxiety for the purpose of alleviating symptoms (with a professional's help), there are other kinds of labels we can attach to our anxiety experiences that are anything but helpful! Labeling ourselves as "weak" or "broken" or "messed up" because we experience anxiety is harmful—and couldn't be further from the truth. Anxiety is a legitimate and potentially debilitating struggle that can have physiological as well as psychological origins. The good news is that, with help and strategies, it can be addressed and alleviated with great success.

5. **Ditch the denial.** Write yourself an honest and encouraging letter. Acknowledge your anxiety, while debunking any harmful labels you might have embraced in the past. What would you say to help someone you love embrace reality in a positive way that moves them forward? Take that same tone and approach with yourself.

   While attaching demeaning labels to your anxiety experience

isn't helpful, ignoring your pain and telling yourself things like "This is ridiculous. I'm fine. I just need to power through this" can be just as detrimental. In a way, Rosie was in denial regarding the extent of her struggle with anxiety, and it took an observation from someone she trusted in her life for her to take action. If you are living with anxiety but have been unwilling to acknowledge your pain and take steps toward greater peace in your life, today is the day to ditch the denial and move forward.

CHAPTER 5

How Anxiety Affects Your Life

The tension-inducing tentacles spread far and wide.

The first time I met Claire, she paused at my office door, head pivoting. Her alert eyes swept every corner of the room before entering. I offered her a seat beside my desk, but she preferred the sofa. It was nearest to the exit, and she could sit with her back to the wall. She pressed her already thin frame as tightly against the sofa's arm as possible and drew her legs and arms together to present the smallest possible target. Only then did she make fleeting eye contact with me.

This is the kind of hyperalert behavior often displayed by combat veterans struggling with post-traumatic stress disorder (PTSD). That makes sense when you consider that survival in a war zone often depends on extreme awareness of one's surroundings and hypersensitivity to the slightest threat. Former soldiers who suffer from PTSD can't turn off that response once the danger is no longer present.

But here's where the story takes a surprising turn.

Claire had never served in the military or worked as an emergency first responder or witnessed an incident of mass violence. She was a part-time bookkeeper operating from an office in her garage and a stay-at-home mom of two teenagers. Claire had been referred to me by her family physician, who was treating her for a gastrointestinal disorder. It's common these days for general practitioners to ask their patients to complete mental health questionnaires when seeking treatment for other conditions, and Claire's responses had strongly indicated she suffered from elevated anxiety.

To be honest, I was glad she showed up at all. Many people who are identified as at risk and possibly in need of help with depression or anxiety never follow through. Those who do turn up at suggested appointments often resist the idea that they actually need any of "this psychology stuff." I quickly learned that Claire was in that camp. When I began asking about her questionnaire and why she thought it might have prompted the doctor's concern about possible anxiety, she responded by shrugging and producing a photograph from her purse.

"I told Dr. Moreno the same thing," she said, handing me the photo. "I've just always been a little high-strung, that's all. Ask anybody."

The photograph was taken at a kid's birthday party, years ago. A half dozen ten-year-olds were clustered around a table where the birthday boy was opening presents. A young girl—unmistakably Claire—sat straight-backed in a chair by the door. She looked with wide eyes into the camera lens and held herself in a small, defensive posture that was eerily similar to what I saw before me that day.

"Who's the boy opening presents?" I asked.

"Roger," she said. "We sat next to each other in class."

"Didn't you like him?"

"Sure, I guess," Claire said, her eyes sweeping the room again. "Just not everybody else jumping around and being crazy. I had enough of that at school."

Nothing "Normal" about It

It was clear to me then that Claire almost certainly did suffer from an anxiety disorder and probably had for a long time. But because anxiety had been a part of her daily life for so long, she had accepted the symptoms as normal. That's just how she is, she said. "High-strung," with nothing to be done but endure.

How tragic! And how unnecessary. Millions of people like Claire live day in and day out with the negative—and sometimes severe—consequences of uncontrolled anxiety without ever recognizing them as such. That's bad enough for each individual, but we must multiply that number by all the others who are also negatively affected: parents, spouses, children, employers, coworkers, friends, neighbors, and even strangers they interact with at the coffee shop or grocery store.

The Anxiety and Depression Association of America provides the following information:

- Anxiety disorders are the most common mental illness in the U.S., affecting 40 million adults in the United States age 18 and older, or 18.1% of the population every year.
- Anxiety disorders are highly treatable, yet only 36.9% of those suffering receive treatment.
- People with an anxiety disorder are three to five times more likely to go to the doctor and six times more likely to be hospitalized for psychiatric disorders than those who do not suffer from anxiety disorders.[1]

Furthermore, anxiety often develops—as it did in Claire's case—early in childhood. As the ADAA declares, "Anxiety disorders affect 25.1% of children between 13 and 18 years old. Research shows that untreated children with anxiety disorders are at higher risk to perform poorly in school, miss out on important social experiences, and engage in substance abuse."[2]

It doesn't take a crystal ball to see that this can add up to real trouble for individuals and for society as a whole.

So what can be done to decloak anxiety disorders and strip them of the false conclusion that they are "normal"? In Claire's case, comparing known symptoms of anxiety with her own life experiences was enough to open her eyes to the possibility that she—and everyone else who had ever labeled her "high-strung"—had been wrong.

In this chapter, that is our goal. As long as the symptoms of anxiety are considered "normal," they will simply be tolerated and left alone. While it may be painful to do so, we will take an unflinching look at these symptoms and the costs they impose on those who suffer from anxiety. By doing this, my hope is that you will come to see, as Claire did, that you may be suffering from an anxiety disorder and that healing is within reach at long last.

Little Left Untouched

Allow me to list some of the many areas of life that are negatively affected by debilitating anxiety. Under each category, I'll provide a brief description and then step aside to let a few of the people I have met over the years speak for themselves. Perhaps in their voices you'll recognize your own pain or that of someone you love—and find hope that relief is available. Untreated anxiety can negatively influence all of the following areas.

Physical and Mental Well-Being

An article published by Harvard Medical School states, "Anxiety prepares us to confront a crisis by putting the body on alert. But its physical effects can be counterproductive, causing light-headedness, nausea, diarrhea, and frequent urination. And when it persists, anxiety can take a toll on our mental and physical health."[3]

That's before you consider how anxiety can disrupt healthy eating and sleep habits and inhibit proper exercise. Furthermore, anxiety has been linked to a number of other disorders, including heart disease, migraine headaches, insomnia, chronic respiratory disorders, and gastrointestinal disorders. Untreated anxiety often makes dealing with associated physical conditions much more difficult.

To make matters worse, anxiety often goes hand in hand with other mental disorders such as depression. The impulse to self-medicate, for example, causes many people who suffer from anxiety to develop a substance abuse disorder or addictions to other harmful behaviors.

Deborah shared this about her experience: "I can't sleep more than three or four hours at a time, because I'm playing back in my head all the mistakes I made that day. So I'm always exhausted. I honestly don't know how I get through a day. Sometimes I can't breathe, and I feel like I will die."

Social Freedom and Enjoyment

People with severe symptoms of anxiety report being terrified to ride in an elevator with strangers. They fear ordering food at a restaurant, answering an unexpected phone call, being caught in casual conversation with a coworker at the office copy machine—or any of a thousand other daily contacts with people that are bound to occur.

What are the chances, then, that they would choose to spend a day at an amusement park with friends, or attend a crowded concert, or say yes when invited to a going-away party for a coworker at a popular nightclub? Anxiety has a way of shrinking a person's world down to a handful of places, activities, and experiences that feel "safe." And safety, to many people suffering from anxiety, is not just a matter of physical security. It's about limiting the possibility of saying or doing something that might invite the vulnerability of ridicule or judgment.

As Marcus told me, "When I feel like I've made a mistake or said something stupid, I'm absolutely haunted by it for days. I relive it over and over, just certain that everybody thinks I'm an idiot. So I just stay away from places where I might have to say something. My anxiety robs me of the confidence to even be in the room."

Romantic Relationships

Given the description above, it's not hard to imagine how difficult it is for a person with an untreated anxiety disorder to even think about dating, much less to actually go out with someone new.

Dating can be nerve-racking for anyone. By definition, it requires you to let your guard down and allow yourself to become transparent to someone else. Being seen as they are—and possibly judged for it—is the very last thing someone suffering from anxiety feels confident enough to do. In spite of desiring romantic fulfillment as much as anyone, a person with anxiety often does everything possible to avoid it.

Courtney related her heartbreaking experience: "There's this guy at work who once asked me out for lunch. I couldn't even answer him. I just turned around and left. That was ten months ago, and I'm still terrified of running into him in the hallway. So I only leave my tiny office when I have no other choice. I literally feel like I will throw up."

Other times, people riddled with anxiety will "mood manipulate" through excessive sexual acting out. They will try to address their anxiety by overcompensating through inappropriate sexual activity. This, of course, does nothing to relieve anxiety, and most often only increases it.

Professional Opportunity and Success

Imagine a company employee who takes the stairs to avoid elevator small talk, rarely enters the break room, never accepts a lunch invitation from coworkers or supervisors, and speaks mostly in monosyllables on those occasions when avoidance fails. This person probably is the first to arrive and the last to leave every day, but their work may be only so-so because they never ask for help or feedback for fear of being thought incompetent.

How would you rate this person's chances for career advancement? Or of being among the first to be laid off when the need arises? It is impossible to overstate the cost of untreated anxiety in the workplace— measured first in misery for those who live like this but also in lost potential, lower wages, and job insecurity. Beyond that, businesses themselves lose the full, productive services of otherwise qualified and competent employees.

According to the World Health Organization (WHO), depression and anxiety have a significant economic impact: "Depression and anxiety disorders cost the global economy US$1 trillion each year in lost productivity." But don't forget that "lost productivity" for the economy also means lost or lower income for individuals and families. Anxiety becomes a very real limit on prosperity and well-being. In a bit of hopeful news, the WHO report goes on to estimate that every one dollar spent on treatment yields four dollars "in improved health and productivity."[4]

Howard summed up the problem like this: "I want to succeed at work. My family depends on me. But I freeze up anytime I'm asked a question or put on the spot. It's like my brain turns into the small end of a funnel and a million things are trying to rush through at once, so nothing comes out. Then later I want to cry because I have anxiety over my anxiety. Being so afraid all the time makes me more afraid. Every time I hear my name called, I think I'm going to be fired."

Parenting

Among the symptoms of uncontrolled anxiety are extreme sensitivity to loud and startling noises, an inability to relax when things are out of place, fear of the unexpected or the chaotic, exaggerated irritability, difficulty sleeping, and excessive fear that something bad will happen to yourself or someone you love.

Anyone who has been around small children will immediately recognize the problem: kids just being kids will trip all of these triggers multiple times each and every day. Parenting can tax anyone's personal resources, but to the person who already struggles to manage symptoms of severe anxiety, it takes positively heroic levels of resolve to be present and nurturing. The stress can take a heavy toll on the whole family. Children often live in a more restrictive environment than is healthy or find their own social options limited by their parent's impulse to isolate. And the experience of trying to be a good parent with one hand tied behind your back has a way of becoming a feedback loop that only exacerbates anxiety.

Then, all of that often combines to put undue pressure on the other parent and, by extension, on the marriage.

Here's Megan's story: "I start every day determined to relax with my kids and be less jumpy and demanding. But I fail. Every scream, every bang, and I nearly come out of my skin. My husband comes home, and I can barely talk. I'm terrified he thinks I'm crazy and a terrible mother."

Civic Engagement

Imagine how a person who is afraid of crowds and who avoids confining spaces at all costs would feel about going to vote on Election Day. How would the prospect of attending a public meeting on an important issue feel to someone reluctant to speak up even when ordering fast food at a drive-thru window? In a very real sense, untreated anxiety has the potential to rob people of their voice in society—and, conversely, to rob society of their unique and valuable perspective.

Anton cringed when he shared this memory: "Some people from the homeowner's association came to our door to ask a few questions about how we felt things were going in the neighborhood. I had a million things

I wanted to say, but all I could manage was, 'I don't know,' because I was nervous about saying the wrong thing. I felt so ashamed when they left."

Spiritual Resilience

People of faith often find it difficult to acknowledge that prayer and other spiritual healing practices must be accompanied by the help and expertise of medical professionals. It is sadly common for those people to conclude that their inability to get the upper hand on their disorder by appealing to God alone is a sign of failure—theirs or God's. As a result, they can lose faith at exactly the moment when they need it most.

Faith and medicine do not stand in either-or opposition to each other. Instead, they work hand in glove, because committing to and successfully sticking with treatment very often requires inner strength and resolve that only trust in God can deliver. Left untreated, anxiety can ultimately cut you off from both sources of help.

In addition, a key part of any spiritual practice is active involvement in a community of like-minded people. As we have seen, attending church or other similar gatherings sounds daunting to someone with an anxiety disorder. With their faith already eroding, and cut off from the community that might offer comfort, these people become vulnerable to deep hopelessness and despair.

Donette put it this way: "I grew up going to church, and I loved it. I sang in the choir and even did a few solos in front of the whole congregation. But somewhere along the way, my anxiety just made it harder and harder, until I finally had to quit. It was either that or spend Sunday mornings hiding in a ladies' room stall."

A Way Out of the Dark

Think back to Claire, whom I told you about at the beginning of this chapter. After our first meeting, when she could only cling to the worn-out conclusion that she simply was what she was, with nothing to be done, she learned to see herself differently. Taking a hard look at all the ways she'd settled for suffering when it wasn't necessary motivated her to engage with treatments that eventually led to lasting improvement and healing.

The good news is that, in both respects, Claire's story is universal. Yes, millions of people struggle with hardships they don't know are, in fact, symptoms of a treatable condition. But millions more, like Claire, have found their way to renewed health and well-being. You get to decide which path you'll take—and I have faith that you will take the path toward healing.

Your Personal Reset Plan

One effect of living with untreated anxiety for years is that you lose sight of what life could be like without it. You adjust to a distorted view of normal. Use these exercises to break that pattern and reclaim your hope for a better future.

1. **Engage with others who experience anxiety.** Self-isolation is often one of the first things people in mental and emotional distress do to protect themselves. It is also one of the most detrimental. Left alone, it's easy for you to conclude, as Claire did, that your condition is simply who you are, with nothing more to be done. Listening to the struggles of others and seeing the similarities between your story and theirs can break that spell. Furthermore, others may have found solutions that will work for you as well, or you'll have something to offer them. It's called community, and it is always a step in the right direction. Answer these questions:

   • Who do I know who has experienced anxiety that I can talk to?

   _____

   _____

   • What online, national, or local groups or communities support people who experience anxiety? (A Google search might help you answer this question.) _____

   _____

2. **Make a wish list of things you would do, if not for anxiety in your life.** Be bold, and be specific. Think back to dreams you had when

you were younger—to learn to sail, take an art-history tour through Italy, write a screenplay, or start a business. Considering these things will help you see more clearly what anxiety has cost you—freedom, enjoyment, opportunity, and achievement. The purpose is not to remind you of pain but to fuel your motivation to do what is necessary to reclaim all that you've lost. Give yourself permission to dream big. You are worth it!

3. **In your journal, explore your reasons for wanting to heal from anxiety.** Write this sentence and then complete it for each reason you can think of: "I yearn to be free of anxiety because . . ." Some examples might include "I want to feel more healthy" or "I want to build better relationships" or "I want to explore the world, not hide from it." In this exercise you are reclaiming two powerful words that you may have lost along the way: "I want."

4. **Pick one thing from your wish list above, and start planning for it to come true.** Your mind may still tell you it's impossible, but that doesn't matter. Make a plan anyway, in detail. Courage (and healing) is found when we act in spite of fear, not wait for it to disappear.

5. **Create a storyboard or collage of imagery that describes what you want from your life.** Yes, this will make you feel like you are back in school—the magazines, the scissors for clipping out images, the smell of Elmer's glue. Let the art embody your desire. Place it somewhere you'll see it every day.

CHAPTER 6

This Is Your Brain on Anxiety

*Anxiety takes a toll on brain performance . . .
and vice versa.*

"I just haven't been at my best," Diane reflected at the start of our second visit.

You met Diane in chapter 3. She had sought help because she was feeling stressed, anxious, and exhausted. Now, as we began our second session, she seemed a bit more comfortable talking with me about her situation. Eye contact came more naturally, and while she loosely held the chair's decorative pillow, she didn't clutch it to her torso as she had the week before.

But the weariness was still evident in her voice. "I slept a little better—one night," she continued, "but I'm still in and out of sleep. I'm not thinking as well as I used to. And I can't seem to shake this nervous feeling in my gut."

I glanced at my notes from our first visit, when I had jotted down several of the stressors that were foremost on Diane's mind:

- pressures at her job
- conflict with a teenager at home
- coordinating transportation to numerous events for two younger children

- her husband's constant travel
- her mother's serious illness
- serving on busy church and community committees

At the end of that session, I had challenged Diane to write down each stressor that occurred to her during the week and ask herself, *What's good about this?* She was to write a thoughtful answer to each question.

I asked, "How did you do on your assignment this week?"

A sheepish smile tugged at the corners of her mouth. "Well . . . good and not so good," she admitted. She leaned over and fished a small notebook from her purse on the floor. She flipped a page, then said, "I only got one: 'Coordinating transportation for my younger children.' I haven't thought of any for the others . . . yet."

"*Yet* being the operative word," I assured her. "You'll get there. But what did you write for the stress that you feel coordinating the children's transportation?"

Aloud, Diane read what she had composed:

Okay, so what's good about the hassle of getting the kids to and from their weekly activities? Well . . . it's a God-given time for natural (hopefully positive) conversation with each of them. A time to encourage and affirm them. To listen to what's on their minds and show how much I love them and care for them. (Gotta change my attitude!)

"That's all I've got." Her voice trailed off.

"But it's a great start!" I said. "That's the idea, Diane. And in the coming days, I'm confident you'll be able to do the same for the others. Now tell me, did it help?"

"Some," she admitted. "A couple of times the kids were particularly squirrelly, and I didn't respond well. But there were two afternoons when I had better prepared myself ahead of time, and I actually enjoyed the experience. I turned the bad stress into kind of good stress."

We both chuckled at that. It was a good start indeed, but as Diane had pointed out at the beginning of this visit, her struggle with worry, stress, and anxiety remained very real. We still had work to do.

Shifting gears, I said, "You mentioned when you arrived today that you don't feel at your best. Tell me more about that."

"Well, like I said, I still have this constant jittery feeling. It's as if I've consumed two gallons of strong coffee. And I don't feel as sharp mentally. It's like I'm preoccupied with a tension that I can't explain. It's all so exhausting."

I continued to probe, and Diane did her best to answer my questions. I assured her that what she was describing was not at all unusual for people struggling with anxiety.

Like Diane, you may not be able to shake that deep-down feeling that something's just not right, that the stress you're under keeps you from being at your best, thinking clearly, and enjoying life. You may even feel that you're losing your mind or losing mastery over thought processes and your ability to cope.

Since your brain controls your mind and body, it's important to understand the relationship between anxiety and brain function. Here are some examples:

- In a study at the University of British Columbia, researchers found that patients with mood and anxiety disorders have significantly decreased activation in regions of the brain that regulate cognitive processes and emotions. Brain scans also showed hyperactivity in the brain regions associated with emotional thought processing.[1]
- A study conducted by scientists at Weill Cornell Medical College "amassed evidence directly linking susceptibility to social anxiety disorder with problems in a neural circuit that runs between a part of the cerebral cortex called the orbitofrontal cortex (OFC) and the BLA, a part of the amygdala, an area deep in the brain involved in processing emotions."[2]
- Research published in the journal *Biological Psychiatry* found that sustained anxiety prevents the brain from growing new brain cells, a process called neurogenesis. Neurogenesis is crucial to the brain's ability to function at its peak as well as to general mental health.[3]

Numerous studies have shown that chronic anxiety can take a negative toll on brain function. And as though that's not enough, anxiety-affected brain chemistry can then circle back to reinforce and sustain anxiety.

It's a vicious cycle that can make you feel helpless, hopeless, and life weary. But a basic grasp of how your brain works under anxiety can better prepare you to break the anxiety cycle.

Understanding how significantly brain function contributes to anxiety will further show that this condition isn't something you can just "get over" through determination or an act of the will. Your brain is a high-powered engine that sometimes overworks or underworks, causing problems such as anxiety.

Even more important, your brain is not static and unchangeable; it is dynamic and adaptable. Certain therapies—many of which we will discuss in the chapters ahead—can reset your brain's performance to maximize its efficiency and minimize its contribution to anxiety.

THE FIGHT-OR-FLIGHT RESPONSE

Generalized anxiety disorder (and other anxiety disorders) is related to the body's fight-or-flight response. The same response that your body has when confronted with a legitimate threat (like meeting a bear in the woods) can be activated by a host of triggers in the anxious mind, flooding your system with three major stress hormones: adrenaline, norepinephrine, and cortisol. While these hormones are helpful when you encounter a legitimate threat, they can be harmful in a constant state of threat.

Adrenaline prepares your body to respond to a threat.

Norepinephrine stimulates the mind to quicken reactions and sharpen focus.

Cortisol is slower acting and stabilizes the body's reactions to a threat.

What Goes On in Your Brain

When stress and anxiety kick in, so does your brain, as several neurological processes go to work at once. Harvard Medical School researchers offer this glimpse into the process:

> Generalized anxiety disorder, like other types of anxiety, probably arises from an excessive activation of the brain mechanism underlying fear and the fight-or-flight response.
>
> When someone confronts a dangerous situation, two brain

circuits become active and relay sensory information about the danger—such as the sight and smell of fire—to different parts of the brain. One circuit extends to the cerebral cortex, the outermost part of the brain, which is used for thinking and decision making. The other circuit involves a deeper structure called the amygdala that is central to emotional processing. The amygdala monitors the body's reactions to the environment, evaluates an event's emotional significance, and organizes responses that a person may or may not be conscious of.[4]

In fact, two parts of the brain play a key role in anxiety: the amygdala and the hippocampus. The almond-shaped amygdala acts as a communications center. It receives messages from the parts of your brain that are responsible for interpreting sensory data and raises the alarm to the rest of the brain if it perceives a threat. This, in turn, causes fear and anxiety.

Another part of your brain, the hippocampus, is responsible for saving threats a person has experienced as memories. Scientists have found that the hippocampus seems to be smaller in people who have suffered serious trauma such as military combat or childhood abuse, and thus it may contribute to anxiety by linking present-day stressors to previous trauma.[5] (However, much research remains to be done about the relation of the hippocampus to anxiety disorders.)

Then what happens? When your brain registers a real or perceived stressor, your natural fight-or-flight response goes into action and floods your system with three major stress hormones: *adrenaline, norepinephrine,* and *cortisol.*

Adrenaline

You have probably heard adrenaline referred to as the fight-or-flight hormone. When the brain senses a dangerous situation, it raises the alarm, which causes the adrenal glands to produce adrenaline in response. Adrenaline (and norepinephrine) account for your reflex responses to stress or danger.

For example, imagine you're on a hiking trail when suddenly a bear comes crashing through the woods toward you. Instinctively, you freeze and prepare to flee, your heart pounds, and your throat goes dry. But then the bear crosses the path and continues on its way through the woods. You're safe, but it sure frightened you, and it all seems a bit surreal. That is adrenaline doing its job—adrenaline prepares your body to act in response to the threat.

Along with increased heart rate, adrenaline also provides a surge of energy, which you might need to escape from the threatening situation. In addition, the adrenaline rush helps you focus your attention on actions to take.

Norepinephrine

A hormone similar to adrenaline, norepinephrine is released from both the adrenal glands and the brain. Like adrenaline, the primary role of norepinephrine is arousal. This means you will feel more alert and aware when under stress or facing a threat. Your reactions will be quickened and your focus sharpened.

Another function of norepinephrine is to shift blood flow away from parts of the body where it might not be needed in the moment to parts where your body has a more immediate need.

Adrenaline and norepinephrine serve similar functions, but in combination they act as a fail-safe for each other. If one hormone is not supplied for some reason, the other will kick in to deliver needed energy to address the dangerous situation.

Cortisol

Cortisol, as opposed to adrenaline and norepinephrine, takes longer— minutes instead of seconds—to deliver and for its effects to be experienced during a stressful event. It helps to stabilize and regulate the body's functions in the midst of a threat.

While this is great when you're facing an immediate danger, unfortunately, when you fret over a problem for a period of time, the body *continuously* releases cortisol.[6]

Again, these three hormones are helpful if you encounter a bear in the woods, but sometimes our bodies produce these hormones in non-fight-or-flight situations, which over time can lead to significant health problems.

NEW PROMISE OF "NEUROPLASTICITY"

A recent development in the study of brain science is neuroplasticity, which means the ability of the brain to change its structure and reorganize its patterns of responding.

As described by William Shiel, MD, neuroplasticity is "the brain's ability to reorganize itself by forming new neural connections throughout life. Neuroplasticity allows the neurons (nerve cells) in the brain to compensate for injury and disease and to adjust their activities in response to new situations or to changes in their environment."[7]

This offers significant hope for the treatment of anxiety (and other issues) because your brain

- does not have to react in a certain way permanently;
- has the ability to change to be more resistant to anxiety;
- is capable of shifting your thoughts, feelings, and reactions;
- has circuitry that can be rewired; and
- can "reframe" stressful or traumatic experiences to bring relief and healing.

Healthy in Moderation

I realize that stress hormones don't make for the most fascinating reading, but it should be helpful and encouraging to note that the stress hormones we've been surveying are not necessarily bad. In fact, they are healthy defense mechanisms carefully designed into our systems. I agree with the psalmist who wrote, "I praise you [his Creator God] because I am fearfully and wonderfully made; your works are wonderful, I know that full well."[8] We can be thankful that our loving Creator has built those systems into our bodies to protect and assist us in the stresses of life.

But as with all good things, too much can become unhealthy. If adrenaline, norepinephrine, and cortisol continue to surge indefinitely, long after the immediate stressor is behind you, the continuing state of arousal can become harmful to both your mind and your body. This is what plagues you with that disquieting sense of unrest in your gut, stresses your mind so you can't think clearly, keeps you from sound sleep, and makes you irritable and weary. This is anxiety.

Which leads to a logical question as we wrap up this quick lesson on what happens in the brain: Does anxiety alter brain chemistry, or does compromised brain chemistry cause anxiety?

The answer is yes.

While there is still much research to be done, current science seems to confirm that both answers are correct. Anxiety, which by definition is a more generalized discomfort or concern over an indefinite, less-defined situation, does indeed cause the brain to try to compensate with a prolonged supply of stress hormones. In this respect, extended anxiety affects brain chemistry. But we've also seen that brain chemistry, when not in proper balance, can extend and amplify existing anxiety with all its undesirable side effects.

So, yes: anxiety affects the brain, and the brain affects anxiety. If not dealt with, it's a vicious cycle. This is what Diane faced in the early days of her therapy.

The Good News

The good news for Diane, and for you, is that "your brain on anxiety" is eminently fixable if treated promptly and appropriately. Reversing the toxicity and harm of anxiety—in fact, your propensity toward anxiety itself—is very doable. But it's not always easy. It requires diligence and discipline as you employ the practical, whole-person strategies we're discussing in this book. (It may even require medicinal help, but that's neither a complete nor a permanent solution, as we'll see in the next chapter.)

My second visit with Diane was drawing to a close. She had jotted some notes as I shared the effects of anxiety on brain chemistry and vice versa and nodded in agreement at how certain information seemed to help explain her own struggles. At the end of our visit, she was eager to proceed with further counseling. She was fully committed to doing whatever it took to control worry and stress, conquer anxiety, and enjoy peace of mind.

She was all in.

Are you?

I thought so.

As mentioned in the sidebar earlier in this chapter, while brain chemistry affects anxiety and anxiety affects brain chemistry, the promise of neuroplasticity—the brain's incredible ability to adapt, reorganize, and rewire itself—means that with a comprehensive, "all in" approach, you *can* reset your anxiety.

Your Personal Reset Plan

Please invest some thoughtful time responding to this personal reset plan. Then, in the next chapter, we'll explore whether medication might play a role in your journey to wholeness and vitality.

1. **Review the descriptions of the three stress hormones.** For ten or fifteen minutes, write in your journal about a time in your life when you found yourself in fight-or-flight mode. Consider the discussion on eustress and distress from chapter 3 (see pages 36–38). Was the time you journaled about eustress or distress? In what ways were the "fight-or-flight" hormones of adrenaline, norepinephrine, and cortisol helpful to you?

2. **Rehearse what new information will assist you moving forward.** What specifically did you learn in this chapter that helps explain what goes on in your brain during anxiety? How will these facts help you in the future? Write out your answer in a succinct sentence or two.

3. **Find a visual explanation of the brain-anxiety connection.** Go on YouTube or another online source and enter the words *neuroscience and anxiety* or *brain and anxiety*. Seeing a visual depiction of the concepts presented in this chapter may help you understand more fully how anxiety affects the brain (and vice versa).

4. **Reread Psalm 139:14, quoted in this chapter.** Or access the entire Psalm 139 online. In what ways does the knowledge that you are "fearfully and wonderfully made" encourage you on your journey to health and vitality?

CHAPTER 7

If You Want to Chill, Should You Take a Pill?

Medication can help, but be cautious about its being a long-term solution.

Most people would find it difficult to imagine a time before pharmaceutical drugs dominated the practice of medicine. These days, it's impossible to watch television, scan the internet, or open a magazine without seeing medication advertisements promising relief from some malady or another.

Yet people tend to forget that the science of pharmacology is less than two hundred years old. Apothecaries have prescribed plant-based remedies for millennia, but the pharmaceutical industry we know today didn't begin its ascent until the mid-nineteenth century. That's when advances in synthetic chemistry provided scientists with the means to systematically alter the structure of existing compounds and tailor their effects on the human body.

No doubt modern civilization owes a debt to early researchers who teased out the secrets of synthetic painkillers, antibiotics, insulin, antiepileptic drugs, and so on. At the turn of the twentieth century, for example, the top three killers in the United States were pneumonia, tuberculosis, and diarrhea—infectious diseases that no longer pose serious threats to Americans today.[1] Pharmacology—along with improved hygiene, education, and our advancing understanding of biological systems—has played a huge role in dethroning a number of diseases and disorders that our ancestors saw as invincible enemies.

Those successes certainly include the more recent development of psychotropic drugs used to aid people who suffer from mental disorders such as schizophrenia, severe depression, and anxiety. Without question, some people benefit significantly from the stabilizing effects of drugs like Xanax, Zoloft, and Prozac.

Still, I know I'm not alone in wondering if the trend toward applying pharmaceutical fixes to every ailment has not swung dangerously out of balance. The deadly and devastating prescription opioid crisis—which has finally begun receiving the regulatory attention it deserves—is just one dimension of the problem. The misuse and overuse of hundreds of drugs may represent an even more entrenched challenge. Consider these numbers gathered by the US Centers for Disease Control and Prevention between 2013 and 2017:

- percent of persons using at least one prescription drug in the past thirty days: 48.4 percent
- percent of persons using three or more prescription drugs in the past thirty days: 24 percent
- number of drugs ordered or provided during doctor visits: 2.9 billion
- percent of doctor visits involving drug therapy: 73.9 percent
- number of drugs given or prescribed during hospital emergency room visits: 368.5 million
- percent of hospital emergency room visits involving drug therapy: 81.1 percent[2]

That's almost half the population using at least one prescription drug and nearly one in four people taking three or more at a time. Further, according to figures compiled by Statista, the total number of prescriptions dispensed in the United States in 2018 climbed to 4.21 billion—and by the end of 2020, prescribed drug expenditures in the United States will likely reach almost $360 billion.[3]

In 2017, *Consumer Reports* published a feature article called "Too Many Meds? America's Love Affair with Prescription Medication." Author Teresa Carr writes,

To be sure, some people—especially those who are uninsured or underinsured—don't get all of the care they need, including medication.

Still, many Americans—and their physicians—have come to think that every symptom, every hint of disease requires a drug, says Vinay Prasad, M.D., an assistant professor of medicine at Oregon Health & Science University. "The question is, where did people get that idea? They didn't invent it," he says. "They were spoon-fed that notion by the culture that we're steeped in."

It's a culture, say the experts we consulted, encouraged by intense marketing by drug companies and an increasingly harried healthcare system that makes dashing off a prescription the easiest way to address a patient's concerns.[4]

The report goes on to describe three broad areas of problematic prescription drug use: taking too many drugs at once, taking drugs that aren't needed, and taking drugs prematurely. The consequences of falling into one or more of these categories in your own use of medications can be quite severe, frequently causing more harm than good.

The Math of Mental Health

What does this mean for our conversation about how best to heal from detrimental anxiety? Only that understanding the proper role of anti-anxiety medication in your recovery is nowhere near as simple as some would like you to believe. To balance the equation requires us to account for many complex factors, not just one.

Here's a series of key questions to help you make an informed decision for yourself:

What Do Anti-Anxiety Medications Do, and How Do They Do It?

Without my getting too technical, drugs that have a mood-altering effect fall into two general categories: benzodiazepines and SSRIs—or selective serotonin reuptake inhibitors.

"Benzos," as benzodiazepines are often called, function like typical sedatives, shutting down neurotransmitters specifically related to thinking and worry. They are fast-acting compared to SSRIs, offering much-needed relief in extreme cases, and they pose little risk of fatal overdose.

SSRIs, by contrast, do not suppress neurotransmitters but rather attempt to bring them back into balance and increase the availability of naturally occurring "good-feeling" chemicals in the brain, such as serotonin, norepinephrine, and dopamine.

What Are the Risks?

It's tempting to think of benzos as "magic pills" because of their ability to offer relief quickly. However, the list of potentially harmful side effects argues for great caution:

- a high risk of addiction with prolonged use, even periods as short as a couple of weeks
- withdrawal symptoms that can include seizures, physical craving, and increased anxiety
- impaired long-term brain function[5]

In addition to these effects, it's worth noting that one kind of benzo called Rohypnol is well-known as a "date rape" drug for its ability to significantly impair or suspend a person's ability to resist unwanted sexual advances.[6]

Benzos may provide momentary psychological and emotional stability to help you regain the upper hand when anxiety symptoms have spun out of control, but sustained use is simply not advisable.

SSRIs have their own risks. Though recent studies indicate that SSRIs may perform better than placebos in controlled experiments—seemingly settling a decades-old debate—doubt still remains as to their broad effectiveness. A 2019 Medical News Today article explains:

To a greater or lesser degree, all the factors below and more have combined to produce a situation where scientists are still not clear whether antidepressants work better than a placebo:

- Pharmaceutical companies are keen to market the drugs they have spent years designing and testing.
- Doctors want to provide medication to those with a reduced quality of life.
- Patients are keen to try anything that might improve their well-being.
- Journals are more likely to publish studies with positive findings.

The latest analysis to form part of this ongoing battle comes from scientists at the Nordic Cochrane Centre in Denmark. This time, the authors conclude that the current level of evidence in support of antidepressants is not sufficient to prove that they work better than placebo.[7]

In any case, SSRIs work more slowly than benzos, taking on average four to six weeks to produce noticeable improvement. They are not considered addictive, but abrupt cessation can cause withdrawal symptoms such as nausea, dizziness, lethargy, and increased anxiety. Other negative side effects include

- health complications when combined with other drugs;
- insomnia, nervousness, sexual dysfunction, and reduced appetite; and
- in some cases, increased thoughts and feelings about suicide.

Again, research indicates that no anti-anxiety medication should be considered a long-term solution or singular fix for mental health disorders.

What about Marijuana as an Option for Anxiety Relief?

As long as we are addressing anti-anxiety medications, this is a good place to discuss marijuana as a potential medical and therapeutic choice for anxiety relief. As you know, marijuana legalization (for both recreational use and medicinal applications) has proliferated in recent years. Attitudes about marijuana have changed considerably among many people as more and more acceptance of the drug has spread through our country.

These days, hardly a week goes by without someone asking me, "I'm thinking about using marijuana to help me calm down—should I?" And often people phrase the issue as a statement, not a question: "I use marijuana to help me relax and stay mellow."

Is this a wise choice and a viable option? We need to acknowledge that this is a relatively new phenomenon, and much scientific research is currently being conducted, with much more to come in the years ahead. Still, early and credible research is emerging that gives us indications about marijuana use as a remedy for mental health issues, including anxiety. Here's a sampling of reports on the subject:

- According to a CBS News report: "New research says marijuana is not helpful in treating mental health problems. There hasn't been a lot of substantive research on using marijuana to treat mental health problems such as depression and anxiety, but the latest science doesn't find many benefits. Medical marijuana can be therapeutic for certain conditions like seizures, but it doesn't appear to be very helpful for mental health issues, according to new research that reviewed 83 studies on medicinal marijuana, synthetic marijuana and marijuana-derived products."[8]
- From a *USA Today* article titled "Is Marijuana Linked to Psychosis, Schizophrenia? It's Contentious, but Doctors, Feds Say Yes": "A number of physicians and parents are pushing back against the long-held assertion of users and advocates that marijuana is a safe, benign and even beneficial drug. . . . Advocates on either side of the marijuana debate have different interpretations of the connection reported in a National Academies cannabis study in 2017 and other studies. In March, *The Lancet*, a British medical journal, reported a two to five times higher risk of psychotic disorders for daily consumers of high-THC marijuana compared with people who never used."[9]
- A *Time* magazine report said, "Even though many consumers turn to cannabis compounds, known as cannabinoids, to soothe issues like depression and anxiety, these substances don't seem to do much for mental health, according to a new research review published in the journal *Lancet Psychiatry*."[10]

As my team of medical and psychotherapy experts and I have studied this issue carefully, we have developed a position for our clients and potential clients. What follows is "The Center Policy Statement of Marijuana Use," which I include here to explain our beliefs on the subject:

> While The Center acknowledges the ongoing debate about using marijuana for certain medical purposes, including terminal illness and certain debilitating health conditions, cannabis remains an unapproved (per FDA) psychoactive substance without substantial evidence that it effectively treats complex and comorbid mental health conditions.[11] The long-term effects of marijuana include impaired brain activity in areas responsible for memory, learning, and impulse control.[12] This runs counter to the goal of actively processing negative emotions rather than suppressing them, and is not in line with The Center's whole-person health and wellness model.
>
> Furthermore, smoking is not a safe means of drug delivery even for patients with specific reasons to use cannabis. Products are not standardized nor held to the same requirements as FDA approved medical treatments.[13] The behaviors, smells, and general atmosphere that accompany marijuana use are serious hurdles to recovery for both the individual and the general therapeutic milieu of The Center.
>
> With the exception of regulated, FDA-approved cannabinoid medications, The Center rejects the recommendation of cannabis as a palliative for its clients. Nor will clients be allowed to use marijuana recreationally during their treatment process. Cannabis use includes smoking, vaping, oils and/or any edible product made with cannabis. In individual discussions with clients who have questions about medicinal marijuana, we direct our staff to recommend the client first establish a long-term relationship with a physician who is well versed in recognizing and treating substance abuse and addiction.

What Are the Alternatives?

Now we've come to the most important question of all. Anti-anxiety medications can offer relief but not long-term *hope*. For that, you need what we at The Center promote and advocate with every client and every mental health issue: the whole-person approach to healing.

Full-Spectrum Recovery

The whole-person philosophy is rooted in the belief that human beings are not machines that can be understood in mechanical terms. Modern medicine has done a remarkable job of describing how the human organism functions, governed by the laws of physics, chemistry, and genetics. We've done less well at accounting for the role that human thoughts, feelings, and choices play in our wellness. We are complex creatures with minds and bodies that are seamlessly interwoven into a single living system, and our maladies cannot be simplistically blamed on any single source of trouble. Even a good auto mechanic knows it is pointless to keep changing fouled spark plugs without searching for underlying causes.

In your quest to heal from anxiety, "underlying causes" can include many factors that our society considers far removed from modern medicine:

- spiritual faith and practices
- a willingness to forgive others and yourself
- integrity in your relationships
- a sense of belonging and purpose in your community
- daily choices about what sorts of images and ideas you feed your mind
- addictions of all kinds, not just those that involve substances

It's true that genetics, innate temperament, and certain imbalances in brain chemistry also have a role to play, and these are the things that medication can help to balance and improve. But the purpose of pharmaceutical aids is not to carry the entire load but to hold physical propensity toward anxiety in abeyance—*while you also do the whole-person work that's necessary for lasting recovery.*

If you have chosen to make medication a balanced and responsible part of your treatment plan, there's nothing wrong with that. Just be sure it's only part of the plan, not its entirety. Throughout the next part of this book you'll find many practical suggestions for how to do that.

Your Personal Reset Plan

It's perfectly understandable why a person in the grip of severe anxiety would reach for a quick fix, available for the cost of a doctor visit and a prescription. But as in many areas of life, the quick fix is also best viewed as temporary. To be sure that the consequences of unbalanced medication use do not become another challenge you have to overcome down the road, take time to evaluate where you currently stand in relationship to prescription drugs and your willingness to change it if needed.

1. **Complete an honest inventory of the drugs entering your body.** Make a list of every medication you currently take, prescription and over-the-counter. Then make sure the list includes alcohol, nicotine products, and any illicit drugs you routinely use. Leave room after each medication to write down more information. No one will see your inventory unless you choose to share it, so be honest. The purpose is to create the opportunity to see clearly whether a problem has begun to form in your life.

2. **Answer these questions for each drug: Why am I taking this? How long have I taken it?** By taking this step, you will remind yourself what you want each medication to do for you and be able to determine whether each medication is accomplishing what you want it to accomplish.

3. **Research potential side effects.** Are you fully aware of the known, potentially negative effects the drugs you take may cause? The truth is, few people are. We are usually so eager for relief that we minimize or even ignore the risks. Even less common is for people to have a clear idea how various drugs interact with each other in the body. Go back to the list you made in step number one and research possible side effects for each medication. Write them down.

4. **Self-assess your experience of these effects.** Next, take an honest look at whether some of these consequences are already present in your life. It is not uncommon for people to start taking new medications in an attempt to alleviate the side effects of other drugs. It's

important at this stage for you to see clearly if any of your symptoms can be addressed simply by reducing or eliminating certain prescriptions. Place a check mark on your list beside side effects that already apply to you:

- blurry vision
- constipation
- dizziness
- drowsiness or fatigue
- dry mouth
- feeling agitated or restless
- headaches
- increased blood pressure
- loss of appetite
- nausea
- sexual problems or erectile dysfunction
- sleep problems
- sweating more than usual
- upset stomach
- weight gain

5. **Ask yourself,** *Am I willing to consider alternative ways to achieve what I want the medication to deliver?* Once you've listed the medications you take, considered their potentially negative effects, and inventoried which of those you may already be experiencing, you may have all the motivation you need to commit to the whole-person approach I advocate so strongly for. That doesn't mean abandoning medication as a potentially helpful tool, certainly not overnight or without the guidance of your physician. But it is an opportunity to add those steps that have greater promise to deliver lasting change.

PART 2

The Pathway to Peace

Overcoming Obstacles
& Finding Freedom

CHAPTER 8

Inventory Your Inner World

Look inward to improve your outlook.

By now I trust that you see for yourself that severe anxiety is not caused by just one thing but results from a poisonous brew made of many ingredients. We've looked at the common contributors—everything from genetics and brain chemistry to temperament and past trauma. Some of the causes are inherited, and others are circumstantial.

So far we've examined these various elements like the parts of a disassembled engine—one at a time. Now let's put all the pieces together so you can see how the components function as a whole and amplify one another in a predictable progression into fearfulness.

First, however, let's be clear on one very important point. The purpose of such a close look at how anxiety can grow in your life from one stage to another is not to give the impression that this is inevitable. It is not a chemical reaction that always behaves the same way, governed by immutable laws. The aim here is to find those places where the power of free will and conscious choice can breach your mind's habitual defenses and put an end to your war with anxiety for good.

The typical progression I'm about to describe flows both ways. The road that led you into captivity to your fear can still lead you out again.

An Unfortunate Beginning

I met Allen after he'd grudgingly admitted to himself that medication alone was not going to solve his lifelong battle with anxiety. His primary care physician had rightly concluded that Allen needed help. Step one was to prescribe a pharmaceutical aid to bring his severe panic attacks under control. She also referred him to a therapist for additional treatment, but he didn't keep the appointment.

"I saw no value in talking about stuff forever," Allen told me. "I just wanted the magic pill." He got the medication but quickly found that, while it helped in some respects, the core of his problem remained intact and as seemingly intractable as ever. It didn't help that over the years Allen had tried to medicate himself with various substances and behaviors that now bordered on full-fledged addictions.

After months of hard work with me, he saw for himself that he had been reluctant to seek long-term treatment because, deep down, he knew what he might have to give up in exchange for wellness. But in the beginning, Allen saw himself strictly as a victim, and the world as a perpetrator. Here's how that happened.

When he was in sixth grade, Allen's class took an end-of-year field trip to the town swimming pool. Everyone was excited—except Allen. He was a timid and cautious boy who didn't like the idea of all the dunking and splashing and horseplay he'd be subjected to. His parents refused his plea to be allowed to stay home that day.

Sure enough, despite the teacher's best effort to maintain order, a simple game of water tag evolved into a territorial division of the pool into shallow end and deep end, the object being to get past defenders into the shallow end. Predictably, Allen was pushed back into water over his head. Not a strong swimmer, he couldn't hope to compete, and he started to sink.

By the time the lifeguard saw him, Allen was very close to drowning. He was hauled out of the water—"like a bag of potatoes," he recalled— and received CPR to clear his lungs of water he'd inhaled and restore his breathing. He remembers looking up at a ring of his classmates' faces, all "morbidly delighted at the excitement."

"Many times I've wished I did die that day," Allen told me.

When he came to me, Allen was understandably terrified of water. But just as powerful was his fear of feeling exposed in any way. If someone glanced his way in the supermarket a little too long, it triggered an intense desire to vanish and never be seen again. He was extremely sensitive to perceived ridicule or judgment. You can imagine the social fortress he had built around himself as a result—and what it cost him in opportunity and enjoyment of life.

Links in a Long Chain

Allen's struggle with fear was not a foregone conclusion. It unfolded along a predictable string of cause and effect. Here are some common stages along the way.

1. A Seed Puts Down Roots.

Something happens in a person's life to trigger a fear response. It can take place in childhood or later in life. Trauma can be acute, as Allen's was, or chronic, such as suffering prolonged abuse. Perhaps the trigger is compounded by a biological predilection toward unregulated fearfulness. Given Allen's childhood personality type, I suspect that was true in his case.

The point is, life hands a person a *reason* to feel afraid, and they run with it.

Tracing anxiety to its root can be enormously empowering. Many people have struggled so long with intense fear, they've forgotten that it certainly had a beginning. There was a time before anxiety took charge of your life, which means your current state is not your only possible state. That's great news!

Left unexamined, however, the root leads to the next stage.

2. You Form an Identity Out of Your Fear.

It was clear that Allen didn't see himself as a person struggling with anxiety. Rather, in his mind, he *was* his condition. Everything in his life was built around it—his home, his profession, his nonexistent social life. He never thought of himself as anything other than his anxiety. When forced to interact with new coworkers, he made sure to inform them early on that he suffered from severe anxiety, "so they could understand who I am." He routinely reminded family members as well.

Follow Allen's story back to its root, and you'll see the beginning of this habit. After the incident at the pool, he remembers that people stopped using his name but rather identified him as "that kid who almost drowned" and "that kid who can't swim." With little emotional resilience to begin with, he succumbed to the temptation to see himself in these terms also. Ultimately, however, it wasn't the judgment of others that stuck; it was his own. To himself he became "that kid who is terrified all the time."

Similar things can happen to adults as well. Ask anyone who has lost a business or a home or endured a public and painful divorce. It is accurate to say of ourselves at such times, "I had a setback" or "I've hit a rough patch." Instead, you'll most often hear people say, "I *am* a failure." That kind of self-judgment is always a choice—and one you go on making every day. If you do, you'll most likely move on to the next stage as well.

3. You Adopt a Dark View of the World.

In this phase of development, it's common for people to start believing that well-being is a myth and that life will never be anything but frightening, unfair, and brutally hard.

Albert Einstein is often quoted as saying, "The most important decision we make is whether we believe we live in a friendly or a hostile universe."

I couldn't agree more! The reason is simple: If you believe the universe is a cruel place—or even just coldly indifferent to your existence, much less the quality of your life experience—then the idea that there is no hope for you can start to seem plausible. If you've struggled for a long time, you might even conclude that a hostile world is the only thing that makes sense. There simply must be some malevolent force working against your health and happiness!

That perspective is a dark lens that filters out every bit of evidence to the contrary—and there is an abundance of it—that life is fundamentally *good* and that healing is *always* possible for those willing to reach for it. I'll say it again: we only reach for what we believe we can have. We only walk through the doors we can see and that we believe will open to us.

With a skewed view of the world, the next step is logical.

4. You Adopt a Dark View of People.

It's human nature to look for someone to blame when we are battling something difficult. In Allen's case, he had plenty of candidates to choose from: his parents, for pushing him too hard to overcome his fearfulness; his teacher, for failing to safeguard him at the pool; his classmates, for treating his accident like an entertaining spectacle. Never mind that many of his judgments may have been wrong or at least wildly incomplete. He believed them to be true.

The real danger to your long-term mental and emotional well-being, though, is what can happen when you move beyond blaming particular people for specific offenses and adopt a dark view of people *in general*. Then you start to push away potential friends and allies who cross your path without giving them a chance. It's prejudice on steroids, because rather than prejudging a single group based on skin color or ethnicity or religion, you reject everyone for simply being human.

The truth is that in the course of your recovery you are going to need help that can only come from other people—for example, a spouse, minister, coworker, or caregiver. Deep distrust of humanity may feel like justifiable self-defense, but is ultimately only self-defeating.

5. You Compensate.

So far, this list has contained only internal responses—how you choose to think and feel in response to your fear. This next stage is where those things turn into action, and you develop a *lifestyle* around your anxiety. There are two primary ways this happens.

The first is *isolation*. Based on all of the above, you build a fortress in which to hide. You limit your exposure to risky situations, which you may define as almost anything that happens outside your four walls. For example, Allen's response to his childhood trauma—more than three decades in the past by the time we met—made him feel very uncomfortable and exposed when strangers made eye contact.

"It feels like being half-naked again, lying beside the pool," he confessed.

So he arranged his routine to visit the grocery store only late at night, when he was more likely to shop alone. He stood during the train ride to work, rather than taking a seat that faced another commuter. And, of course, he avoided any social setting that might make him the focus of attention. All of that added up to a self-imposed quarantine that kept him well away from anything that might bring healing and joy back into his life.

That kind of isolation cuts you off from another important source of help: others who struggle with an anxiety disorder. In an article for the Anxiety and Depression Association of America (ADAA), Dr. Sarah Bloch-Elkouby offers this encouraging reminder:

> Don't forget, there are no human beings who live their life
> without experiencing hardships. Mental illness is much more
> common than you may think. Most of us go through difficult
> experiences and struggle with some form of distress. Your struggle
> makes you more human; not less.[1]

The second major method of compensating for the pain of severe anxiety is *self-medication*. Let's be clear: not all attempts to distract yourself from your fear, or deaden the sensation of it, are harmful. Perhaps you have learned that a daily walk in nature helps you manage your feelings and keep your balance, for instance. Problems arise when the methods themselves pose further danger to your mental and physical well-being. Anything can become an addiction, even physical exercise. But some things are virtual ticking time bombs: alcohol and drug abuse, gambling, pornography, internet and social media connection, overeating, overspending, and so on.

The ADAA reports that 20 percent or more of people who suffer an anxiety disorder also struggle with a substance abuse disorder.[2] Based on the thousands of individuals my team and I have treated at The Center, we believe the percentage is actually much higher.

Allen was afraid of alcoholism because it ran in his family and he'd seen for himself the devastation it can cause. Instead of reaching for booze, he rationalized taking prescription sleep medication to combat his insomnia and in time developed a stubborn addiction to it.

It's a short distance from compensation to the next stage.

6. You Habituate.

Now comes the culmination of this progression from the inciting event or chronic fearful condition to severe anxiety. In this stage the cement hardens on all that led you here, and your struggle with anxiety becomes just the way things are.

The best word to describe what makes this so damaging is *payoffs*. That is, the identity, lifestyle, and compensating habits you've formed around your fear begin to deliver certain perceived benefits that you become very reluctant to give up. It is simply easier and more comfortable to stay where you are than to do the heavy lifting needed to get well. For instance, tackling anxiety head-on might also mean confronting a stubborn addiction or working to heal broken relationships or figuring out who you are *without* your anxiety-based identity. The prospect of change becomes yet another thing to fear.

When I met Allen, he had checked every box on this list. He had lived a life of isolation and self-medication, still as fearful and bitter as ever. But for some reason a lifetime of dysfunction had finally led him to desperation and a hunger for change that was more powerful than his condition. That made him ready for the final stage—or perhaps it's better to call it the first, if you want to work through this process in reverse: undoing the damage and restoring hope every step of the way.

7. You Decide to Heal—Whatever It Takes.

This is common knowledge among those who have experienced addiction recovery: until a person is truly ready to deal with every aspect of their dependency—to take a whole-person approach—progress will be limited, and no amount of external intervention will change that fact. In many respects, the same can be said of recovery from severe anxiety.

Yes, medication can calm the storm to facilitate effective treatment. But ultimate success will always depend on the indispensable factors of desire, determination, and dedication to a brighter future—things that only you can provide. If you are armed with them, there is absolutely no reason you can't roll back the effects of years of letting fear run your life.

Your Personal Reset Plan

Taking inventory is not easy—ask anyone who runs a restaurant, warehouse, or retail outlet. It means cleaning out dusty cabinets you haven't opened in a while and taking stock of things you'd just as soon forget about. But it's the only way to know what you have and, more importantly, what you need.

That's doubly tough when the attic you are rummaging around is your mind and the "things" you are counting are slippery thoughts and emotions. Grab a pen and paper as you begin your inventory. Here's a checklist of categories to get you started and ways to reclaim them from fear:

1. **Your identity.** *Who am I?* is not a question with a single answer. We all have different personas for different settings and relationships. The person your coworkers think you are might be unrecognizable to your children, for example. The purpose of this inventory item is to take stock of who you might be without the hobbles of anxiety. As you make the following lists (and any others you can think of), be aware of items you are tempted to leave off because of your fearfulness. Include everything that comes to mind as if you were 100 percent free of fear.

   - Five things I would love to do for fun
   - Five things I want to have (Think big! Be outrageous!)
   - Five places I'd like to go
   - Five things I'd love to give someone else

2. **Your outlook.** When taking stock of your true outlook about the world and other people, it's best not to think about it too hard. These are deeply held beliefs that we often learn to hide from view, even from ourselves. It's not politically correct to be too caustic with our responses, so we learn to keep them to ourselves.

   To get around this, finish this sentence: "The world can be

counted on to . . ." Just let your hand hover over the page and write your answers anywhere and in any way you like. No one will see, so be honest.

Do it again with this variation: "People can be counted on to . . ."

Look at your answers. Are these *your* beliefs, or the answers your fear would give?

3. **Your compensating habits.** This one hits close to home, because it is not easy to see your weaknesses, much less to make an honest accounting of them. Nevertheless, this is a key part of your recovery. List those things you can honestly say you'd have a hard time giving up, even if the prize was a shot at freedom from fear. (If you are really determined to reach the truth, ask the question of someone close to you.)

   Once you have the list, for each item, add three small steps you can take today to let them go.

4. **Your payoffs.** What benefits do you receive from the identity and lifestyle you've built around your anxiety? These can come in all shapes and sizes, and it takes courageous honesty to see them at work in your life. For example, you receive a payoff when you use your anxiety as a shield against taking responsibility for carrying your own weight in relationships or at work. You receive a payoff when anxiety becomes an excuse for behavior you know to be harmful to yourself or others. Dig deep and list those things you might be reluctant to lose as you heal.

5. **Your desire to move on.** Gut check time: how badly do you want to heal? This is a freewriting exercise, with no filters and no need to get it "right." Start with "I want to be free of my fear because . . ." Keep going until you reach the reasons that touch you deeply.

CHAPTER 9

Put Down the Shovel

Identify unhealthy habits that intensify anxiety.

Many people create or contribute to their anxiety without realizing it.

In other words, there are probably things you're doing right now that are contributing to feelings of anxiety in your life.

Yes, your anxiety may be linked to genetics, or childhood trauma, or brain chemistry. But as we saw in the last chapter, there may be lifestyle choices you're making today that are very likely adding fuel to the fires of anxiety.

In the pages ahead, I want to help you recognize unhealthy habits that are intensifying your anxiety and then help you take steps—today—to change those habits.

Before we delve into some of the bigger changes you can embrace that will help you live in greater peace, I want to give you a quick win or two.

As the saying goes, "When you want to get out of a hole, stop digging." We'll work on filling in that gaping hole in future chapters. Right now, I simply want to help you put down the shovel.

Small Habits Add Up to Big Anxiety

Doug did the same thing every morning. His routine was made up of a series of ingrained habits that he had never even considered trying to change.

Every morning when his alarm went off, Doug hit his snooze button several times before rolling out of bed feeling irritated and rushed. Rummaging through the perennial pile of clothes on a chair in his room, he'd find something cleanish to wear and hurry toward the kitchen to grab his morning coffee. Then he would spend ten minutes hunting for his keys before rushing out the door.

More often than not, the fuel needle in Doug's car hovered near E, and he would sweat over whether to stop for gas on the way to work. If he didn't run out of gas, he'd hit the vending machine in the lobby, grabbing a prepackaged sticky bun before landing at his desk, feeling anxious and dreading the start of the workday.

Whatever deeper issues are at work in Doug's life, there's no doubt that his daily habits that include procrastination, clutter, caffeine, poor nutrition, and inadequate planning are creating copious amounts of anxiety in his life. In fact, until he addresses these sloppy habits, identifying the root causes of any anxiety disorder may prove hard to do.

Think about how you start your day. Are you setting yourself up for emotional, physical, and spiritual success? If you're not getting enough sleep, if you're hoarding or living in clutter, or if you're starting your day revved up on energy drinks and sugar, you're going to feel the effects. In fact, habits like these will increase anyone's anxiety—with or without the presence of a true anxiety disorder.

Habits Are Helpful—If They're the Right Kind

Habits are a useful brain function. Your brain puts repeated actions on autopilot so it can focus on new situations that require decisions, creativity, and solutions—and this is extremely helpful. After all, if you had to put the same energy into figuring out how to brush your teeth every morning as you do, say, figuring out an alternate route to work when the highway is closed, you would be exhausted by midmorning. If you had to concentrate on how to operate your computer at work each morning, you would be distracted from the report your boss asked you to create.

The problem is that once patterns form, we rarely give them another thought, and it's hard to see their effects. We continue doing the same thing over and over without stopping to conduct a mental audit, evaluating whether a particular habit is still serving us well. In fact, it's possible that a habit that served us well at first is now creating havoc in our lives. But as long as we continue on autopilot, or in denial, we will go on experiencing the havoc without ever analyzing its source.

Analyzing your morning routine is a good place to start. Before we continue in this chapter, I would encourage you to write down your typical morning habits. Think about the things you do most mornings, and ask yourself whether these habits are contributing to peace or distress in your life.

Patterns That Can Make You Anxious

Let's take a look at four life patterns that you're going to want to ditch—and the science behind why those habits are making you more anxious than you need to be.

Procrastination or Avoidance

When it comes to anxiety and procrastination, we are reminded of the chicken and the egg. Which came first? The fact is that procrastination is both a *result* and a *driver* of anxiety. In a study of over two thousand men and women in a German community, procrastination was consistently linked with higher stress; more anxiety, depression, and fatigue; and reduced satisfaction with life. In addition, there are numerous studies on procrastination among students that establish the connection between procrastination, anxiety, depression, and reduced social integration.[1]

Procrastination means putting off tasks because of anxiety . . . which will only increase future anxiety. Because anxiety and procrastination are circular—anxiety prompts avoidance, which creates more anxiety, and so on—disrupting behavior anywhere in the circle can be helpful.

In other words, reduce your anxiety, and you may find that you procrastinate less; *or* stop procrastinating, and you may very well find that your anxiety drops.

How can you stop the habit of procrastinating? Here are some strategies:

- *Make a list of things you've been putting off.* Do one thing on that list right now. With one item off your list, schedule a time later today or first thing tomorrow to tackle another item on the list. Repeat this process until you've worked through your list.

- *Move beyond perfectionism.* Anxiety over getting things just right can sometimes make it hard to move forward at all. To overcome this tendency, factor a few "practice runs" into your plans and accept that giving it your best is more important than getting it perfect. When we embrace the idea that failure is one of the natural steps along the way instead of a final and humiliating destination, we may find that procrastination flees.

- *Set a timer.* Some brains work better under pressure. Be in control of a sense of urgency you create for yourself by setting a timer and giving yourself a limited window to accomplish a task quickly. Sometimes having to work under a deadline distracts the brain from engaging in the negative self-talk that can keep us putting off something we know we should do.

Clutter and Disorder

Studies continue to show that the more clutter we have in our homes, the greater our stress, anxiety, depression, and procrastination. In a study of thirty-two families, for example, researchers at UCLA's Center on Everyday Lives of Families (CELF) discovered that clutter not only adversely impacted people's mood, but it also affected their self-esteem.

The link between clutter and stress was particularly strong in women, the study determined. Women surrounded by a high density of household objects—including a messy kitchen sink and a jam-packed closet—had higher levels of the stress hormone cortisol. In the study, even the number of magnets and papers on the front of the refrigerator was linked to greater clutter throughout the house—and increased anxiety.[2]

The studies confirm what common sense would suggest. Clutter creates unnecessary stimuli for our brains, keeps us frustrated looking for car keys and other obscured items, and adds to feelings of guilt, irritation, or shame.

Clutter even adds to our waistline. In a 2017 study at Cornell University, participants offered snacks while in a messy, disorganized kitchen ate twice as many cookies as those in an organized kitchen.[3]

And in a series of four fascinating studies conducted by researchers James Cutting and Kacie Armstrong, it was determined that cluttered backgrounds in movie scenes make it harder for viewers to interpret the emotions expressed on the faces of the actors and actresses.[4] Dr. Cutting explained, "Clutter distracted the viewers and made the task of recognizing the emotion more difficult."[5] These intriguing findings raise the question, Could living in a cluttered home impact our perception of and relationship with those around us?

No wonder living in a mess adds to our stress!

There are countless books and blogs that will give you tips on the mechanics of getting rid of clutter in your life. But perhaps one of the most important shifts you can make is to replace a "consumer" mindset with an "experience" mindset.

According to CELF, while American families produce 3 percent of the world's children, they buy 40 percent of the world's toys.[6] Whether we're talking toys for kids, digital gadgets for adults, clothes, or household knick-knacks, an unchecked "consumption mindset" is a recipe for clutter.

Begin to think of "fun" and "reward" in a new light. Shift your focus from spending money and acquiring objects to embracing experiences and connecting with people. Spend time in nature, go for walks, and converse with people you love and with those whose paths you cross. These experiences cost nothing, accumulate nothing, and will reduce your anxiety and enrich your life in ways that clutter never will. (In chapter 18, we'll explore how simplifying life improves well-being and reduces anxiety.)

Eating Patterns

The connection between sugar and anxiety is still being researched. According to Uma Naidoo, MD, the director of nutritional and lifestyle psychiatry at Massachusetts General Hospital, "[Researchers] suggest eating whole foods and avoiding processed and ultra-processed foods that we know cause inflammation and disease." The reason is that "there is anatomical and physiologic two-way communication between the gut and brain via the vagus nerve. The gut-brain axis offers us a greater understanding of the connection between diet and disease, including depression and anxiety."[7]

Sarah Wilson, author of *First, We Make the Beast Beautiful* (a memoir about coping with anxiety) and *The Anti-Anxiety Diet* program, couldn't agree more. According to Wilson, eliminating sugar from her diet is a major player in how she manages her anxiety. She writes,

> There are many competing theories as to why collective anxiety is
> on the rise, but the most recent and compelling science suggests
> that anxiety is not merely a chemical imbalance in the brain,
> as we've been told for two decades, but that it is also a result of
> inflammation and imbalances in the gut. . . . If you have fire in
> the gut, you have fire in the brain.[8]

Indeed, a 2011 study conducted with 1,782 young adults showed a "significant relationship between consumption of processed foods and anxiety."[9]

We are just now beginning to understand the relationship between gut health and mental health, and what we are learning is that there is constant communication going back and forth between your brain and your gut—and, more specifically, the bacteria that live in your gut. Your diet plays a huge role in the balance of good and bad bacteria in your gut, and that balance plays a game-changing role in emotions like depression and anxiety.

We're going to take a deeper dive into diet and anxiety in a coming chapter and talk about *what* to eat to balance your gut and your emotions. But right now I want to identify three poor *habits* that may be fueling poor food choices:

- *Lack of preparation.* Having healthier fare prepped and on hand—before you're hungry and heading for the pantry—is one of the greatest habits you can develop for healthy eating success. If you're in the habit of satisfying your hunger with whatever fast or processed foods are easily at hand, your brain, body, and emotions will pay the price.

- *Burning the candle at both ends.* Not getting enough sleep has a profound impact on not only your appetite but also on your brain's ability to signal when you've had enough to eat. In addition, a study published in the *American Journal of Clinical Nutrition* found that when twenty-one volunteers took actions to improve their sleep habits, they gained an average of 1.5 hours of sleep each night, and their daily consumption of sugar went down by as much as ten grams a day.[10]

- *Not staying hydrated.* Some people confuse thirst and hunger symptoms, which can lead to reaching for snacks instead of the water bottle. It's not hard to do since some hunger symptoms (headache, dizziness, nausea) and thirst symptoms overlap.

  What's more, numerous research studies have demonstrated a clear link between dehydration and mental health issues, including anxiety.[11] Thankfully, this is a problem with a simple solution: drink more water. Get into the habit of drinking water based on a healthy fluid allowance, rather than reaching immediately for food.

  So how much water consumption will help you to thrive? You have probably heard the mantra that you should drink at least eight eight-ounce glasses of water each day (sixty-four ounces). Well, there is a lot of truth to that saying. Don't forget that our bodies are composed of approximately 60 percent water. We need a lot of water to keep our biological machine humming along in good health.

  Actually, I believe we all need a bit more water than that, depending upon body weight. I advise my clients to drink the equivalent of half their body weight in ounces of water each day. For example, if you weigh 176 pounds, you should drink eighty-eight ounces per day—the equivalent of eleven eight-ounce glasses of water. The trick is to start early in the morning and have a water container near you during the day, even while you are driving.

Negative Thought Patterns

Many factors can create and exacerbate anxiety, from past trauma to brain chemistry to lifestyle choices. Another factor that must be addressed is falling into a habit of negative thought patterns.

The more we worry, the more our brains become wired to worry. Psychologist Guy Winch explains:

> When we encounter painful experiences we typically reflect on them, hoping to reach the kinds of insights and epiphanies that reduce our distress and allow us to move on. Yet for many of us who engage in this process of self-reflection, things go awry. Instead of attaining an emotional release we get caught in a vicious cycle of rumination in which we replay the same distressing scenes, memories, and feelings over and over again, feeling worse every time we do. We become like hamsters trapped in a wheel of emotional pain, running endlessly but going nowhere.[12]

There's a common saying in the sciences that "neurons that fire together wire together." It means that the more we repeat neural patterns associated with any given behavior or thinking, the more those neural patterns become ingrained—even hardwired—in our brains.

The more we complain, worry, or rehearse anxiety-producing thoughts, the easier our brains default to those same negative thoughts in the future.

The fact is, we all have an inner voice that serves as a constant commentary or "news feed" about our moment-by-moment experiences. When these messages are negative or pessimistic, they will contribute to anxiety. But you control the on-off switch for that voice. It has had its own way for so long that it may take work to get back the controls, but you can. Begin by identifying the thoughts streaming through your brain. Are they negative or positive, helpful or harmful? Intentionally replace negative abstractions with positive affirmations. (We will discuss this process further in chapter 11.)

Cortisol and Anxiety

The habits we've just examined—procrastination, clutter, poor eating habits, and negative thought patterns—are all proven stressors that increase cortisol, which in turn ramps up anxiety.

Ways to decrease cortisol include getting more sleep, doing yoga, practicing deep breathing, listening to relaxing music, getting exercise, eating healthy, having healthy relationships, having fun—even owning a pet.

And, of course, breaking the four anxiety-producing patterns we've identified in this chapter.

But as anyone who has tried it will tell you, busting bad habits can be easier said than done.

Proven Habit-Busting Strategies

How do you change a bad habit—especially habits that may be contributing to your feelings of anxiety? Here are four strategies you can use to tackle any habit.

Disrupt a Familiar Pattern

Do you have a habit of heading for the pantry for a predinner snack the moment you walk in the front door from work? Change the familiar patterns associated with your habit. For example, have a healthy dinner waiting for you in the slow cooker so you can skip the unhealthy snack and eat as soon as you walk in the door. Or squeeze in a walk around the block between getting out of your car and walking through your door. Or take a baggie of fresh veggies or nuts with you to work for a snack when you leave the office. You'll arrive home satiated enough to prepare a healthy dinner.

Because habits are automated responses, shaking up the familiar can help you ditch the automation and have more power over your choices.

Visualize Better Behavior

Practice new habits in your imagination, and they will be easier to practice with your actions. Visualize yourself starting to go down the path of an old habit, then change the picture in your mind's eye and envision a new ending, with yourself making a healthier choice. Do this often.

Search and Replace

Once you identify a habit you want to change, don't simply try to stop the old habit. It's much easier to practice a new habit in its place. For example, instead of telling yourself, *I'm going to stop my old habit of going to bed at midnight*, create enjoyable new habits around going to bed at ten instead. Treat yourself to a new pair of pajamas, play relaxing music in your bedroom while you get ready for sleep, and turn off your electronic devices an hour or two before that. In general, you'll find it easier to nix an established habit if you have new behaviors you can practice.

This is why experts recommend combating negative thinking by intentionally thinking grateful thoughts. In fact, researchers at the University of California discovered that people who worked every day to practice gratitude experienced greater energy, less stress, and less anxiety. In fact, "gratitude blocks toxic emotions," says UC Davis professor Robert Emmons.[13]

Journal about It

Writing is a powerful tool when it comes to setting new goals. It's also a great way to process thoughts and feelings, increase self-awareness, and bring attention to subconscious, automated behavior—like bad habits—so they can be changed. Write about the habit you want to change, addressing things like triggers, behaviors, and ramifications. Then journal about the new behavior you want to embrace. When you write about the new behavior, describe it in detail and then journal about your motivations and the benefits of embracing the new habit.

When Habits Turn into Addictions

Sometimes unhealthy patterns evolve into addictions, which come in all forms. Addictions leave us feeling out of control and always bring with them a rise in anxiety.

When we think of addictions, we often think about hard-core substance abuse like nicotine, alcohol, or drugs or about addictions to spending, gambling, or pornography.

But the truth is that we can become dependent on even seemingly innocuous behaviors (like checking our phones). However "harmless" the activity may seem, if we are driven by a compulsion, our anxiety is going to rise.

How do you know that you're in an addiction's grasp?

DIGITAL ADDICTION AND ANXIETY:
WHAT TO WATCH FOR

In recent years, we've heard a lot about digital addiction, sometimes called internet addiction or Problematic Internet Use (PIU). Though a relatively new phenomenon, psychologists, researchers, and social scientists agree that addiction to digital devices is an actual addiction with similar symptoms and repercussions to other addictions, including substance abuse.

What's more, numerous studies published in respected, peer-reviewed scientific journals have demonstrated the link between digital addiction and mental health issues, including anxiety. For example, a study reported by the Anxiety and Depression Association of America said,

> In a recent analysis of 2006 patients, 181 (9.0%) of which had moderate to severe problematic internet use, it was found that attention-deficit hyperactivity disorder (ADHD) and social anxiety disorder were associated with high PIU scores in young participants ([under age] 25), whereas generalized anxiety disorder (GAD) and obsessive-compulsive disorder (OCD) were associated with high PIU scores in the older participants respectively.[*]

Given the prevalence of digital addiction in our society, let's look at the signs and symptoms so you can evaluate whether these are evident in yourself or someone you know:

- anxiety
- depression
- insomnia
- feelings of guilt
- feelings of euphoria when using digital devices
- inability to prioritize or keep commitments
- isolation

- defensiveness
- avoidance of work
- agitation
- mood swings
- fear
- loneliness
- boredom with routine tasks
- procrastination
- weight gain or loss

Many studies and surveys are currently used to measure the extent of digital addiction. I appreciate the work of Dr. Kimberly S. Young, who has created an assessment called the Internet Addict Diagnostic Questionnaire

---

[*] Vera Nezgovorova et al., "Problematic Internet Use and Its Impact on Anxiety, Depression and Addictions: Patient-Centered Approaches and Digital Applications and Interventions," Anxiety and Depression Association of America, accessed October 3, 2020, https://adaa.org/learn-from-us /from-the-experts/blog-posts/professional/problematic-internet-use-and-its-impact.

(or IADQ). This eight-question questionnaire is modeled on questionnaires for other addictions to determine how severe an addiction is. If you answer yes to five or more of these questions, it could point to an addiction:

- Are you preoccupied with using the Internet? Do you think about your previous or future online activity?
- Do you have the need to be online longer to be satisfied?
- Have you made repeated but unsuccessful attempts to cut back, stop or control your Internet use?
- Do you become moody, restless, irritable or depressed when you stop or decrease your Internet use?
- Is your time spent online longer than what you originally planned?
- Did your online use negatively affect a significant relationship, education, career or job?
- Do you conceal the extent of your Internet usage from your therapist, family or others?
- Does the Internet serve as an escape from problems or relief from a bad mood?*

---

* Dr. Kimberly Young's questionnaire appeared in "Computer/Internet Addiction Symptoms, Causes and Effects," PsychGuides.com, American Addiction Centers, accessed October 3, 2020, https://www.psychguides.com/behavioral-disorders/computer-internet-addiction.

- You continue the behavior even when there are negative ramifications. For example, finding yourself unable or unwilling to detach from your phone despite the complaints of family and friends.

- When you try to stop the behavior, you feel anxious or uncomfortable— or if you manage to stop for a few days or weeks, you return to the behavior despite your desire to stop.

- You feel the need to be secretive. Hiding how frequently you engage in an activity is a huge red flag. Furthermore, the shame and stress related to keeping secrets can create anxiety for anyone, with or without an anxiety disorder.

Finding freedom from anxiety while living under the control of an addiction is unlikely, if not impossible. The good news is that addiction recovery is possible, and there are myriad resources that can help you kick even the most tenacious habits.

Your Personal Reset Plan

If you want to experience a true reset in your patterns, follow these actions that will empower you to *review, reenergize, renew, resist,* and *redirect.*

1. **Review your daily and weekly routine.** Take twenty minutes to make a list of the habits you engage in automatically. Some may be harmless or even helpful. But some likely aren't, causing you to think and act in ways that create anxiety. Put a check mark next to automatic habits that are helpful. Draw a circle around automatic habits you would like to change.

2. **Reenergize.** Review the circled habits from your list. Which of these may be linked to added anxiety in your life? Circle these a second time.

   Journaling is energizing because it involves mental, emotional, and spiritual processing and engages our bodies as well. After journaling about a struggle—and potential solutions—we often have greater clarity on what is really going on and powerful insights to move us forward.

   Looking at the list of double-circled automatic habits you want to change, journal about the ramifications of these habits. As you journal, identify a minimum of three positive habits or behaviors you could develop to replace the habit you want to change.

3. **Renew thoughts and behaviors.** Practicing positive replacement habits is a great way to break a pattern that is adding fuel to the fire of your anxiety. With many ingrained behaviors, it's not realistic to stop cold turkey. You'll find more success if you choose new, healthier routines to replace the old, unhealthy ones.

   In the previous action point, you identified three replacement habits for each harmful habit. Now identify what would need to be true to turn the new habits into automatic habits. How can you set yourself up to be successful at consistently practicing the new habits?

4. **Resist the old.** There are many ways to resist the pull of old habits you are trying to break, but a proven strategy is to find an

accountability partner who can encourage you along the way. This is a powerful tool for changing habits. Do you know someone who has found freedom from the habit you wish to change? Consider asking that person for tips and encouragement on your journey to better habits.

5. **Redirect your thoughts regarding your future.** To begin to think more hopefully about the future, commit to keeping a gratitude diary for two weeks. Every day, write for ten or fifteen minutes about the things that brought you joy, relief, and gratitude. What three things are you thankful for each day? Studies show that a daily practice of gratitude results in lower stress, less depression, less hopelessness, improved sleep, and increased optimism.[14]

CHAPTER 10

Make Peace with Your Past

Healing hurts and heartaches will put you on the path to peace of mind.

Rachel took a deep breath and reminded herself that she was safe.

It was something she told herself on a daily basis. Some days the reassuring self-talk helped; other days it didn't.

Rachel was in her late thirties, but the trauma of being sexually assaulted in high school never felt far away. She often wondered how an event two decades past could feel so present, but the truth was that the rape felt like a pivot point at which her entire life had turned and spiraled in a completely different direction. And her constant companion on this unfamiliar and dimly lit path was anxiety.

Hurts and heartaches from years past are a common origin of anxious thoughts and feelings. Rachel longed to feel safe, and fears of being otherwise stirred anxious feelings inside of her.

Thomas also struggled with anxiety, but his anxiety was rooted in fears of abandonment and betrayal stemming from the trauma of having his bride of six months leave him for his best friend. Even though he had recently become engaged to another woman, he was unable to manage his anxiety, which was sometimes expressed in anger. If his fiancée arrived home from work even ten minutes late, Thomas became anxious and accusatory. His fiancée had finally had enough and was considering breaking off their engagement.

Just as anxiety can be rooted in past trauma that has been perpetrated on us, it can also be rooted in our own past failures or mistakes. When we've failed in the past, the thought of trying again can leave us feeling overwhelmed. *What if I blow it this time too?* we ask ourselves. Whether we regret a failure experienced in a relationship, on the job, or while in pursuit of a dream, we frequently feel anxiety at the thought of taking the same risk again.

What do all of these scenarios have in common?

In each of these circumstances, freedom from anxiety begins with finding healing from a past hurt, heartache, trauma, or failure.

Assessing the Lies We Believe and the Truths We Avoid

Healing from our past almost always begins with abandoning lies and denial and reaching for truth. We begin down this path to healing when we are willing to tell ourselves truths about the past, the future, and the present.

Tell Yourself the Truth about the Past

Sometimes our anxiety stems not so much from an event itself but from our *assessment and interpretation* of the event.

For example, going through a relationship breakup is traumatic enough. But when you interpret the experience to mean you're not worthy of love and you're going to be alone forever, it's no wonder that the memory evokes anxiety.

Separating fact from opinion is critical when it comes to finding healing for past hurts and heartaches. A breakup is a fact. In contrast, what you tell yourself about the breakup, what you believe the broken relationship says about you, and what you fear this turn of events means for your future must be evaluated to see whether they fall into the category of fact or unfounded opinions.

One indication that your interpretation of a past event is unfounded is the presence of extreme language. For example, if that breakup causes you to use words like *always*, *all*, or *never*—as in "I'll *never* find love" or "*All* men (or women) are jerks and abusers"—you've strayed from the facts.

For Thomas, separating fact from fiction is critical not only to his healing but also to the health of his current and future relationships. This is because an inaccurate assessment or interpretation of a past hurt can have profound and even tragic ramifications for the future.

Tell Yourself the Truth about the Future

Marwa Azab, PhD, asserts that "anxious people differ significantly from non-anxious ones in how they assess future events." She then describes several ways that anxious people miscalculate:

- They overestimate the likelihood of negative future events.
- They underestimate how much power they have over changing negative situations.
- They over-plan to accommodate all possible future scenarios. . . .
- They are blind to available safety options.

Dr. Azab also says that instead of recalibrating their expectations after a success, anxious people continue to expect the worst.[1]

When we have experienced past hurts and heartaches, our perception of the future can become warped. Tailoring our view of the future based on unhealed wounds from the past is a recipe for even greater heartache. If your past hurts and heartaches are informing your current expectations, they are going to impact your future perceptions, experiences, and behaviors.

The link between current expectations and future outcomes has been documented by scientific research. In fact, researchers have discovered that past experiences create identifiable changes in the brain that help shape future thoughts and responses. In a study conducted by neuroscientists at MIT, researchers concluded that our past experiences alter the strength of synapse connections between neurons. "The brain seems to embed prior experiences into synaptic connections so that patterns of brain activity are appropriately biased," explains Dr. Mehrdad Jazayeri, the senior author of the study.[2] In other words, these altered connections impact how we think and even respond.

Tell Yourself the Truth about Where You Are Today

There's no doubt that pessimistic interpretations, catastrophic leanings, and victim mentalities can keep us stuck in the morass of past hurts. At the same time, unrealistically rosy thinking and denial don't help either.

Making peace with your past may involve acknowledging painful truths before being able to put them behind you. For example, admitting that you're struggling with depression is an important milestone on the path to getting help. Acknowledging other uncomfortable truths—that someone betrayed your trust, that you're still grieving, or that you're not coping well, for instance—are also first steps toward wholeness.

When you're in the grip of a past hurt or heartache, denial is not your friend and in fact is a huge obstacle that can keep you from making peace with the past.

When your interpretations of the past, expectations for the future, or acceptance of painful truths are off track, you may need help dividing the facts from the fiction you've bought into. Working with a professional counselor can help you identify the counterproductive thought patterns that are keeping you mired in the painful past instead of moving into your brighter future.

The First Stage of Trauma Recovery: Embracing Self-Care and Safety

Recovering from trauma isn't an overnight process. There are stages in the healing process. In the early 1990s, Dr. Judith Herman identified three stages of recovery that continue to be acknowledged and used by experts in therapeutic fields today.

The first of these stages is safety and stabilization, which involves creating a safe environment from which to continue to pursue healing. Sometimes this means addressing chaotic coping behaviors such as addictions, substance abuse, or other self-harming behaviors. This can mean taking steps to get relief from results of the trauma, including depression, panic attacks, or anxiety. It can also mean getting help with regulating emotions like fear, anger, or aggression.

In this first stage, you're making self-care a priority. You are creating equilibrium in your body, emotions, environment, and relationships. You're not necessarily delving into past memories or processing past trauma. Not yet, anyway.

For Rachel, stabilizing meant learning some grounding techniques to help her focus on the present rather than past dangers or future concerns.

A counselor instructed Rachel to try this exercise: when feelings of anxiety arose, instead of reliving the past or giving in to fear over the future, Rachel was to redirect her thoughts and attention to what she could currently experience through her senses.

One afternoon as Rachel was driving with her nine-year-old daughter in the car, she found herself overwhelmed with feelings of vulnerability, fear, and anxiety. Acknowledging that there was nothing in her present environment to warrant those feelings, she began focusing on what was actually happening at that moment in the car rather than what had happened in the past or what dangers might lurk in the future.

"I'm driving," she said aloud. "The sun is shining through the window onto the steering wheel, and I can feel the warmth on my hands."

By now she had drawn the attention of her daughter in the passenger seat.

"I can hear music from the radio," Rachel continued. "We just passed a house with a red barn. Out of the corner of my eye I can see my daughter staring at me as if I'm crazy." Rachel laughed then, as did her daughter.

Allowing herself to focus on a present environment where she was not in current danger did not dismiss the very real danger and trauma she had experienced as a young woman. Nor did it deny that at any given moment, life can become unsafe or unfair.

What this grounding exercise helped Rachel experience, however, served as a milestone in her recovery journey. It gave her a way to create space in which she could take a break from past pain or future worries and simply live in that moment. And for someone who struggles with anxiety, that's a profound gift indeed.

Here's another example of someone who found a way to create space for herself free from emotions that would have impaired her ability to function in a highly stressful situation.

Gabby's wealthy mother had passed away unexpectedly from a heart attack one year earlier. Gabby's brother—the executor of their mother's estate—had spent the last twelve months in the family home, sorting valuables into numbered lots. A date was established for Gabby to meet her brother at the house and take turns choosing boxes. A list of the contents of each box—each containing a mash-up of unrelated valuables—had been faxed to Gabby just twenty-four hours before the distribution.

That same night Gabby, stressed and anxious to the point of tears, called a friend.

"The last time I was in my mother's house was the day she died," Gabby said. "My brother hasn't allowed me in the house since then. Now, tomorrow, I'm supposed to show up and focus on which 'lots' of her belongings I want to claim. But I know the moment I walk in that front door, I won't be able to think straight. Her absence will overwhelm me, and I will be hit with a year's worth of grieving that has been delayed. That's because I haven't been able to visit her home and get used to the fact that she's not there. I'm so anxious about the whole thing that I know I won't even be able to sleep tonight."

Gabby's friend suggested making a date with her grief.

"Your grief is real and deserves to be experienced, not ignored," the friend said. "Pick a date and time a few days in the future—say, next Tuesday at noon—and when grief shows up tomorrow at your mother's house, speak to it. Explain that you must spend the day focusing on a difficult task, but that your grief deserves your attention and that next Tuesday at noon you have a date. Let your grief know that in just a few days, you'll be free to give it the time and attention it deserves. And then keep that date. Really *do* spend time with your grief. Cry, remember, journal—whatever helps you finally begin to process the losses of this past year."

These are examples of women who have found ways to create stabilization and safety for a few hours or days. These examples are microcosms of the kind of stabilization and safety that can be created on a larger scale.

Sometimes taking care of yourself means learning how to give yourself respite from powerful emotions that, if unrelenting, can keep you off-balance, anxious, and coping badly.

From this state you are better prepared for the healing work ahead.

The Second Stage of Trauma Recovery: Remembering and Mourning

Gabby's Tuesday date with her grief fell into this second stage. She had much to process and grieve related to the loss of her mother and the loss of a safe relationship with her brother, whose greed allowed him to take advantage of his sibling.

Processing past trauma means putting words and meaning to what we've experienced. It can require spending time with challenging or painful memories. It might involve journaling about the impact of the trauma on our life today. Often the guidance of a counselor or support group is helpful on this part of the journey.

One of the tools that can help during this stage of the healing journey is a therapy technique called Eye Movement Desensitization and Reprocessing (EMDR). The treatment involves engaging in rapid side-to-side eye movements while focusing on memories, emotions, and beliefs related to past trauma. This integration of movement and memories stimulates positive changes in how the brain accesses and processes unresolved past trauma.[3]

Since Dr. Francine Shapiro introduced EMDR therapy in 1989, researchers have studied the effectiveness of the therapy. After a systematic review of current research on the treatment, Shapiro reported that twenty-four out of twenty-five randomized controlled trials supported the positive effects of EMDR therapy.[4]

Helping the brain rewire "stuck" memories and emotions related to past traumas can create a bridge between mourning and moving into a brighter future. And that, of course, is what the final stage is all about.

The Third Stage of Trauma Recovery: Reconnection and Integration

In this stage, you begin to focus on reconnecting with meaningful relationships and activities. You also begin to integrate the past trauma into your story so that it becomes a *part* of your story, not what defines you as a person. Finally, instead of feeling trapped in an endless loop of painful memories and emotions, you can focus on activities that help you feel empowered and engaged with life.

Integrating trauma as a part of your life narrative can be assisted by something called expressive journaling. Dr. James Pennebaker is a ground-breaker in the development of journaling as a way of facilitating healing and integration. His prescription? Write your deepest feelings about an emotional event in your life for fifteen to twenty minutes a day for four consecutive days.

Dr. Pennebaker recommends connecting the past trauma to events—positive or negative—that occurred both before and after. Using words and phrases like "and then," "because," and "as a result of" can help you anchor the past trauma to a specific place in the timeline of your life. As you identify events that contributed to the trauma—and evaluate how the trauma has impacted your life since then—you are helping your brain process the trauma and bring a sense of closure to that event in your life.[5]

For many people, moving through these three stages of trauma recovery prepares them to say, "A horrible thing happened. Without dismissing the impact of that hurt or heartache on my life, I can say that I am a stronger person as a result of what happened, I have learned how to create space and care for myself, and I am empowered and free to live a life with meaning and purpose." And that is a wonderful thing.

Your Personal Reset Plan

Past hurt and trauma can have long-lasting effects, but they don't need to define you. Try the following exercises as part of your reset plan to make peace with your past.

1. **Intentionally consider how you interpret past hurts and heartaches.** Is it possible that you believe lies about your worth or your future as a result? Write a list of lies you tell yourself that are keeping you stuck in the pain of the past. If you're not sure, spend twenty minutes writing down what you believe about yourself or your future, then call a friend and ask him or her to help you evaluate your statements. If you find beliefs that are demeaning, or expectations that are falsely pessimistic or limiting, rewrite them to reflect a healthier, more accurate perspective.

2. **Create space to rest and regroup.** The next time you feel flooded with anxiety or other challenging emotions, find ways to disrupt the onslaught. Try the exercise Rachel used: ground yourself by speaking aloud and identifying something you can currently see, touch, hear, taste, and smell.

3. **Focus on self-care.** Write down three specific ways you can nurture and nourish yourself. (You'll find many ideas presented in the pages of this book.) When you learn how to care for yourself and stabilize your environment, you can more confidently remember and mourn, knowing that if you become emotionally flooded, you can care for yourself by stepping back, stabilizing, and regrouping if needed. That said, are there past traumas, hurts, and heartaches you need to remember and mourn?

4. **Reread the statement at the end of this chapter.** This chapter ended with this affirmation: "A horrible thing happened. Without dismissing the impact of that hurt or heartache on my life, I can say that I am a stronger person as a result of what happened, I have learned how to create space and care for myself, and I am empowered and free to live a life with meaning and purpose."

   Read these words aloud if you can. Envision yourself in a place in your healing journey where these words are true and you can say them with passion and conviction.

5. **Give the right kind of counseling a fair chance.** As you might suspect, I am a big believer in engaging in therapy with a skilled, experienced practitioner. There are many reasons to pursue counseling, and for our discussion here, an excellent reason is to reduce your anxiety. Tending to your hurting heart and taking steps beyond a painful past will bolster your emotional health in many ways.

CHAPTER 11

Practice Mind over Mood

Change how you feel by changing how you think.

If our minds are oceans, then anxiety is a tsunami. Debris and toppled boats litter the water. The currents are wild and unpredictable. Who could navigate such a climate?

Anxiety is fueled and fostered by the way we *feel* about our *thoughts*. We all experience countless thoughts throughout the day. They trickle into our awareness like a steady stream. And for some people, this stream is more like a raging river. As we notice our thoughts, we judge and categorize them.

- *That wasn't a kind thing to think.*
- *I can't believe I thought that.*
- *I know I shouldn't fantasize about that.*
- *If anyone else knew what I thought, they'd be appalled.*

These are all examples of value judgments we make about our thoughts. The combination of swirling thoughts and shame make for the perfect mental storm. But it doesn't have to be this way. In the pages ahead, we'll uncover practical ways to stop automatically judging our thoughts, viewing them with curiosity instead. Ultimately, this practice will help calm the inner storm and reduce your anxiety.

Mindfulness: Focused and Present

Mindfulness is getting a lot of buzz these days. It seems like everywhere we turn, mindfulness is being touted as the secret to a content and happy life. But what is mindfulness exactly? Is it simply paying attention? Or is it something more? The answer is both.

In fact, my team and I at The Center integrate mindfulness practices into the dialectical behavior therapy (DBT) technique we use frequently with clients struggling with anxiety and other issues. That's because mindfulness is a valuable strategy for regulating emotions, achieving stability during a crisis, and resolving interpersonal conflicts.

Because mindfulness is a term widely used these days, it's important to understand where this practice came from and how it has become so popular in our modern culture. Historically, mindfulness has been associated with the practice of yoga. Practitioners of yoga have tapped into the power of mindfulness for centuries. However, when most people think of yoga and mindfulness, they assume it must entail "clearing the mind" or "emptying the brain of all thoughts." It's true that emptying or clearing the mind is sometimes encouraged, but that's not exactly what I mean by mindfulness in this context. Instead, mindfulness can be understood as becoming aware of our physical and mental surroundings in the present moment. No more, no less. An astute reader will notice that this definition is simple yet broad.

For centuries, Western philosophy has been dominated by dualism, the belief that the mind and body are separate entities. Dualism often suggests that the mind is superior to the body, which serves merely as a vessel for the more valuable and elite mind. It seems that this philosophy might finally be losing its grip on the Western imagination, at least in part due to the work of Dr. Jon Kabat-Zinn, who pioneered the Mindfulness-Based Stress Reduction program at the University of Massachusetts Medical School in the late 1970s. Kabat-Zinn's work brought mindfulness into mainstream culture, detaching it from its strictly religious roots. Mindfulness operates under the belief that human beings are an inextricable blend of mind, body, and emotions.

WHAT CURRENT RESEARCH SAYS ABOUT MINDFULNESS

Over the past decade or so, considerable scientific research has been conducted focusing on the health benefits and healing attributes of mindfulness. Here is a sampling:

- Researchers at the University of Bergen analyzed nineteen studies of mindfulness-based therapies and their effects on anxiety. They concluded that MBTs "are associated with robust and substantial reductions of anxiety symptoms." They also discovered that "MBTs are successful in reducing symptoms of depression." This matters for our discussion of anxiety because major depressive disorder often goes hand in hand with generalized anxiety and social anxiety disorders, affecting 20 to 40 percent of those who suffer from them.[*]
- Researchers from Johns Hopkins University examined forty-seven credible meditation studies and found that "mindful meditation can help ease psychological stresses like anxiety, depression, and pain."[†]
- Mindfulness-based stress reduction (MBSR) has been shown to relieve chronic stress and anxiety, whether or not the person is healthy. One study reported that, among patients who completed a ten-week MBSR program, "the majority . . . reported significantly decreased physical and emotional distress, improved quality of life, a greater sense of general well-being, increased optimism and increased feelings of control." Another study revealed that individuals diagnosed with irritable bowel syndrome—which often accompanies anxiety—"experienced significantly fewer symptoms of both IBS and anxiety when they engaged in two brief (15 min) daily sessions of mindfulness meditation."[‡]
- Harvard University researchers "found that just eight weeks of MBSR by participants decreased brain cell volume in the amygdala, which is the part of the brain responsible for anxiety, fear and stress." The results demonstrate that MBSR "helps the brain to process in areas related to individual self-reference, perspectives and the regulation of emotion."[§]

---

[*] George Hofmann, "Using Mindfulness to Treat Anxiety Disorders," Psych Central, July 8, 2018, https://psychcentral.com/blog/using-mindfulness-to-treat-anxiety-disorders/. Original research source: Jon Vøllestad, Morten Birkeland Nielsen, and Geir Høstmark Nielsen, "Mindfulness- and Acceptance-Based Interventions for Anxiety Disorders: A Systematic Review and Meta-Analysis," British Journal of Clinical Psychology 51, no. 3 (2012): 239–60, https://www.ncbi.nlm.nih.gov/pubmed/22803933.

[†] Julie Corliss, "Mindfulness Meditation May Ease Anxiety, Mental Stress," Harvard Health Blog, Harvard Health Publishing, January 8, 2014, https://www.health.harvard.edu/blog/mindfulness-meditation-may-ease-anxiety-mental-stress-201401086967.

[‡] James Lake, "Meditation and Mindfulness for Anxiety," Integrative Mental Health Care (blog), Psychology Today, August 23, 2018, https://www.psychologytoday.com/us/blog/integrative-mental-health-care/201808/meditation-and-mindfulness-anxiety. Original research source: L. Keefer and E. B. Blanchard, "The Effects of Relaxation Response Meditation on the Symptoms of Irritable Bowel Syndrome: Results of a Controlled Treatment Study," Behaviour Research and Therapy 39, no. 7 (2001): 801–11, https://www.ncbi.nlm.nih.gov/pubmed/11419611.

[§] Justine Cooke, "Using Mindfulness to Overcome Anxiety," Visions 12, no. 2 (2016): 8, https://www.heretohelp.bc.ca/visions/mindfulness-vol12/using-mindfulness-to-overcome-anxiety. Original research source: Britta K. Hölzel et al., "Mindfulness Practice Leads to Increases in Regional Brain Gray Matter Density," Psychiatry Research 191, no. 1 (2011): 36–43, https://www.ncbi.nlm.nih.gov/pmc/articles/PMC3004979/.

Furthermore, the distinction between these three is probably less clear than most of us would like to believe. Who hasn't gone to the doctor complaining of stomach pains only to discover that stress, not an ulcer, was the culprit? The opposite can also hold true. The mind has a profound impact on the body, even to the point of alleviating pain. This is why I am such a passionate advocate of a whole-person approach to relieving anxiety (and promoting wellness in many ways). I have learned over many decades of work as a mental health practitioner that every person is made up of physical, emotional, spiritual, and intellectual components. An individual's wellness depends on these aspects working together in a healthy, harmonious way.

Mindfulness helps to integrate those seemingly disparate components. Mindfulness means paying attention moment by moment to our bodily sensations, physical surroundings, emotional state, thoughts and ideas, and spiritual beliefs and contemplations. Medical journalists Shelley Kind and Stefan Hofmann record some of the benefits:

> *Research has shown that mindfulness helps us reduce anxiety and depression. Mindfulness teaches us how to respond to stress with awareness of what is happening in the present moment, rather than simply acting instinctively, unaware of what emotions or motives may be driving that decision. By teaching awareness for one's physical and mental state in the moment, mindfulness allows for more adaptive reactions to difficult situations.*[1]

This practice can profoundly reduce anxiety. Instead of hurtling forward into an unknown future or rehashing the past, the mind becomes trained to stay fixed on the present moment. This is a powerful step toward ending rumination and fostering a peaceful mind.

Optimism: More than "Happy Thoughts"

Optimism is a key ingredient for every content and successful person. In fact, developing a hopeful, positive, optimistic attitude is far more potent for wellness than many people recognize.

One need look no further than the nursery in a maternity ward to discover that optimism is alive and well, even in our complicated world. Each new life is celebrated by parents, grandparents, and friends—all of whom believe this infant is imbued with God-given talent that will lead to a great life. Furthermore, no matter how bleak the political and economic land-scape, people go on getting married, starting families, taking vacations, and fostering new relationships. We celebrate milestones both small and large.

While optimism is its own reward, its benefits far exceed a cheery outlook. Studies show that optimism has real, tangible health benefits (again, the mind and body influence one another). Research indicates that optimistic people rebound from illness and surgery better than people who report possessing a more cynical outlook on life. But can a person who isn't naturally optimistic develop a sense of optimism? Absolutely. Optimism isn't just something a person is born with; optimism can be learned and exercised, like a muscle.

Both optimism and pessimism have to do with how we think about our circumstances and the causes of adversity. Take Jack, for example. His car broke down on the way to work. Immediately, his mind started swirling with pessimistic views. He thought to himself, *If I weren't so irresponsible, this wouldn't have happened. I should've been more prepared.* Jack believed his entire day would be ruined because of this setback—an example of a universally pessimistic view. And since Jack kept on chastising himself and blaming his "usual bad luck," he did indeed have a lousy day.

Now consider Jill, whose car broke down on the way to work that very same morning. Jill is a practical person who neither wears rose-colored glasses nor blames herself for every little thing that goes wrong. She accepts that sometimes difficult things occur that are beyond her control, and she doesn't allow setbacks to negatively impact how she views herself. After inspecting her flat tire, Jill thought to herself, *Well, these things happen. It's no big deal. I'll call a tow truck and catch a ride into work.* Jill accepted the situation, dealt with it, and moved on with her day. Of course she wasn't thrilled with the hassle and coming repair costs, but she kept the predicament in perspective and made a conscious choice to remain positive.

Optimism is, at its core, a way of reframing obstacles. Here are a few strategies for developing your optimism muscle:

- Instead of dwelling on your problems, focus on finding solutions. Brooding over a problem won't change anything. Identifying solutions is empowering and will help you feel self-sufficient and capable the next time a similar problem presents itself.

- Practice gratitude, even (and especially) for the small things. If you haven't started a gratitude journal yet, now would be a great time to do so. Make a list of five things you're thankful for each night. Soon enough, your mind will naturally look for reasons to be grateful.

- Look for the opportunities in your misfortune. Part of what makes a difficult situation so hard to handle is the sense that you are powerless, but that is rarely (if ever) the case. If you forgot your big work report at home on its due date, you now have the opportunity to practice humility and ask your boss for an extension. If you lost your wallet, you have the opportunity to reevaluate your organizational habits and develop ones that work better for you. The options are truly endless.

Self-Talk: The Stream of Messages You Send Yourself

In the 2000 movie *What Women Want*, viewers get a peek into the minds of the women the main character (portrayed by Mel Gibson) encounters on a daily basis. And what he discovers startles him. He is surprised to find that the women he interacts with have a constant, never-ending stream of inner dialogue. The joke resonates with audiences because it's true. And of course it's not just true for women—it's true for all of us.

We talk to ourselves all day long. We become so familiar with the sound of our own internal voice that we sometimes don't even recognize it as a voice anymore. But the way we talk to ourselves matters tremendously. Our inner voice impacts the atmosphere in our minds, how we view ourselves, and how we perceive the world around us. Anxiety occurs when our inner critic turns up the volume. Some of us were born with a critical inner voice; others experience a slow shift over time, and our inner critic comes out during seasons of stress.

Take a quick inventory of your own inner voice. Do the following thoughts resonate with you?

- *I'm going to blow it!*
- *I never get things right.*
- *I shouldn't even try.*
- *I deserved to fail.*
- *I only bring people down.*

If any of those sound familiar to you, your inner voice could use a tune-up. Most of us fall into the trap of believing that our thoughts are the by-product of a healthy mind. We consider our thoughts an extension of ourselves, and we don't question whether our thoughts are good for us. But that's not exactly the case. Thankfully, we can reduce anxiety by simply changing our internal conversation.

Challenge yourself to notice critical, fearful thoughts. At first, noticing them is enough. After a few days, commit to adding positive thoughts throughout your day. There's no need to chide yourself for experiencing negative thoughts. In fact, doing so may make matters worse. Simply adding more compassionate thoughts is enough to begin to reduce anxiety.

Here are a few such thoughts to get you started:

- *I deserve the good things in my life.*
- *Perfection isn't required.*
- *I've succeeded at many things before.*
- *One bad moment does not make a bad day.*
- *God loves me just as I am, even with my shortcomings.*

The way you talk to yourself sets the tone for how you'll engage with the world and the types of interactions you'll come to expect with others. If you can't talk to yourself kindly, how can you expect others to? Many people see a significant reduction in anxiety by learning to speak to themselves with more compassion.

Cognitive Defusion

One powerful tool in the process of healing anxiety is cognitive defusion, the ability to distance ourselves from our thoughts without becoming ensnared by or entangled in them. Many of us automatically judge our own

STRATEGIES TO PRACTICE MIND OVER MOOD

Mindfulness

Mindfulness involves being present in the current moment. Rather than being anxious about the future or regretting the past, we focus on what is immediately present—our own bodily sensations, physical surroundings, emotional state, thoughts and ideas, and spiritual beliefs and contemplations.

Optimism

Optimism is a key ingredient for every content and successful person. At its core, optimism is a way of reframing obstacles. It can involve focusing on solutions instead of problems, practicing gratitude, and looking for opportunities in misfortune.

Self-Talk

The way we talk to ourselves sets the tone for how we'll engage with the world and the types of interactions we'll come to expect with others. Talking kindly to ourselves will make it easier to accept and look for the kind things others say about us.

Cognitive Defusion

Cognitive defusion is the ability to distance ourselves from our thoughts without being entangled in them. Through cognitive defusion, we try to observe our thoughts without judgment, letting them come and go like the tide.

Metacognition/Labeling

Metacognition is the act of observing our own thoughts and then developing thoughts *about* those thoughts. By labeling our anxious thoughts and emotions, we create a safe space for them to come, and then—importantly—to go. Becoming more specific about our emotions will help us to notice patterns and feel less intimidated by overwhelming, unnamed feelings.

thoughts, determining them to be good or bad, acceptable or unacceptable. By doing so, we commit ourselves to avoiding or fighting those thoughts. And as a result, we face a monster of our own creation—an exhausting and impossible feat.

Instead, try to imagine your thoughts like the waves of the ocean, and your mind is the boat you have with which to navigate them. The goal of any skilled sailor is not taming the waves but gracefully and skillfully staying above them. The same is true for how we navigate our own thoughts.

Cognitive defusion is the act of observing your own thoughts without judgment, letting them come and go like a tide.

This process may seem foreign at first, but the truth is that we are not plunged into our own thoughts, nor do our thoughts possess some compulsory power over us. We can separate ourselves from our thoughts and, in effect, resist succumbing to the undertow of anxiety. Cognitive defusion is a major component of mindfulness and meditation, and it can be practiced like any other skill. Set aside five minutes each day and practice allowing your thoughts to ebb and flow. Resist the urge to condemn them; simply allow them to *be*. When this becomes difficult to practice, try using defusion statements like the following:

- *My thoughts are neither good nor bad. They just are.*
- *My thoughts don't determine the kind of person I am. How I act on my thoughts is what matters most.*
- *I can let go of this thought and welcome the next.*

The application of cognitive defusion is called cognitive distancing and involves practices that help make defusion practical and concrete. Cognitive distancing is an important step along the way toward healing anxiety because the brain effectively "seals" what you know emotionally when you apply it physically. Here are some examples of cognitive distancing:

- Write down your uncensored thoughts in a thoughts journal. The purpose of this exercise is not to judge yourself or the quality of your thoughts but to practice knowing, naming, and distancing your sense of identity from them.

- Write your thoughts as they come to you on a whiteboard and read them from across the room. This activity serves to literally separate you from your thoughts. Notice that you are not attached to your thoughts. In fact, the thoughts you write on the board will be done and over by the time you read them back to yourself; that's how quickly thoughts come and go!

- Imagine or pretend that your thoughts are happening within another person's mind. Replace your own name with someone else's and write the following sentence: "I notice that Susanne is thinking . . ." This activity will help you to gain a less passionate and clearer perspective on your thoughts.

Metacognition: Label Your Thoughts

All of us have anxious thoughts sometimes—it's part of being human. Anxiety is normal from time to time. But instead of *fighting* anxiety, changing our approach to being curious about our anxiety will bring about peace. So when we sense anxious thoughts arising, instead of pushing them away or giving in to them, we can practice metacognition and labeling.

Metacognition is the act of observing our own thoughts and then developing thoughts *about* those thoughts. For example, at the end of a long workday, when you find yourself dreading the next day and feeling like a failure, try expressing curiosity about your own thoughts. That might mean saying out loud, "Here comes Dread. It's here to teach me something. What can I learn from this feeling?"

In essence, we need to create a safe space for our own anxious thoughts to come, and then—importantly—to go. Anxiety often feels like it's going to last forever. But the fact is that every emotion has a shelf life. Anxiety triggers chemical reactions in our body that last under one minute and which will likely resolve on their own—unless we reactivate them by worrying. This is why it's so important to become dispassionate observers of our own feelings.

Labeling is an extension of metacognition. It allows us to name our emotions, become more familiar with them, and thus let them come and go. Many of us have a limited emotional vocabulary. Expanding our ability to recognize and differentiate our emotions will be helpful in getting to know our feelings better and giving ourselves power over them. For example, try replacing the word *anxious* with the following: *uneasy, fretful, disturbed,* or *tense.* Becoming more specific about our emotions will help us to notice patterns and feel less intimidated by an overwhelming, unnamed feeling. Try observing your emotions and greeting them by name.

Labeling your emotions is also helpful as you try to talk with loved ones or professionals about them. For example, if you've ever felt tense around your spouse, emotional labeling will help you be more specific and measured with him or her. Perhaps you're not anxious at all—perhaps you're angry. And underneath your anger, you might be afraid. Emotional labeling allows us to become more self-aware and to manage our own responses. We can then adapt to our circumstances and negotiate with other people.

The mind is one of the greatest assets God gave us to thrive, flourish, and prosper. Our minds can empower us to discover creative innovations, solve difficult problems, and make decisions that lead to a fulfilling life. But sometimes our minds—our thoughts and impressions and perceptions—work against us. When our thoughts are negative, distorted, or out of balance, we become filled with doubt, distrust, and despair. And anxiety.

This leads to very good news. It is within your power and ability to control and shape your thoughts to be comforting, reassuring, and life-giving. The theme of this entire chapter is distilled down to this: you are not a slave to your anxious, pessimistic thoughts. You are in charge of your thoughts, and you can direct them to help you rather than hinder you, to propel you forward rather than hold you back.

Your Personal Reset Plan

This chapter looked at several techniques to help you overcome negative thoughts rather than *be* overcome by them. Try some of these activities to begin putting these techniques to use in resetting your anxiety.

1. **Read a book (or a blog post or article) about mindfulness.** This is such an important technique for calming your brain and soothing your emotions that it warrants further exploration. Many people misunderstand what mindfulness involves, assuming it means doing yoga or sitting cross-legged on the floor while meditating. There are many ways to incorporate a mindful approach to life, and reading a helpful book will give you ideas. I have included book suggestions in appendix 6 (see pages 249–252).

2. **Identify several specific aspects of your life that you feel especially positive and optimistic about.** Do this in your journal or with a counselor or a close friend. These aspects might be your work,

parenting, marriage, spiritual growth, or creative pursuits. Be as specific as possible, and celebrate the good things in your life. One powerful way to relieve anxiety is to *choose* to focus on the positive parts of your life rather than dwelling on the things that are less than ideal.

3. **Examine your negative thoughts.** Write down a sentence or two that reveals a specific thought that's been troubling you. Then try to identify what might have triggered the thought. Did a coworker make a snide remark about you? Did a news report particularly upset you? Did a review of your bank statement send you into a panic? Once you know the source of the troubling thought, you're in a better position to look at it realistically and to reframe it in positive terms.

4. **Try a simple cognitive distancing exercise.** On a piece of paper, write down a negative belief you feel is holding you back and weighing you down. Now take the piece of paper, fold it up, and throw it in your blazing fireplace (or put it through your shredder, or cut it up into small pieces and throw it away). As you do, say to yourself, *This belief has been with me for a long time—but not anymore. I am choosing to let it go and replace it with a more positive and more accurate belief about myself.*

5. **Envision your best possible self and life.** For the next two weeks, spend fifteen minutes thinking about and writing about enjoying the best possible circumstances in your future. Ponder your goals and dreams, and envision that everything works out to be the very best situation. Then spend another five minutes visualizing this best future life as vividly as you can, with lots of details. This exercise is more than just a feel-good pep talk for yourself; you will be retraining your mind and redirecting your thoughts. A study published in the *Journal of Behavior Therapy and Experimental Psychiatry* demonstrated that this exercise boosted the participants' level of optimism.[2]

CHAPTER 12

Manage Your Emotions to Alleviate Anxiety

*Navigate your thoughts and feelings
to chart a new course forward.*

First-century Roman slave–turned-philosopher Epictetus once said, "As you think, so you become. . . . Our busy minds are forever jumping to conclusions, manufacturing and interpreting signs that aren't there."

That's as good a description as you'll find of one of the most powerful reasons why breaking free from the grip of anxiety can seem so hard to do. In short, our own mental habits reinforce the enemy from within. Most of the time this happens quite beyond our conscious awareness, like a program running in the background on your computer, out of sight, but very much in charge of your experience.

The good news is, it's possible to *become* aware of how your thoughts and beliefs are shaping who you are—and to deliberately take back control of your life. You can flush out your hidden negative assumptions and conclusions and replace them with thoughts that serve your recovery and support who you want to become.

A Proven Hypothesis

Mental health professionals have a name for this approach: cognitive behavioral therapy (CBT). That's a fancy-sounding title that acknowledges the link between our thoughts (cognition) and our actions (behavior). When our thoughts and beliefs are out of whack, the theory goes, then our behavioral responses will be too. Then, through our actions, we'll go on perpetuating and reinforcing whatever condition is causing us trouble, with no end in sight. Here's how psychologist Vara Saripalli describes CBT, writing for Medical News Today:

> Some forms of psychotherapy focus on looking into the past to gain an understanding of current feelings. In contrast, CBT focuses on present thoughts and beliefs. . . . According to CBT, people's pattern of thinking is like wearing a pair of glasses that makes us see the world in a specific way. CBT makes us more aware of how these thought patterns create our reality and determine how we behave.[1]

Experts at Mayo Clinic assessed the treatment's application and effectiveness this way: "CBT can be a very helpful tool—either alone or in combination with other therapies—in treating mental health disorders, such as depression, post-traumatic stress disorder (PTSD) or an eating disorder. But not everyone who benefits from CBT has a mental health condition. CBT can be an effective tool to help anyone learn how to better manage stressful life situations."[2]

That's an important point. We're talking about mental habits that can spin out of control no matter who you are or what is troubling you. For instance, distorted thinking may be playing a negative role for people struggling with potentially threatening medical conditions, anger, grief, shame, divorce, workplace stress, parenting worries, and so on. "Dysfunctional assumptions"—the name given by psychologists to negative and inaccurate self-talk—come in all shapes:

- Career: *Things never work out for me, so why bother trying anymore?*
- Health: *Odds are good I'll get cancer at some time in my life.*

- Parenting: *The world is full of bad people who want to hurt my kids.*
- Finances: *I'm no good with money. I never will be.*

If done properly, CBT can help you become your own psychotherapist. It leads you to see these underlying principles at work and to confidently apply them to yourself in any situation. That helps explain why people pursuing CBT often experience much more rapid progress than those undertaking traditional talk therapy.[3] In fact, numerous studies have confirmed that CBT performs at least as well as common anti-depression medications in mitigating symptoms and has a more lasting effect.[4]

A Story of Distortion

Micah lived in a studio apartment above his sister's garage. He had moved in "temporarily" after graduating high school—just until he could choose what to do with his life.

I met Micah a few weeks before his thirtieth birthday, and right after his sister Ruth had put her foot down. It was one thing to stand by while her brother turned twenty with no clear direction, but she would not be a part of letting him start his thirties that way. If he didn't seek help, she said, then he could look for other living arrangements. It was immediately apparent to me what had kept Micah's life frozen in place for so long: he suffered from severe social anxiety, particularly around women.

Micah described himself in boyhood as a "scrawny, sensitive kid, nothing but big ears and bony elbows." As often happens, however, around age sixteen, Micah started to emerge and transform. Not exactly a "cool kid" yet, he nevertheless was no longer the obvious school "dork." That emboldened him to ask a girl from chemistry class to the Valentine's Day dance in his senior year. She had her own reputation for awkwardness, something Micah felt gave them common ground. Unbelievably, she said yes. Things were looking up.

But there was another dimension to Micah's life that challenged his confidence regularly. He'd grown up with an angry, alcoholic stepfather who had an uncanny ability to sense when Micah was growing stronger and to know precisely what was needed to put him back in his place. The night of the dance, the man saw Micah leaving the house in sport coat and tie and followed him with the kind of subtle taunts that emotionally abusive people excel at. Today we call it "gaslighting," sowing self-doubt without ever being overtly confrontational.

"She must be a real winner," he said, with skillfully disguised sarcasm.

That night, for some reason, it was too much for Micah. He lost his composure and talked back. You can imagine how that was received, and the escalation left Micah enraged—and in tears.

"I hope you don't let your girl see that," his stepfather said of his emotions.

Micah had regained outward control by the time he picked up his date, but she sensed he had been crying and asked if he was upset.

"I wanted to prove the old man wrong, about myself and about her," Micah shared with me after a few sessions of digging. "So I told her everything." Sitting in the school parking lot, all his pain came flooding to the surface, and he cried again.

You can probably guess what happened next. The young woman—who had her own set of adolescent emotional struggles—was completely unprepared to handle Micah's. Shortly after they went inside, she claimed she was suddenly not feeling well and asked him to take her home. She was not cruel, just anxious to remove herself from her own discomfort.

A League of Dysfunctional Assumptions

That was the last date Micah had ever had. The event was charged with such high-voltage emotional energy that it defined everything about his life for over a decade. In particular, it caused him to form some powerful conclusions about "the way things are." Here's what he told himself:

- *My stepfather was right about showing emotional weakness to women.*
- *He must have been right about everything else as well, especially his low opinion of me.*
- *I am the person he said I am.*
- *No woman would want a person like me.*
- *The only way to escape that pain is to avoid women entirely.*

With thoughts and beliefs like that talking in his ear, it's not hard to see how Micah came to be living alone above his sister's garage like it was a fortress. His list of beliefs about himself, others, and the world had provided fertile ground for a full-blown anxiety disorder—and the hypersensitive, protective behaviors that came with it.

However, Micah—like so many others struggling with mental, emotional, or behavioral problems—could see only his anxiety. He felt it to be simply who he was and had never recognized the link between his mistaken beliefs, his behavior, and his experience of life.

Understanding that relationship, it turns out, is one of the most powerful tools available to anyone looking to heal from anxiety. Give it a moment's consideration, and you'll quickly see for yourself what good news this is. If much of the fear and anxiety that plagues you is the result of misguided or flat-out false assumptions you've made, then changing how you think can directly change your life!

How Does It Work?

Though every situation is different, CBT generally follows four basic steps:

1. Identify the Conditions or Situations in Your Life That Are Troubling You.

In order to set clear, measurable goals, you must be honest and specific about the problems you are eager to solve. People who have struggled for years with severe anxiety can have very distorted ideas about what's wrong, often gleaned from the well-meaning advice of friends and family or from a host of dubious internet sources.

In Micah's case, he was convinced that if he could come to grips with his troubled relationship with his stepfather, it would break an emotional logjam and take care of the rest. While that was certainly an aim worth pursuing, it was too vague and amorphous for the CBT process. The real issue was that severe social anxiety was having a significant negative effect on his life, even to the point of causing his sister to threaten him with eviction. The goal he identified for himself was to understand the assumptions reinforcing his anxiety and to alter his fearful behavior in life-affirming ways. *That* was something he could work with.

2. Notice Your Thoughts, Feelings, and Beliefs about Your Problems.

Next, you'll take inventory of your internal dialogue with yourself and of beliefs that are so deeply ingrained you're barely aware of them anymore, if at all. Once we form certain judgments, it's no longer necessary to overtly repeat them over and over to ourselves. They simply become a given that silently, but surely, shapes how we behave. A skilled counselor will help you see these at work by listening carefully and encouraging you to hear yourself clearly as well.

As with many people dealing with chronic anxiety, Micah at first found it difficult to identify specific thoughts and feelings that fueled his distress. He just knew he felt anxious much of the time and that his emotions were "like a big, tangled ball of twine." With guidance, by sorting through his feelings and by journaling to gain clarity, Micah came to recognize that he frequently told himself he was a "loser" and a "screwup." He considered himself "pathetic" when trying to interact with others, and he believed he was better off avoiding people as much as possible, for his sake and theirs.

3. Identify Which Thoughts Are Negative or Inaccurate— and Are Perpetuating the Problem.

Often the hard part, once you've taken stock of your thoughts about something, is to see which thoughts are destructively negative or even outright wrong. That's because, over the years, your mind has become quite adept at rationalizing and defending its cherished perspective on things. It can explain until Armageddon all the reasons why anxiety is the only logical response to conditions in your life, based on the "evidence."

In this stage of CBT, it's your job to step outside your own thoughts and feelings and force your everyday mind to *prove* what it believes. You get to act as the judge in a court case and decide what is admissible and what isn't. That requires a solid commitment on your part to really get to the bottom of things and to face the truth, no matter how uncomfortable it may be to do so.

This step was not easy for Micah because the labels he bore and the messages he had told himself for so long had become ingrained—a part of his identity. But in time he saw that challenges in his communication with people, especially women, did not mean that he was a loser and a screwup in all aspects of his life. When he saw those labels for what they were—lies he was told and came to believe himself—he recognized the destructive toll they were taking on his attitudes and actions.

4. Replace Negative or Inaccurate Thoughts and Feelings.

Now comes the payoff. You've seen the link between your thoughts, behavior, and life experience. You've honestly assessed where your dysfunctional assumptions lie. Finally, you get to put the power of your mind to work on your behalf for a change—by consciously deciding what you think and believe about your life.

Here's how it worked for Micah:

- He accepted that anxiety was causing dramatic negative consequences in his life.
- He paid attention to his thoughts and feelings for a time.
- He challenged the ones that were unhelpful or wrong: *Is it really true that just because one young girl wasn't ready to handle my emotional state, all women would react that way?*
- He replaced those thoughts with ones that were more true and affirming: *I don't have to adopt anyone else's view of me. There are plenty of people who will accept me exactly as I am.*

Back in the Driver's Seat

It would be misleading to say this process is easy or delivers instantaneous results. Like almost everything in life, your reward will be proportionate to your resolve and readiness to heal. But I can confidently say that if you make CBT a part of your anxiety treatment plan, you will do far more than gain relief. You'll lay the foundation for a lifetime of health and wellness. You'll know firsthand that your life is yours to shape and to grow as you please.

"As you *think*, so you become."

Your Personal Reset Plan

CBT is an approach to healing that is best undertaken in partnership with a trained and committed therapist. It often takes the observational skill and neutral perspective of a trusted guide to navigate the tricky terrain of your own thoughts.

However, here are some things you can do to prepare yourself for that journey:

1. **Keep a journal.** Writing is a powerful way to shrink larger-than-life fears and judgments down to a manageable size and to make them stand still long enough to submit to scrutiny. The beauty of journaling is that no one need ever see what you write, so you are free to honestly express yourself. There are no "wrong" answers. Just you and your desire to be well.

2. **Carry blank index cards and a pen everywhere you go.** As you move through your day, notice your thoughts and feelings. Quickly jot down the essence of it on a card, along with any circumstances that triggered it. Don't hold back. You are forming the habit of awareness, so be bold.

3. **Rewrite cards on which you have recorded your negative or inaccurate thoughts.** As you record your thoughts, you'll start to notice which ones are "dysfunctional assumptions." Take out a new card and write a new belief you'd like to replace the old ones with. Be as specific as possible. Tear up the old one. With this exercise you are quite literally designing your new self.

4. **Share your thoughts with someone you trust.** So far, by noticing your thoughts, recording them, and rewriting them, you've still remained in the privacy of your own mind. However, there is real power in speaking these things out loud as well. It's important to choose someone who will listen but not judge; who will support you without the need to add their voice in intervention. Sometimes just hearing yourself say the distorted beliefs that have been your mental default for years is enough to help you see through them—and to know what you'd like to believe instead.

5. **Be patient. You will certainly have good days, full of clarity and insight.** Then there will be others that seem to set you back to square one. Don't despair! You are challenging mental habits that have had free rein for perhaps many years. Set small goals and realistic expectations. Celebrate every incremental win, and you'll soon notice that the wins outnumber the setbacks many times over.

CHAPTER 13

Bolster Your Body

*Here's how to reset your physical strength
and wellness.*

I appreciate the words of theologian and educator Anthony Coniaris, who said, "The truth is that the body and the soul live so close to each other that they often catch one another's sicknesses, illnesses and diseases."[1] So true! I have seen this principle at work in the thousands of clients I've worked with for over three decades. All aspects of our being—body, mind, and spirit—are inextricably intertwined and affect one another, for better or worse.

As you've wrestled with anxieties large and small, you have likely also realized that your body and mind have a symbiotic relationship. When you feel worried or anxious, your heart might race and your blood pressure increase. You might experience tension in your stomach and notice your muscles tightening and fists clenching. This is the initial fight-or-flight response that we've discussed previously, and sometimes this response is a good, helpful thing. But unabated, the anxiety response can eventually wear you down, give you headaches, make you feel tired and weary, and even cause serious illnesses.

The car you drive may help illustrate this point. If your vehicle needs servicing, it may have a high idle that needs adjustment. Even when you're stopped at a light, the engine revs too high, and you practically have to stand on the brakes to keep from lurching into the vehicle ahead of you. Keep driving the car in this condition, and your gas mileage will plunge as your engine wastes gas. You'll use too much fuel, wear out your brakes, and eventually burn out your engine.

A life of anxiety is like living on high idle. It's a waste of fuel and not good for you. Like the engine and brakes of your car, your body bears the consequences of the frequent anxiety-driven state of fight or flight. Chronic anxiety doesn't give your body the respite it needs to relax, renew, and rebuild. Over time, the emotional problem also becomes a serious physical one. In a ruthless, vicious cycle, the anxious mind leads to a weakened body, and a weakened body is compromised when trying to help the anxious mind.

The Physical-Emotional Connection

Father Anthony Coniaris, quoted above, continued his description of the physical-emotional connection in terms we can all identify with:

> Sometimes the ills of the body have their root in the mind, in our emotions, in our soul. Thus, when the spirit is healed, the strength of the body is restored. . . .
>
> The body is the sounding board for the soul. For example, worry can cause knots in the stomach, anger can increase blood pressure and stress can cause heart disease. Troubled relationships reflect the dynamic between soul and body. There is reason for the often-used sayings, "He is a pain in the neck" or "she gives me headache." Anxiety, worry, resentment and unhappy family relationships all take their toll on the body.[2]

A healthy spirit (mind, emotions, soul) is vital to a sound body; likewise, a sound body is vital to a healthy spirit. Thus, it makes sense that in treating the anxious mind, we must also keep the body healthy and strong, providing the mind a sound, stable foundation on which to rebuild the whole person.

In the pages ahead, I'm going to share five essential strategies that will help you bolster your body and fortify your physical wellness—to renew your physical vitality and keep your engine and support systems properly tuned so your body will sustain you as you confront the stresses and anxieties of life. As you put these strategies to work, it won't be long before you start to feel better, stronger, and more able to tackle the challenges before you.

1. Check Your Fuel Quality

A friend of mine recently purchased a gas-powered lawn mower. Before wheeling it away from the lawn center, he asked the salesman to put a little gas in the tank to test the engine. Then, only a few seconds after my friend pulled the starter cord, the engine sputtered and died. He tried again with the same result. The salesman quickly diagnosed the problem: "You know what? This gas has been sitting in this container for several months. It's old. Let me get some fresh gas." He brought out a new container, and the engine started right up. My friend has had no trouble with his mower since. The fundamental problem was bad fuel.

In a similar way, our bodies were created to require proper fuel. But in the name of convenience, our culture pushes thousands of processed, prepackaged foods bearing lengthy lists of ingredients that require a doctorate in chemistry to pronounce, let alone comprehend. Then there are the ubiquitous fast-food places on every other corner, where you don't even have to leave your vehicle to purchase bags full of saturated fat, real and artificial sugar, caffeine and double caffeine, and empty calories.

It has become far too easy—and, let's face it, too delicious—to imbibe bad fuel and deprive our bodies of the good fuel we need to be at our best. So in order to conquer anxiety and be stronger than the stresses of life, we must start with a strategic improvement of the fuel we feed our bodies.

First comes *water*. The adult human body is up to 60 percent water, and the blood that courses through your arteries and veins is 92 percent water. You *need* water, and large amounts of it throughout the day, for your organs, skin, and blood to function properly. Even mild dehydration can make you feel weak and affect your mood. So start each day with sixteen ounces of water, and try to consume this amount at least four or five more times throughout the day, easing off a few hours before bedtime.

A healthy diet needs a frequent variety of *fresh fruits and vegetables*. I'm not talking about a mere apple a day or a couple of salads a week—though those are a good start. Each and every day, your body needs multiple servings of fresh fruit and fresh veggies. Recent studies have determined that you should consume a total of *nine* moderate servings of fresh fruit and vegetables with your meals and snacks throughout the day.[3]

Building a healthy body also requires *whole-grain foods*, not highly processed ones. Swear off nutrition-free white breads and shift to whole-grain breads. Leave the ever-present sugared cereals behind on the grocery shelves, and treat your body to steel-cut oatmeal or unsweetened granola with fresh berries.

Good fuel also means *lean meats and fish, eggs, and low-fat dairy products*. Deep-fried meats or fish should be minimized; grilled or baked is far healthier. Fish and fish oil provide healthy fats, as do unprocessed nuts and seeds such as raw almonds, walnuts, and sunflower seeds. If you have trouble digesting milk, you'll want to consider lactose-free products such as almond milk.

Unfortunately, grocery-store "fresh" may camouflage the fact that your store purchases contain GMOs (genetically modified organisms) or that the crops were treated with pesticides and other chemicals. For this reason I suggest that you look for the "USDA Organic" certification label on as many foods as possible. (Note that the term *natural* is overused and under-regulated. It doesn't assure you of the purity you're looking for.) Yes, organic foods typically cost a little more, but more and more grocery chains are increasing their certified organic offerings, and their prices are becoming more affordable.

I also recommend a *broad-based nutritional supplement* including vitamins, minerals, and amino acids. I live a busy, complex life, and I just don't have the time to figure out all the food combinations I'd need to make sure I get enough selenium, calcium, magnesium, and zinc, to say nothing of the alphabet of vitamins my body needs. A quality nutritional supplement conveniently assures me that I'm getting the balanced nutrition that even a healthy diet may lack. (We'll address nutritional supplements more thoroughly in chapter 15.)

ANTI-ANXIETY NUTRIENT RESET CHECKLIST

To regulate your emotions and relieve anxiety, it's essential to ensure that you are consistently consuming nutrients that will fortify your body. In fact, you might be surprised to learn that specific foods have been shown to reduce anxiety. These include

- leafy greens, such as spinach, kale, and Swiss chard. These foods are rich in magnesium, which is important because a lack of this nutrient has been show to increase anxiety-related behaviors.
- legumes, nuts, seeds, and whole grains. These foods are also rich in magnesium.
- omega-3 fatty acid foods, including wild Alaskan salmon, tuna, sardines, mackerel, anchovies, chia seeds, flaxseeds, walnuts, and soybeans.
- antioxidant-rich foods, such as pinto, black, and red kidney beans; apples, prunes, sweet cherries, plums, blackberries, strawberries, cranberries, raspberries, and blueberries; walnuts and pecans; artichokes, kale, spinach, beets, and broccoli.
- foods rich in zinc, such as oysters, cashews, liver, beef, and egg yolks.
- probiotic-rich foods such as pickles, sauerkraut, and kefir.
- avocado and almonds, which are rich in vitamin B.

The Magic of Moderation

Now for the really hard part. What about that life-giving fluid lovingly referred to as coffee and those sweet treats that taste *sooo* good as a snack or dessert? It goes without saying, but I'll say it anyway: coffee and other caffeinated beverages don't calm you; they rev you up. You know this; your body knows this. Caffeine increases your heart rate and blood pressure and makes you jittery and nervous, which only compounds anxiety. Caffeine can stay in your system for as long as eight hours, so you can imagine the accumulated effect of consuming multiple cups of coffee throughout the day. Ease off the habit by cutting your consumption to just one or two cups with a healthy protein breakfast in the morning, and avoid those highly sugared, highly caffeinated "energy" drinks altogether.

Sweet treats? Sugar is a potent, mood-altering substance. It tastes so good, but watch any group of children after they've consumed birthday cake, ice cream, and soft drinks, and you'll see manic activity followed by a plunge into sluggish grouchiness. This reaction may be more pronounced in children, but it happens in adults, too. Refined sugar can make you climb the walls. Your blood glucose levels spike to an artificial high, then rapidly plummet, which only exacerbates the physical and emotional effects of the anxiety you're working so hard to overcome. Avoiding dramatic ups and downs in your blood glucose levels will help stabilize your mood, calm your system, and improve your overall energy. Again, with sweet treats, moderation is the key, and only after a healthy meal.

What kind of fuel have you been putting into your body? You won't conquer anxiety unless you upgrade the quality of your food and beverage intake. Why not start today?

2. Get Moving

Research has shown that focused physical movement is healthful to your body's cardiovascular system, strengthens bones and fortifies muscle, reduces fatigue, and calms the worrisome thoughts and jittery feelings that may be building up inside you.

A big reason for the soothing effect is that regular exercise increases the release of essential chemicals and hormones that have a major impact on brain health and mood. These chemicals include *serotonin*, a natural mood stabilizer; *norepinephrine*, which affects alertness, focus, and memory; and *dopamine*, a neurotransmitter linked to pleasure and motivation. Perhaps the most noticeable mood benefit of exercise comes from the enhanced release of *endorphins*—chemicals produced naturally by the nervous system that are often called "feel-good" chemicals because they can act as a pain reliever and happiness booster. Endorphins are primarily made in the hypo-thalamus and pituitary glands, though they may come from other parts of the body as well. The well-known "runner's high" that is felt after vigorous exercise is due to an increase in endorphin levels.

But it doesn't take a marathon-like effort on your part to realize the positive effects of endorphins. Scientists have found that regular, moderate exercise decreases overall levels of tension, elevates and stabilizes mood, improves sleep quality, and improves self-esteem.

Psychologists studying how exercise relieves anxiety have reported that just five minutes of aerobic exercise can begin to stimulate anti-anxiety effects, and that a ten-minute walk may be just as good as a forty-five-minute workout. In one study, researchers found that those who engage in regular exercise were 25 percent less likely to develop an anxiety disorder over the following five years.[4]

Even more encouraging is that some studies indicate that regular exercise is as effective as medication in reducing anxiety symptoms—and the results can stay with you. According to the Anxiety and Depression Association of America, "One vigorous exercise session can help alleviate anxiety symptoms for hours, and a regular schedule may significantly reduce them over time."[5]

These findings indicate that exercise is the perfect activity when you need a healthier coping strategy. When anxiety is weighing heavily, it's far too easy to self-medicate with comfort foods, alcohol, smoking or vaping, pharmaceuticals, excessive TV, or other forms of escapism. But focused physical movement is the healthy coping strategy; it helps you feel better in the moment, both physically and emotionally, as it creates lasting benefits for the health and well-being of your brain, mind, and body.

Start Gently . . .

If you've been relatively sedentary lately, please don't let the idea of focused physical movement scare you. You can and should start small . . . and slowly. Of course, you'll want to check with your physician before engaging in any exercise program that's more vigorous than what you're currently doing.

To start getting good exercise, you don't need to load up on overpriced designer workout attire, purchase expensive weights or machines, recruit a personal trainer, or spend hours (and dollars) at a fitness center—although a trainer and gym could help you down the road. You can start small simply by

- parking your car farther from your workplace or grocery store;
- taking the stairs instead of the elevator;
- grabbing fifteen-minute walks outside during breaks;
- walking the dog in the mornings and evenings; and
- picking up the pace a bit, wherever you walk.

Any focused physical movement that gets your heart beating faster and lungs breathing more deeply will stimulate blood circulation, oxygenate your body and mind, and produce the endorphins and neurotransmitters that help you feel both relaxed and energized.

... Then Build Gradually

As soon as you are able, you will want to step up the physical movement both in quantity and quality for even greater benefits to your overall health and in overcoming anxiety. The US Department of Health and Human Services' *Physical Activity Guidelines for Americans* recommends that you aim for at least

- two and a half hours weekly of *moderate-intensity aerobic activity* (a.k.a. "cardio" exercises such as brisk walking, hiking, running, bicycling, and elliptical). This weekly time target is equivalent to just thirty minutes daily for five days per week or forty-five to fifty minutes daily, three days per week.
- two days per week of *muscle-strengthening ("resistance") activities* that work all major muscle groups (legs, core, back, chest, arms, and shoulders). You could start with simple graduated exercise bands that stretch and resist as you pull on them, then gradually move up to dumbbells, barbells, or weight machines.[6]

Again, let me emphasize that you take exercise one step at a time, especially if you're just starting or starting over. Begin gently to safely awaken those dormant joints and muscles. Push just hard enough to elevate your heart rate and breathe more deeply. (A good rule of thumb for cardio activity is the "talk test": you should be able to carry on a conversation with a real or imagined companion.) Then build gradually, adding both time and resistance. Within just a few weeks, you'll begin to notice significant, positive changes in your overall sense of well-being. Your outlook and self-confidence will be on the upswing. And, perhaps best of all, your days and nights will become calmer as exercise helps you overcome anxiety and brighten your spirit.

Dr. John Ratey, MD, associate clinical professor of psychiatry at Harvard Medical School, sums it up nicely:

As a psychiatrist who studies the effects of exercise on the brain, I've not only seen the science, I've witnessed firsthand how physical activity affects my patients. Research shows aerobic exercise is especially helpful. A simple bike ride, dance class, or even a brisk walk can be a powerful tool for those suffering from chronic anxiety. Activities like these also help people who are feeling overly nervous and anxious about an upcoming test, a big presentation, or an important meeting.[7]

3. Sleep on It

Studies show that more than one-third of all American adults and more than two-thirds of teens don't get sufficient sleep on a regular basis. And our busy schedules are only part of the sleep-deprivation equation. Sleep apnea can cause fragmented sleep and reduce oxygen in the blood, which play a huge role in depression and anxiety.

When you don't get enough sleep, your body, brain, and emotions are negatively affected, and you experience undesirable symptoms including the following:

- decreased overall activity in the brain, impacting focus, learning, memory, and productivity
- impaired driving alertness and response times
- interference with healthy heart function
- compromises in how your body repairs joint and muscle injuries
- reduced production of the hormones your body uses to control appetite, leading to increased obesity
- a "shorter fuse," meaning that your usual mental and emotional filters are compromised and you feel crabby and irritable, less able to respond patiently and diplomatically to the day's challenges

After working with thousands of patients who struggle with anxiety, I know that poor sleep is almost always a part of the problem. You may sleep poorly because you're anxious; then, because you've slept poorly, your anxiety is worse and your ability to cope is compromised, resulting in poor sleep—another vicious cycle. Licensed professional counselor and author Dr. Kathleen Smith, PhD, agrees:

Which comes first, the anxiety or the disruption of sleep? Researchers have found that the relationship between sleep problems and anxiety is bidirectional. This means that sleep problems can cause anxiety, and anxiety can disrupt sleep. And just like anxiety, sleep problems can impact how you function emotionally, mentally, and physically.[8]

If poor sleep is part of the problem, it follows that improving the quantity and quality of your sleep will be part of the solution. In order to support your battle to overcome anxiety, your body and mind need all the refreshment and strength that good sleep brings. If quality sleep has been elusive for you, you'll find the following behaviors to be of significant help. And note that good sleep hygiene is not limited to bedtime; it starts during the daylight hours.

During the Day

Get some sun. One of the many benefits of sunlight is that it helps the body and mind maintain a healthy sleep cycle. Your *circadian rhythm*, or internal clock, is dependent on receiving intervals of light and darkness during a twenty-four-hour period. Exposure to natural light during the day is especially critical if you don't get outside much. Try for at least one fifteen-minute walk outdoors each day. (If you're going to be outside more than twenty minutes, be sure to use sunscreen.)

Move your body. The regular physical movement addressed earlier not only helps relieve anxiety; it brings sleep benefits as well. The energizing endorphins that surge throughout your body during and after exercise help your sleep-wake cycle get back on track, alleviating insomnia. (But because of those energizing endorphins, you'll want to exercise during the day or right after work, not right before bedtime.) And the deep breathing and exertion of exercise help relax your muscles as well as your mind, which improves your sleep quality.

Limit caffeine and alcohol. We've already addressed the caffeine issue, but it's worth another mention here. Too much caffeine or consuming it too late in the day can increase anxiety and inhibit sleep. And drinking alcohol before bedtime can increase your heart rate. You don't want either, so go easy on these products, especially in the evening.

Grab a short nap. While some experts advise against napping at all, I encourage my clients to catch up on slumber anytime they can. A brief midday nap of thirty minutes or less can reduce tension and improve mood, alertness, and performance. Consider it a quick "reset" of your mind and body to better take on the rest of your day.

Before Bed

Limit screen time. Our phones, tablets, and TVs emit light that keeps our brain awake, and as Dr. Smith states, "checking email [or texts] or doing work right before bed can also trigger anxious thoughts and make it difficult to calm your brain."[9]

I go a step further and recommend keeping your cell phone either outside your bedroom or across the room—definitely not on your bedside table. You need to keep it far enough away so you're not hearing the buzz or seeing the screen light up from incoming texts, calls, or emails while you're sleeping.

Create and follow a regular, relaxing bedtime routine. What relaxes you? A warm shower or candlelit bath? Reading a novel or the Bible? Easy-listening music? This is your unwinding time, so keep it soothing and sacred. Do some slow, deep breathing to relax. (There's more on breathing in appendix 4.) Smile and call to mind the blessings of your day, for indeed, there were some *good* things about your day. Focus on them.

Try to go to bed about the same time each evening. A consistent bedtime routine signals to your body and mind that it's time to sleep.

Create a comfortable, sleep-friendly environment. To help you sleep, you should have a quality mattress, and your bedroom should be cool and dark. You may find earplugs, a white-noise machine, a fan, and even a blindfold to be helpful. If you let pets sleep in your bedroom and they keep you awake or awaken you in the night, you may want to rethink the accommodations for your roommates.

Don't watch TV, study, email, text, or read in bed. When you engage in these activities in bed, your brain associates your bed with wakefulness, not with sleep. You want your brain to connect the bed with sleepiness and sleep, and banishing these practices from your bed will definitely help you fall and stay asleep.

At Night

Don't lie awake in bed for more than ten minutes. If you've awakened in the night and can't go back to sleep within ten minutes, get out of bed and sit in a chair, in the dark, until you feel sleepy. Then return to bed. But resist the inclination to check Facebook, turn on the TV, or turn on a light to read. The light will confuse your internal clock and stimulate your brain. Stay in the dark and do some slow, deep breathing to further relax until you're ready to go back to bed.

Of course, despite these recommendations, you may still experience an occasional bad night. That's okay; it happens to all of us. Just get back on track tomorrow. And the next day. By continuing to follow these guidelines, you'll establish some healthy sleep-hygiene habits that will, in the long run, refresh your body and mind and promote emotional wellness.

INDICATORS OF SLEEP DISORDERS TO WATCH FOR

- difficulty falling asleep
- waking up frequently during sleep
- fatigue and low energy during the day
- loud snoring or gasping during sleep
- waking up feeling exhausted
- waking up with chest pains or shortness of breath
- irritability
- lack of concentration
- depression
- weight gain
- diminished work or school performance

4. Take the Right Vitamins

I've already mentioned the importance of a quality vitamin-mineral–amino acid supplement, but it bears repeating as we wrap up this chapter on taking care of your body. Vitamins and minerals, or *micronutrients*, have been called the building blocks of good health. A balanced diet of healthy foods, such as we've examined in this chapter, goes a long way in providing the micronutrients you need; however, they may not cover all the bases or in sufficient amounts. For example, a deficiency in magnesium can trigger anxiety and even panic attacks, and supplementation can provide long-awaited relief. A quality vitamin-mineral–amino acid supplement will help round out your nutrition and give your body and brain the nourishment they need for the day ahead.

5. Do a Gut Check

Recent studies have indicated that anxiety and other mood issues may not be all "in your head" after all; they may also be in your gut. One report says that "gut microbiota—the trillions of microorganisms in the gut which perform important functions in the immune system and metabolism by providing essential inflammatory mediators, nutrients and vitamins—can help regulate brain function through something called the 'gut-brain axis.'"[10] These microorganisms, also called the gut microbiome, have been shown to affect everything from your digestive health to your heart functions to your immune system. And the activity of these bacteria has significant influence on the brain itself, including the function and dysfunction of neurotransmitters (such as those mentioned earlier in this chapter) that affect your mood.

Here's a condensed version of how this works.

The *vagus nerve* is your body's biggest nerve, running from the brain down to the gut, where it branches into a vast information network of neurons. This two-lane highway, along with our immune system and hormones, is known as the *gut-brain axis*. Originally, scientists thought this was for the brain to more closely monitor and control digestive functions. But recent studies have revealed that 90 percent of the fibers in the vagus nerve are actually sending messages *from* this intricate system of neurons *to the brain*. Some of those tiny microorganisms send messages to your brain that directly influence your level of anxiety, happiness, satisfaction, and even depression.

As you know, some foods are extremely beneficial to your overall health as well as your mental health. Likewise, some foods are detrimental, resulting in an unbalanced gut microbiome that, we now know, negatively affects your brain and your mood. In our whole-person approach to healing chronic anxiety, we want to focus on the foods and supplements that promote healthy gut bacteria.

For example, studies reveal that certain strains of bacteria reduce cortisol levels, which decreases stress and therefore decreases anxiety. This research tells us that the introduction of certain "good bacteria" to the gut may relieve stress and anxiety specifically by reducing the output of cortisol.

Our Greatest Cause of Gut Imbalance

According to the Centers for Disease Control (CDC), for every one thousand people, approximately eight hundred to nine hundred antibiotics are dispensed. And, the CDC informs us, nearly 50 percent of antibiotic use in US hospitals is unnecessary or inappropriate.[11] Because of the overuse and misuse of antibiotics, certain diseases are becoming resistant to the drugs, causing a proliferation of the diseases they were formulated to treat.

With so many people taking so many antibiotics, we're looking at our greatest cause of gut microbiome imbalance. Think of how an antibiotic works. You ingest it, and it chases down infection-causing bacteria and eliminates them from your system. The problem is that many antibiotics, especially broad-spectrum treatments, also indiscriminately take out much of the good bacteria your system needs.

And gut imbalance can be difficult to overcome. The most aggressive antibiotics can damage your system so thoroughly that some good strains of bacteria can't even grow back—sometimes not for years, and sometimes not at all, without being intentionally reintroduced.

Thus it's now common for doctors and pharmacists to alert patients to potential digestive side effects like diarrhea, but they don't often take the conversation further. The latest research linking gut imbalances to anxiety and depression will, I hope, change that soon. Until it does, you can become more personally vigilant about your use of antibiotics, only taking them when absolutely necessary and balancing their use with prebiotics and probiotics.

Prebiotics and Probiotics

Prebiotics are substances that support the growth of certain healthy microorganisms, while probiotics are made up of the microorganisms themselves. Just one probiotic supplement contains billions of good bacteria.

A delicious example of a healthful probiotic food is organic unsweetened yogurt, which offers millions of healthy microorganisms to help you restore and maintain gut balance. You can also find good probiotics in capsule form at your grocery or health-food store.

Prebiotics pave the way for probiotics to work. They are not microorganisms; they are nondigestible nutrients that help good bacteria grow and flourish. Most prebiotics are fibers or carbohydrates that can be taken as supplements or found occurring naturally in foods.

No, your anxiety is not all in your head. It's in your gut, too, and I hope this "gut check" will help you make sure you're receiving the micronutrients, prebiotics, and probiotics most of us need to keep the gut microbiome as balanced as possible.

Your Personal Reset Plan

Hopefully this chapter has encouraged you that there are specific steps you can take to strengthen your body and reduce anxiety by strengthening the body-mind connection. The following reset plan will help you get started:

1. **For the next two weeks, keep a food log.** List all the foods and beverages you consume and when. Keep a small notebook in your pocket or purse, and quickly jot down every item you eat and every beverage you drink and at what time you consumed it. As you go, what are you learning about the fuel you put into your "engine"? What are you learning about what you consume, at what time of day, and why you eat or drink it? What is the effect on your energy? Your mood?

2. **Determine three positive changes you'll make in your eating and drinking habits starting now.** Write them down and review them throughout the day. After two weeks, evaluate how your new and improved habits make you feel physically, mentally, and emotionally, then add three more positive new habits over the following two weeks.

3. **Conduct a "sleep audit."** Keeping in mind what I've shared about sleep, honestly assess the daytime, evening, bedtime, and nighttime habits that may be negatively affecting the quantity and quality of your sleep. What three bad habits will you begin changing today? Why?

4. **Starting today, block out a fifteen-minute walk break on your daily schedule.** Schedule your walk for at least once a day; twice is better. Step outside if at all possible, soak in some sunlight, swing your arms as you walk, and breathe deeply. If the weather outside is frightful, then walk indoors and use the stairs. After you return to your workstation, assess how you feel. Is your gut less tense? How's your outlook and energy level? Then, determine your plan to attain the targeted levels of aerobic and resistance exercise in the future and go for it.

5. **Research what types of prebiotics, probiotics, and mood-improvement supplements might be best for you.** By no means am I trying to push The Center's products on you, but they are an option for you to consider. Our team of experts has worked with a nutritional-supplement company to produce a range of products that we believe are very helpful. Another option is to visit your trusted health-food store, one that has a good nutrition section, preferably with a nutrition specialist on staff.

CHAPTER 14

Fortify Your Filters

*Screen out negative messages
that amp up your anxiety.*

Anxiety can be fueled by a surprising number of influences in our lives. Extreme trauma, genetics, childhood experiences, ongoing stressors, how we manage our health and diets—even seemingly innocent daily habits can all contribute to feelings of anxiety or full-blown anxiety disorders.

Some of these factors, like genetics or many forms of trauma, come into our lives without our permission. Other factors, like our daily habits or what we consume, are things we choose.

In this chapter I want to talk about a category of factors we may not actively choose but over which we have a good amount of control. I'm talking about negative messages that come into our lives. The truth is that we are bombarded with detrimental messages from every direction on a daily basis. But this doesn't mean we are helpless or handcuffed in our ability to manage what amplifies our anxiety. Equipped with helpful information and the purposeful intent to fend off these messages, we can fortify our minds against them.

Negative Messages from Negative People

Some people in our lives build us up with encouragement, affirmation, and validation. Other people, unfortunately, do just the opposite, sending us negative messages that shake our confidence and cause us to question ourselves. Parents, bosses, neighbors, or spouses can communicate messages to us that leave us feeling hurt, angry, or anxious.

Leslie lives under the weight of constant disapproval communicated to her daily from her aging mother. No matter how hard Leslie tries to please her mother, nothing she does ever seems to be good enough, and her mother inevitably responds with complaints and criticism. Leslie, age thirty, still visits her mother every week and stays in touch by phone on the other days, but after every interaction, she feels anxious and unsettled. And even on days she has no contact with her mom, Leslie finds it hard to keep her brain from replaying the older woman's critical comments.

We don't have to be related to people to have their negativity impact our mood, self-esteem, and peace of mind. Have you ever read a criticism or rebuttal in the comment section of a post you made on social media and felt uneasy and off-kilter for hours?

Twenty-nine-year-old Dan says interacting on social media definitely increases his anxiety. "After I post a thought, I find myself waiting anxiously for responses, nervous that someone may disagree or even attack me over what I've shared," he explains. "And I don't even post or repost controversial stuff. I'm just talking about sharing an idea or opinion. People seem freer today than ever to slam and dump on other people."

Dan makes a strong point, and he, of course, is not alone in feeling that using social media has its drawbacks to go with its benefits. In fact, studies show that half of teens and four out of ten adults say they have been bullied online.[1]

Can these negative messages increase feelings of anxiety? You bet they can.

Negative Messages Streamed Nonstop via Technology

In addition to negative messages from people in person or online, we are pummeled by a never-ending stream of intense and alarming messages from the news and social media. Through our ever-present computers and handheld devices, we are privy to political scandals and acts of violence from every corner of the globe. Social causes, crimes in the community, a friend's layoff, updates on the cancer treatments of a friend of a friend, rants about trending news topics—all these things and more are delivered to us in a constant stream of information that stirs up anxiety in both its content and its incessant quantity.

Even good news shared on social media can create anxiety. An acquaintance is on a blissful vacation—again. A friend got another promotion. Someone else is celebrating the loss of forty pounds. A neighbor is expecting baby number four. If you are reading posts like these and you feel overworked, hate your job, struggle to manage your weight, or are grieving infertility or the loss of a child, these happy posts can send you spiraling into an insecure and anxious place.

In fact, research conducted on young people and published in the *Journal of Affective Disorders* shows that the more time spent on social media, the higher the risk of experiencing an anxiety disorder.[2]

Negative Messages We Tell Ourselves

There is yet another source of negative messages—ourselves. Unfortunately, we are more than capable of adding to the influx of negativity with our own self-talk. Sometimes, as in the case of Leslie, we repeat to ourselves the negative messages we've been told by others.

In other cases, the negative messages we tell ourselves come from our interpretation of experiences, events, and interactions with others. A comment that wasn't intended to hurt can be misconstrued, and suddenly we have new fodder for the damaging messages we tell ourselves:

- *I'm not lovable.*
- *I'm hopeless.*
- *I'm an outsider.*
- *I always disappoint people.*
- *I'll never get it right.*
- *I deserve the pain in my life.*
- *I'm broken and will never be whole again.*
- *I can't control how people treat me. I'm a victim.*

The list is endless. The messages we tell ourselves are powerful and can play a huge role in ratcheting up our anxiety.

Reducing the Emotional Chaos from Negative Messaging

When it comes to reducing negative messages in your life—and reducing the anxiety that comes with them—you are not without options. Here are four strategies to help you filter out the harmful messages coming into your life.

1. Realize You've Got the Power.

The first step is to realize that you are in charge and have the ability to handle messages in a healthy, helpful manner. You don't have to continue living at the mercy of every message that comes into your life, no matter how damaging.

Adopting an "I'm in charge" attitude is extremely important for dealing with anxiety. With it, you'll be prepared to take the next two steps. Without it, you'll continue to feel helpless to stop the barrage and hopeless at escaping the tension you feel as a result.

Roger struggles with anxiety and many days feels bombarded and besieged by the influx of stimuli that come into his life. Emails, push-back from overbearing clients, bad news from his accountant, his own self-deprecating self-talk, stressful news from the media or social media . . . all of these sources leave him feeling overwhelmed.

One day, feeling anxious and depressed, Roger decided to leave his office and take a walk around the block. And during his walk he tried something new. He began to talk aloud to himself. His impromptu pep talk went something like this: "I'm in charge of my day. I'm in charge of my schedule. I'm in charge of my attitude. I don't have to live my life reacting to everything that comes my way. I can be proactive. I can choose to meet deadlines on time so I have happier clients and less stress. I can choose to block out times in my calendar to plan or think. I can choose to check my email twice a day instead of twenty times. I get to choose my responses to everything that comes my way."

He says that recognizing he has more control in his life than he thought he did is empowering. It also created a shift in the way he thinks about himself, his day, and his overall life.

By the time he got back to his desk, his anxiety was greatly reduced, replaced with new direction and energy. And he hadn't actually taken any actions or made any practical changes yet. But his shift in mindset and perspective was a game changer. He wasn't at the mercy of all the negative messages. He could choose something different.

2. Reduce and Eliminate the Noise.

With the right mindset in place, now it's time to take steps to filter out some of the noise. Oh, we can promise ourselves all day long that we're going to spend less time on social media, turn off the news, or find more positive friends. But promises like these are little more than good intentions unless we establish boundaries that are specific and measurable. Here are some examples:

- Don't let social media be your go-to break. It's natural and healthy to take breaks during the day. Regardless of how you spend your days— as a teacher, laborer, full-time parent, corporate employee, or self-employed entrepreneur—you're busy and productive, and sometimes you need to take a breather. During those times, it's all too easy to turn to phones and social media. Instead, take a walk, make yourself a cup of tea, call a friend, meditate, lift weights, read a chapter of a book, or listen to uplifting music. Make your break a positive experience.

- Most phones have features that allow you to set limits on your screen time. Use them.

- Break the habit with a social media "fast." Set a goal—whether one day, several days, or a week—and resist the urge to check social media sources.

- Turn off social media notifications on your phone. You'll be less inclined to check for new posts and information if you are not being notified continually.

- Steer clear of drainers. Who are the people who are communicating toxic messages to you on a regular basis? Identify them. When possible, reduce the time you spend with them. If this leaves gaps in your social calendar, add in activities that will allow you to meet new people and make more positive friends.

- When you can't reduce your exposure to a negative person, speaking up may reduce the negativity they spew at you. For example, tell the gossipy coworker you don't want to hear about all the office drama anymore. Gently explain to a parent who keeps mentioning your weight that you need a break from that conversation, and you'll gladly talk about anything but that. Let a spouse know that belittling comments are unwelcome, and the next time you hear them, you'll remove yourself from the conversation.

- Unfollow or hide the posts of negative people on social media. Remember, you have more control over what you allow into your life than you give yourself credit for.

- At night, charge your phone in a different room so you're not tempted to check email, social media, and news sources right before going to sleep or when waking up in the morning. Create a safe, technology-free space—especially during the vulnerable hours right before sleep. Do it by cutting off the delivery system through which a majority of negative messages reach you—your phone.

Put filters in place that protect your peace. Make yourself less accessible to the sources of negativity that fuel your anxiety.

3. When Negative Messages Get Past Your Filters, Be in Control of Your Response.

Even with healthy filters in place, unwanted and unhelpful messages are sure to get through. You will still encounter offensive or oppressive communication from people, news sources, social media, and even your own thoughts.

When negative messages enter your space, give yourself permission to reject them and the emotions those messages evoke in you. In fact, responding with affirming messages to yourself, out loud, can help. Say things like, "I reject that criticism. There's no truth in it." Or "I reject the fear

I'm feeling since hearing about the latest violent act on the news. I can be informed without being afraid."

Sometimes we don't need to reject the message itself as much as we need to reject a misguided interpretation of the message, as in this example: *I reject the idea that because someone was displeased with me, I'm somehow a bad person. Everyone makes mistakes. I'll make amends as needed, but I can do so without feeling anxious and overwhelmed.*

When negative messages are coming from our own self-talk, it's important to practice recognizing those messages and calling them out. After all, if you heard a friend or child telling hurtful untruths about themselves, wouldn't you step in with the truth?

When we communicate disparaging messages to ourselves, they're hard to refute, aren't they? But when you imagine self-destructive words being spoken by someone you care about, it's easy to think of positive truths to refute the negative perceptions. Don't love yourself any less.

4. When a Negative Message Is Rooted in Something You Need to Address, Do It.

Let's be honest: not every negative message deserves to be rejected or dismissed altogether. Sometimes a message comes as an indicator that there is something we need to consider and address. Do we need to apologize? Make amends? Express appreciation? Talk through a conflict?

When we know the message is in response to something we need to address, anxiety might be increased and prolonged when we procrastinate or ignore the matter. Anxiety is relieved, however, when we take necessary and proper action to address the root of the matter. Evaluating communication openly and carefully might reveal appropriate—and healthy—action that should be taken.

There's no need to live in an anxious state over things you could have done better, especially when there is something you can do now to make things right.

Even amid so much in our world that is uplifting and inspiring, we are subjected to disagreeable and damaging information every day. But we don't have to live at the mercy of the barrage of negative messages. We have the ability—and the responsibility—to filter, reject, manage, or correct.

When you do so, you may be surprised by the result. After all, feeling helpless is a great contributor to anxiety. But when it comes to negative messages, we are anything but helpless. Taking charge of this area of your life will definitely have a positive impact on your peace of mind.

Your Personal Reset Plan

You won't be able to control all the negative messages in your life, but there is much you can do that is within your control. Use these reset plan ideas to get your filters working this week.

1. **For one week, track your usage of social media and traditional media.** Your phone and other devices might have a time-tracking function; if not, keep a written log. Like many people, you might be surprised at just how many hours each week are spent absorbing messages, images, and news from media sources. Your log can look something like this:

Day of the Week	Social Media on Phone	Social Media on Computer	Television
Monday			
Tuesday			
Wednesday			
Thursday			
Friday			
Saturday			
Sunday			
TOTAL			

2. **Add a column to the above log that says "negative messages."** Each day, write down three negative messages that you were exposed to via technology. Sometimes we become oblivious or inured to the harmful communications we receive because of the constant and overwhelming volume confronting us every day. Therefore, it's useful and informative to know precisely where discouraging messages

are coming from. Then you can make the wise decision to avoid sources of upsetting and worrisome messages.

3. **Write down three actions that will protect you from negative messages getting to you through technology.** Many ideas are included in this chapter. Select three actions suggested in these pages (or add your own) and commit to practicing them over the next few weeks. Set a time frame. At the end of that time, evaluate if the reduction in screen time or access had a positive impact on your peace of mind.

4. **Replace negative messages with positive affirmations to tell yourself.** On ten or twelve index cards, write your own list of affirmations. Every morning, thumb through your cards and speak the affirmations aloud. If you can pair your affirmations with a physical activity (walking, lifting weights, even simply standing taller and speaking to yourself in the mirror), they will be even more empowering.

5. **Fortify your filters even more.** The essential premise of this chapter is that an avalanche of messages is threatening to bury you every week, if not every day. But the good news is that you have the ability and the power to choose which messages you will take in and which you will turn away. Think through the filtering strategies I have presented in the preceding pages, and then expand on these ideas to fit your unique situation. Be as specific as possible, implementing the filters as soon as possible or writing out a reminder on a sticky note to follow through on your plan. There are numerous ways to fortify your filters. Use your creativity and strategic thinking to protect yourself from anxiety-producing information infiltrating your mind and heart.

CHAPTER 15

Rewire & Reset Your Brain

Calm your mind and calm your anxiety.

When Janet finally realized that her anxious feelings were not easing up, she scheduled an appointment with her doctor. There, the intake nurse noted Janet's elevated heart rate and blood pressure and asked Janet to itemize what she had been experiencing:

- a persistent but vague sense of apprehension
- tension throughout her body and especially in the stomach
- difficulty falling and staying asleep
- obsession with a stressful event or conversation that recently happened or that could happen in the near future

When her physician arrived, he asked Janet a few more questions; listened to her heart and lungs; did the usual checks of the ears, nose, throat, and adrenals; palpated her abdomen; and conducted a few more cursory exams. Within seven minutes he pulled out his pad and wrote a prescription for a popular anti-anxiety drug.

The medication seemed to help—at first. But it wasn't long before Janet realized that her prescription generated a potpourri of undesirable side effects, including drowsiness, nervousness, and restlessness—an unsavory, contradictory combination. Her insomnia actually worsened, accompanied by morning sluggishness and headaches. The drug's harsh side effects soon outweighed its intended effectiveness as Janet's anxiety symptoms crowded back into her mind and body, dominating her well-being.

A Common Occurrence

Janet's experience is not unusual—in fact, it happens often. As I've said, there may be times when traditional anti-anxiety medication is appropriate and even helpful, but I believe its best use is short-term. Medication typically treats immediate symptoms while leaving the root causes untreated. This is why, at our clinic, my colleagues and I take a whole-person approach to health care, including the treatment of anxiety. Instead of simply relieving the symptoms, we seek out the underlying causes and pursue lasting solutions.

When we treat a client at The Center, we consider everything we're covering in this book, including what the client feeds the body and mind. When we addressed the essentials for a strong body in chapter 13, we looked at the types of food/fuel your body requires to function effectively. Here, I want to address another type of essential fuel your body and brain need in order to support a state of calm and steadiness amid the everyday stresses you face.

Had Janet sought whole-person treatment first, she may have been able to avoid the added physical and emotional trauma brought on by the prescription's side effects. Fortunately, she came to see us at The Center. After giving her a thorough workup, we were able to employ the healthier strategies I'm sharing with you, including the nutritional ideas you'll learn in the pages ahead.

A Big Word—and How It Can Help You Big-Time

As words go, *neurotransmitters* is complicated and a mouthful, but don't let the term scare you. Neurotransmitters are often referred to as the body's chemical messengers. They "regulate numerous physical and emotional processes such as cognitive and mental performance [and] emotional states. . . . Virtually all functions in life are controlled by neurotransmitters"—and your brain requires the proper nutrients each day to maintain the appropriate levels of neurotransmitters to regulate your anxiety.[1] The four major neurotransmitters that regulate mood are *serotonin, gamma-aminobutyric acid* (GABA), *dopamine,* and *norepinephrine.*

Serotonin (often called the "happiness neurotransmitter") and GABA are considered "inhibitory" or "calming" neurotransmitters, and dopamine and norepinephrine are the "excitatory" or "stimulating" neurotransmitters. Reduced levels of serotonin are associated with both depression and anxiety. GABA plays a role in balancing excitement or agitation with feelings of calm and relaxation. Dopamine is commonly associated with the "pleasure system" of the brain, providing feelings of enjoyment and reinforcement to motivate us to do, or continue doing, certain activities. And norepinephrine involves your brain and body's reactions to stress, including your heart rate and blood pressure.

Proper function of the brain and nervous system requires a healthy balance between these and other neurotransmitters. An imbalance can lead to widespread health problems such as those Janet was experiencing, including persistent anxiety, brain fog, jitteriness, sluggishness, and insomnia.

The good news is that a simple, targeted urine test, interpreted by a qualified professional, can reveal neurotransmitter imbalances. And for each neurotransmitter that is out of balance, natural remedies such as vitamins, minerals, and amino acids can help restore proper balance and give your brain and body the nutritional benefits needed to relieve symptoms of anxiety and keep you stronger and stable physically, mentally, and emotionally.[2]

Getting and Staying in Balance

At this point I want to caution you to consult a nutrition-wise, integrative health-care professional regarding nutritional supplementation, as not all supplements are safe or effective. For example, according to the National

NEUROTRANSMITTERS

Neurotransmitters are the body's chemical messengers. They help to control the body's physical and cognitive processes, including emotions. Neurotransmitters play a big role in regulating anxiety. Ensuring you have the right nutrients helps to maintain the appropriate levels of neurotransmitters in your body. Four main neurotransmitters are key to anxiety:

Inhibitory (Calming) Neurotransmitters
- Serotonin—the "happiness" neurotransmitter; reduced levels are associated with depression and anxiety
- Gamma-aminobutyric acid (GABA)—balances excitement or agitation with feelings of calm and relaxation

Excitatory (Stimulating) Neurotransmitters
- Dopamine—associated with pleasure, provides feelings of excitement
- Norepinephrine—is involved in brain's reaction to stress (including heart rate and blood pressure)

Center for Complementary and Integrative Health, *kava* was an accepted anti-anxiety choice before researchers found that it can cause liver disease. Another natural anti-anxiety remedy, *passionflower*, does not have sufficient evidence to support claims of its effectiveness.[3] However, the supplements I've listed below do show promise in calming anxiety and are worth discussing with your health care professional.

- *Oxytocin* is a neurotransmitter that is sometimes called the "love hormone" for its ability to reduce stress and anxiety and promote feelings of self-worth, assurance, trust, and love. According to Joseph Mercola, DO, one of America's foremost proponents of integrative medicine and healing, "The more oxytocin the pituitary gland releases, the better able you are to handle life's stressors. Oxytocin decreases the level of stress hormones (primarily cortisol) your body manufactures and lowers your blood pressure response to anxiety-producing events."[4]

    Mercola explains that loving, supportive touch, such as hugs, can increase oxytocin levels. He and other integrative-medicine practitioners surmise that oxytocin may help explain why pet owners often carry less stress and heal more quickly from illness. "Just a few minutes [of] petting your dog or cat can promote the release of your body's 'happiness' hormones, including oxytocin," says Mercola.[5] A warm hug or a caring touch such as an empathetic arm around the shoulder can help increase oxytocin levels in both the giver and the receiver. Oxytocin supplements are available in capsule or pill form, and also as a nasal spray.

- *GABA* is an inhibitory or calming neurotransmitter that inhibits certain brain signals and decreases activity in your nervous system, thus producing a soothing effect. Studies have also shown that GABA can help reduce blood pressure and help users fall asleep faster and enjoy improved sleep quality. As a bonus, GABA enhances the production of endorphins, those feel-good brain chemicals that boost mood. Unfortunately, GABA isn't available from many food sources, so you may need a good GABA supplement to bolster your body's supply.

- *Vitamin D* deficiency has been connected in multiple studies with mental health conditions. A vitamin D deficiency can lead to other vitamin deficiencies, which can compound the anxiety and stress you're already battling. One way to get enough vitamin D is to spend fifteen to twenty minutes in sunlight each day, which is why vitamin D is called the sunshine vitamin. Combined with the benefits of a brisk outdoor walk, you'll likely detect the benefit of the increased serotonin that vitamin D brings. You can also get more vitamin D by eating fatty fish such as salmon and by taking vitamin D supplements.

- *Fish oil* contains high amounts of the omega-3 fatty acids EPA and DHA, antioxidants conducive not only to heart and circulatory health but also to serotonin production. Salmon, sardines, and anchovies are brimming with healthy fish oil, and supplements combining EPA and DHA are also effective.[6]

- *5-HTP* is a nutrient-neurotransmitter and boosts levels of serotonin in the brain. As a result, 5-HTP can improve overall mood as well as relieve chronic anxiety, depression, insomnia, and the urge to stress eat. Research also suggests that 5-HTP may help ease some other stress-related conditions such as PMS, migraines, and fibromyalgia.

- *B vitamins* are critical for anyone experiencing chronic stress or anxiety. Vitamin B1 fortifies the body's immune system and its ability to handle stress. Vitamin B3 plays a key role in serotonin synthesis. Vitamin B5 is important for the adrenals and therefore helps with moderating stress. And multiple studies have linked vitamin B12 with reduced anxiety and stress levels. Thus, a quality B-complex supplement will ensure that you get all the B vitamins you need.

- *Vitamins A, C, and E* are all essential antioxidants and have been proven to help manage anxiety symptoms. Your body draws on all three, and especially vitamin E, during times of stress. Imbalance can cause oxidative damage that compromises your nervous system and increases anxiety. Ample fresh fruits and vegetables plus a good multivitamin taken daily will help ensure sufficient antioxidants.

- *L-theanine* is an amino acid found in green and black tea. It has a calming effect, reduces the physiological response to stress, and increases dopamine, serotonin, and the inhibitory neurotransmitter glycine. Studies show that L-theanine induces alpha brain-wave activity, which makes people feel more relaxed without making them sleepy.

- *Magnesium* is a mineral essential to nearly every system in your body, and it also has a calming effect. Going through a stressful period without sufficient magnesium can create a deficit that, if not corrected, can cause more stress that depletes even more magnesium from your system. Magnesium is found in whole wheat, spinach, quinoa, almonds and cashews, dark chocolate, and black beans. High dosages of magnesium can cause diarrhea, so if you take a supplement, start with a lower dosage.

- *Chamomile* is a daisy-like flower that has been used for thousands of years as a natural remedy for anxiety symptoms. It is widely accepted for its calming qualities and used in the form of teas, essential oils, or supplements.

- *Lavender* has long been used as a soothing stress remedy, and it has shown relaxing effects on the central nervous system. A 2017 study found that people who used lavender aromatherapy before surgery had lower anxiety than those who did not.[7] Lavender tends to be found in anxiety supplement blends with other herbs. Lavender essential oil can be inhaled with the use of an essential-oil diffuser.

- *Lemon balm* is closely related to lavender and is most often consumed in a tea, but it is also available in capsule form. Studies have shown that it supports a calm mood and sleep quality.

- *Holy basil* is an Ayurvedic adaptogen long used to counter stress. A growing body of preliminary research suggests that holy basil calms the brain and acts as a natural anti-anxiety agent and antidepressant but without the potentially harmful side effects common to pharmaceuticals often used to treat anxiety.

- *Bacopa* may be best known for its brain-boosting benefits, but it also has been found to reduce anxiety and produce a feeling of calm and tranquility. This is due to bacopa's ability to regulate the uptake of serotonin, to prevent dopamine receptor dysfunction, and to support the activity of GABA. As a bonus, bacopa also improves the quality of sleep.

- *Schisandra* has a long history of use as an adaptogen and mood lifter in traditional Chinese medicine. Because it increases dopamine levels in the brain, schisandra is often used to enhance focus and motivation. Studies have found that this ancient herb also restricts the amount of cortisol in the brain during times of stress.

- *Valerian* is an herb native to Europe and parts of Asia, but it also grows in North America. Medicine is made from the root. Valerian root is most commonly used for sleep disorders, but its calming effect also makes it viable for anxiety and psychological stress. It comes in capsule form, as a component in herbal blends, and can also be consumed as a tea.

Many or most of the above supplements can be found combined in proper balance in a quality multivitamin-mineral–amino acid supplement. That's a great place to start. Then you can gradually add other mind-calming supplements if you desire.

In harmony with the other strategies you're reading in this book, a regimen of carefully selected and monitored supplements can help put and keep your neurotransmitters and other key amino acids and chemicals in balance—in effect, rewiring and resetting your brain by giving you a stronger, calmer physical-mental-emotional foundation to help overcome the anxieties of life.

As said before, a really good time to start is now. So, within the next twenty-four hours, begin taking the action steps below.

Your Personal Reset Plan

Of course, neither your stomach nor your pocketbook can handle all the supplements suggested in this chapter. So start now, but start slow. Begin with the basics; then, with the guidance of your nutritionist or other nutrition-minded health care professional, add one or two supplements at a time and monitor how your body and mind respond.

1. **Start taking a high-quality daily multivitamin-mineral–amino acid supplement now, if you're not already.** In addition to a healthy, balanced diet, this supplement will provide your body and mind with the key nutrients on which all the other supplements can build. It's your non-optional foundation.

2. **Seek out a qualified nutritionist or nutrition-minded, integrative-medicine professional.** Do an internet search for integrative medicine practitioners, doctors of osteopathic medicine (DOs), or nutritionists in your area. Check credentials and references. Ask friends and coworkers if they know of a professional who practices holistic, whole-person treatment for anxiety and other health challenges.

3. **Do not stop taking any anti-anxiety medication until a qualified health care professional tells you it's safe to do so.** Most likely, any cessation will need to be done gradually. Or your health care provider may want you to continue taking the prescription and adding nutritional supplementation to the protocol—at the very least, a quality multivitamin-mineral–amino acid supplement.

4. **Research and ask about a neurotransmitter imbalance test.** It's a simple urine test that can be done at home. The findings will help your health care provider determine priorities for your supplement strategy and treatment.

5. **Begin slowly adding a key supplement or two every two to four weeks.** Again, work closely with a trusted health care provider in the selection, purchase, and ingestion of supplements. Remember that most supplements take time to show noticeable effects. Keeping a journal of what you take and when, and what seems to help and what doesn't, will help you keep your supplement list to the most user-friendly and effective products.

CHAPTER 16

Find Strength in Soul Care

Nourish your spiritual life to find serenity.

James was a molecular biologist working at a research facility in Southern California. His company ran clinical trials to test promising new drugs in the war against prostate cancer. A quiet man who lived alone, he kept to himself almost to the point of invisibility to everyone around him. He had no official contact with the patients participating in the studies he helped administer, but from his office window he could see them trudge in and out of the clinic each day. He studied the steady stream of men with morbid concentration. Most of them, he thought, seemed to drag an aura of hopelessness behind them like a long, sticky shadow.

And it was excruciating for James. His mother and her sister had both died of cancer a decade ago, followed by a cousin on his father's side of the family. Other extended family members too. Cancer, James concluded, was clearly a ticking bomb he carried in his genes. Fear became a constant companion, a toxic presence in the pit of his stomach. He barely slept because when he closed his eyes, he saw himself in the line, counting his steps from the car to the clinic door and back and wondering how close each one was to being his last.

"I had put myself on death watch," he told me. "Like I was my own hospice caregiver."

You can guess by now that James suffered from uncontrolled anxiety, which meant that his fear of developing cancer was by no means the only thing that haunted him. He lived near a police precinct, and every wailing siren set his entire nervous system on high alert. He could barely bring himself to speak to a coffee shop barista, much less get close enough to anyone to develop a friendship. He expected to be fired from his job any day, certain that he was the topic of every hushed conversation among his coworkers.

Then one day he *did* get laid off. Cost overruns, his boss said. Cutbacks that came down from above. So sorry.

"I wasn't the only one losing my job that day," James said. "But the words hit me like a personal diagnosis. You're terminal. Might as well get in line with those men outside the window."

So James made a decision. He drove to the beach after dark, careful to obey all traffic laws. It was chilly that night, so the parking lot was empty. In what he thought would be a coded last message to the world, he steered toward the forbidden blue "handicapped" space. But he changed his mind at the last moment and parked dutifully beside it instead. He turned the car off and left his keys in the ignition. James got out and walked along the shore, as far from the lot as he could manage, down to a section of beach that was known for dangerous currents. A posted notice warned against swimming.

James sat down and took off his shoes and socks. He placed them neatly beside himself on the sand. In his mind, he was already counting his steps to the water.

"I had no doubt the end had finally come," he told me weeks later. "I knew I was absolutely alone, and the churning black water was the exact color of my future."

James stood up to go—and nearly "died of fright," he recalled, when a dog barked loudly just a few feet away. He spun around and saw a scruffy black-and-white mutt, with tufts of hair drooping from its ears. James hadn't seen or heard the animal approach. He quickly sat back down, scanning in every direction for the dog's owner, but no one was around. As if on cue, the dog sat too, not threatening, but looking right at James.

"I told him to go away and even threw a handful of sand," James said. "But he just sat there, tongue hanging out, not a care in the world."

James got up again to enter the water and get on with it. The dog jumped to its feet as well, running in semicircles and then crouching playfully between James and the water, daring him to give chase. Determined, James headed again toward the surf. The dog barked twice, forcefully. James looked back to see the animal sitting beside his shoes, ears forward, waiting. And something inside him snapped.

"I'm a secular scientist, so I was taught to look at a dog and see only molecules and proteins and some DNA running everything like software," said James. "But not that night. If that dog had spoken to me in English, I could not have been more startled than I was by the sudden feeling—no, the certainty—that I was *not* alone."

James sat down in the sand and cried for the first time in years. The dog approached and sat beside him, occasionally licking his face. After a time, James looked up and felt the same sense of "presence" in the stars overhead and the palm trees and the soft rhythm of the surf.

"I remember asking the dog, 'Who *are* you?'" James said. "At which point he just shook himself and trotted away. Was he a messenger? An angel? I'll never know. But I do know I was different after that."

Faith as Fuel

You know, of course, that James did not walk into the ocean that night. He did not, as he had intended, attempt to end his life in the dark water. Instead he "woke up," he told me, and for the first time considered the possibility that spirituality is not just "superstition" or "wishful thinking." Maybe, he conceded, there is more to life than can be measured in a laboratory after all. Or, at least, that what he saw under his microscope pointed to deeper mystery than he'd been taught to believe.

Scientist, author, and philosopher Carl Sagan once wrote, "Science is not only compatible with spirituality; it is a profound source of spirituality."[1] And spirituality, in turn, is a profound source of healing and comfort to people, like James, who must fight their way through the challenges posed by anxiety. Many of the same obstacles he faced remained, and he still had to commit to a systematic treatment program. But after that night, James was equipped with something that had been missing until then, the one thing that fuels our willingness to commit to everything else: *hope*.

The truth is, each of us reaches only for those things we believe are real and possible, including our own wellness. Without hope, we stop even asking the right questions, much less digging for answers. Nurturing spirituality in your life—wherever you find it—instills hope by restoring your faith in fundamental ideas that our materialistic society makes it easy to forget.

Here is a short list of the most important ones:

- *You are not alone.* Of all the negative beliefs about themselves and the world that haunt people who struggle with depression or anxiety, "I'm on my own" is especially toxic. Spiritual awareness allows you to see the world for what God intended it to be—loving, nurturing, and embracing. You may at times feel lonely, as we all do, but you are not alone on this journey through life.

- *You are loved.* It probably wouldn't be much comfort to realize you are not alone if God turned out to be cold and impersonal. Thankfully, that is emphatically not the case. Let these words from the Psalms reassure you, as they do me: "The LORD is compassionate and merciful, slow to get angry and filled with unfailing love. He will not constantly accuse us, nor remain angry forever. . . . His unfailing love toward those who fear him is as great as the height of the heavens above the earth. He has removed our sins as far from us as the east is from the west. The LORD is like a father to his children, tender and compassionate to those who fear him."[2]

- *You have a purpose.* Modern secular philosophy holds that none of the above is real. Random chemistry, it says, with no purpose at all, is the creator of everything you are. Without purpose, what's the point of growth? Of sacrifice? Of selflessness? What's the point of working to be well? Spirituality answers these questions by recharging your life with meaning.

Armed with these foundational ideas—and others that you will discover for yourself, when you look for them—you'll be far better equipped to meet the challenges that lie ahead on your road to healing.

Your Part to Play

In the New Testament, Jesus summed up the astonishing and life-changing potential of spirituality like this:

> Keep on asking, and you will receive what you ask for. Keep on seeking, and you will find. Keep on knocking, and the door will be opened to you. For everyone who asks, receives. Everyone who seeks, finds. And to everyone who knocks, the door will be opened.[3]

These words make it clear: you can approach God for help, and he is eager to meet you exactly where you are. But an often-overlooked dimension to this marvelous relationship is that it's not passive. The passage quoted above is filled with action verbs. *Ask. Seek. Knock.* And, to those we must add one more: *persist*. If you do, what you seek will be yours. That is, there is both a *promise* and a *prerequisite* contained in Jesus' words. God is eager to give, but we take an active role when we keep on asking, seeking, and knocking.

With that in mind, here are some active steps you can take to grab hold of spirituality as a source of healing.

Pray

The best way to define prayer, I find, is to begin by listing the things it is not. Prayer is not begging for a blessing. It's not flattering a deity who is hungry for praise. It doesn't happen only on your knees or at church or at certain times of the day.

Prayer *is* an expression of a loving relationship between you and your heavenly Father. It has as many forms and faces as there are people, all of them "right," so long as prayer strengthens your connection with God. If you don't know how to begin to pray, a good first step is to earnestly ask God for help in knowing how to begin!

Practice Gratitude

For many people—especially those who are locked in a constant struggle with mental or physical illness—choosing to be grateful is even harder to manage than prayer. When difficult and draining symptoms dominate your daily experience of life, the thought of being grateful can seem like a cruel joke.

But gratitude is not simply a response we feel when things go right. It's a deliberate attitude we choose even when they don't. It is the decision to consciously acknowledge all the many things in our lives that are good, enjoyable, and beneficial. Because no matter how trying your circumstances, there is always *something* you can notice and appreciate. Research has shown that when you do, there is a demonstrable link between gratitude and improved mental outlook.

Psychologist Alex Korb examined several scientific studies on the link between gratitude and mental health:

> Feelings of gratitude directly activated brain regions associated with the neurotransmitter dopamine. Dopamine feels good to get, which is why it's generally considered the "reward" neurotransmitter. But dopamine is also almost [as] important in initiating action. That means increases in dopamine make you more likely to do the thing you just did. It's the brain saying, "Oh, do that again."
>
> Gratitude can have such a powerful impact on your life because it engages your brain in a virtuous cycle. . . . And the dopamine reinforces that as well. So once you start seeing things to be grateful for, your brain starts looking for more things to be grateful for. That's how the virtuous cycle gets created.[4]

The key to gratitude is to start small. If you are stuck in traffic and late for work, don't try to conjure up gratitude for traffic jams. Instead, be grateful for your car, or its air conditioner that keeps you comfortable while you wait. Notice your surroundings, and actively pick something to appreciate—the pleasing architecture of a nearby building, trees lining the sidewalk, a street musician caught up in the rapture of playing, the brightly colored hot-dog stand on the corner. It's your choice: you can see only the clock and the gridlock, or you can let gratitude lift you above the stress.

What has gratitude got to do with spirituality? Everything, because gratitude is a form of prayer. We are thankful *to someone*. Thirteenth-century German mystic Meister Eckhart summed it up: "If the only prayer you ever say in your entire life is thank you, it will be enough."

Forgive

People who seek our help at The Center are often surprised when we ask about broken or embittered relationships in their lives. They fail to see the link between their mental distress and unresolved conflict with others. But our experience has removed all doubt that hanging on to offenses and emotional wounds is an effective (and unfortunate) way to punish *yourself*. As the old adage goes, "Before you embark on a journey of revenge, dig two graves."

The sticking point for most people is a burning desire for justice. They can't bear to let someone "get away with" some hurtful offense. But letting someone off the hook is not the essence of forgiveness at all. Rather, it's about your own experience of life's inevitable conflicts and whether you want to go on reliving the pain of them—and suffering for it—or to let go and move on.

Here's a mental picture I came across years ago and have reminded myself of many times when it was my turn to forgive. In the South, children will sometimes catch crawfish from the creek by baiting a paper clip on a string with a morsel of bacon. The poor creature clamps on and won't let go, even when hauled out of the water to its doom. Forgiveness is about giving up the need to be right and setting yourself free!

Beyond the personal benefits of forgiveness, however, lies something deeper, something that opens the door to transformative spirituality. Forgiving those who have harmed you is a way of practicing your new spiritual belief that you are not alone and that you yourself are loved. It is your chance to say, "Who am I to make others pay in full for their mistakes when my own don't seem to count against me because I am so loved?" It's a mental and spiritual posture that invites healing.

Develop Generosity

A few pages back, I wrote that a foundational tenet of spirituality is the idea that you have a purpose. Another way to say that is, you have something to give. We all do. It's tempting to imagine what that something might be in epic terms, like medical breakthroughs or contributions to art and culture. That potential always exists, but it's a mistake to discount the world-changing power of more "routine" gifts. These are acts of generosity that easily go unnoticed—a kind word, a helping hand when you could easily walk away, an anonymous gift to someone who needs a boost.

When you struggle with symptoms of anxiety, it's easy to get trapped inside yourself, wrapped up in your own difficulties. But the truth is, everyone struggles with something. To make giving a part of your spiritual practice means cultivating attentiveness to those struggles and being prepared to contribute what you can. In this way, you lighten someone else's load while setting the table for your own healing. In a *Time* magazine article titled "The Secret to Happiness Is Helping Others," science journalist Jenny Santi writes,

> Scientific research provides compelling data to support the anecdotal evidence that giving is a powerful pathway to personal growth and lasting happiness. Through fMRI technology, we now know that giving activates the same parts of the brain that are stimulated by food and sex. Experiments show evidence that altruism is hardwired in the brain—and it's pleasurable. Helping others may just be the secret to living a life that is not only happier but also healthier, wealthier, more productive, and meaningful.[5]

A Real Game Changer

Soul care will not solve the challenges of anxiety overnight. Like every other tool you've learned in this book, it's a choice that takes dedication and determination. However, nurturing the spiritual dimension of your life unlocks the inner resources that make everything else easier. If you must choose only one thing to do for yourself right now, let it be these words of Jesus to a worried and anxious crowd: "Seek the Kingdom of God above all else, and live righteously, and he will give you everything you need."[6]

Your Personal Reset Plan

People often resist soul care more than just about any other healing path. We can only speculate about the reasons why. Perhaps we are too attached to negative patterns of thought and belief, and we worry what we'll lose if we give them up. Whatever the reason, resisting the spiritual dimension of health and well-being misses out on the ultimate goal: *a life worth living.*

If you're ready for that, then here are five actions to consider.

1. **Ask for God's guidance.** One of the most mistaken ideas about spiritual renewal is that you must find your way through the door on your own. As I pointed out earlier, *you are not alone.* That means help is available, even if what you need is help finding help. Ask. You'll be amazed at the result.

2. **Join with others on the journey.** Some help comes in the form of people who have walked the road ahead of you and can share what they've learned. One reason churches exist is to provide a gathering place for people—like you—looking for answers and support. Find one that appeals to you, and join the community.

3. **Start a gratitude journal.** Every day, record at least five things you notice in your life for which you are grateful. As you saw earlier, these things need not be grandiose. Are you grateful for the affection your dog shows you every morning? Write it down. How about grape jelly for your breakfast toast? The color of autumn leaves outside? Soon, you'll realize five items are far too few for a single day. And you'll notice that focusing on the things you love about life leaves less mental space for dwelling on things you hate or fear.

4. **Make it real.** As you consider your own spiritual health, look for tangible ways to act it out in the world. That may mean volunteering for a few hours serving meals to people who are homeless or offering to babysit while your single-mom sister gets time to herself. If you need to start small, consider this: the kindness you show in one genuine smile at the coffee shop or bus stop is sometimes all it takes to change a stranger's day.

5. **Forgive someone.** Pick one person against whom you've held a simmering grudge. Don't start with a really big offense that would be hard for anyone to let go. How about the landlord who took three weeks to fix a leaky toilet? A rude coworker who snapped at you unnecessarily? You'll know the one that works for you. Now take out a sheet of paper and write that person a royal pardon. All charges dropped. What you've done is free yourself from bitterness, always a toxic emotion. And you've acknowledged that everyone—including you—could use a little forgiveness now and then.

CHAPTER 17

Become Bold & Brave

Can you really be free from worry?
The answer is yes!

Among the many things Jesus told people in his day, one message is repeated again and again: *Don't be afraid. Don't worry. Put down your burden and rest.*

No matter who you are, that sounds like a very positive and healthy way to live. We all fear something and from time to time get caught in the whirlpool of worrying about life's what-ifs. But to people who struggle with extreme anxiety, life without fear can sound far too good—and very hard to believe. When every day is one long battle with crippling dread, simply hearing the words *fear not* can hit you like fingernails on a chalkboard. "Yeah, right," you respond. "That's easy to *say*! But it can't be done."

The bad news in that is you are unlikely to work toward something you believe to be impossible, and what we don't attempt, we can't achieve. But here's the good news: you haven't come this far in your search for healing only to slam the door now. Reading this book is proof that you are ready to enter new territory and think things you've never thought before. You're willing to consider that you've been wrong about what is possible and what isn't—that the way you've been living until now is not the only way you *can* live. You're tired of being bullied and backed into a corner by fear, and you are ready to fight back. If that describes you, then begin this chapter by repeating these words out loud and as often as it takes to let them sink in:

> I have not yet faced my fears and mastered them, but that doesn't mean I *can't*! It *is* possible to get my life back and to build a healthier, happier future for myself.

Don't worry if it's hard to muster much confidence at this point. That will come as we start filling in the blanks and answering the obvious question: *How?*

Afraid of Fear

On March 4, 1933, in his first inaugural address to the nation, President Franklin D. Roosevelt stated, "Let me assert my firm belief that the only thing we have to fear is . . . fear itself—nameless, unreasoning, unjustified terror which paralyzes needed efforts to convert retreat into advance."

The country was in the midst of the Great Depression, and for most people, there seemed plenty to fear. They'd lost jobs and homes. They had watched helplessly as trusted banks collapsed, taking their life savings with them. Unemployment and hunger reached unprecedented levels, with little reason to believe an end was in sight. But when Roosevelt took the podium that day, he understood that none of those things posed the greatest threat to the nation's future. With enough courage and determination, the nation's challenges could all be faced, managed, corrected, and overcome. *Without* courage—that is, if fear were allowed to take over and dominate national discourse and action—the damage would be incalculable.

In that moment of crisis, the president told people that paralysis was the by-product of fear itself, not the actual challenges facing society. He urged them to resist fearing the feeling of fear so much that they retreated into isolation and avoidance instead of taking bold and necessary action.

To anyone who has ever felt the grip of uncontrolled anxiety, President Roosevelt's language sounds very familiar: *nameless, unreasoning, unjustified terror. Paralysis.* His message of hope is just as true today as it was then, and not just in the realms of social order and economics. Understanding his point is also essential on your journey of healing from anxiety. Here it is, plain and simple: when you are paralyzed by anxiety, what you actually fear is the feeling of being afraid. It isn't heights, enclosed spaces, social awkwardness, or any of the myriad "triggers" people believe to be the source of their fear. What we are desperate to avoid in all those cases is how lousy fear feels. Writing for *Psychology Today*, Dr. Susan Biali Haas puts it like this:

> When it comes down to it, anxious people fear the feeling of fear. That's the most scary part—the way you feel when something makes you really anxious. This leads to avoidance, which then leads to more avoidance, which leads to a progressively smaller, more limited life. . . . Avoidance is a bad strategy for your brain's fear center. When you feel fear and run away or avoid, you miss the chance to "habituate" your amygdala (fear center) to the thing you're afraid of.[1]

I hope you noticed the incredibly good news in this idea. If it were true that the prospect of drowning is the source of your fear, then you'd have little choice but to avoid beaches and pools at all cost. But it turns out that the nearness of water has no permanent role to play in your health and well-being. It is possible to "habituate" your brain—to literally overwrite old and frightening memories with new ones—and to stop letting your fear of being afraid push you into a life of avoidance.[2]

Sounds great, right? Here's the problem: reprogramming your brain's fear response is not easy. It requires you to do the one thing that all of your anxious reflexes have shielded you from thus far: to stop running away, to turn and face your fear head-on. In other words, it takes *courage*.

Bravery under Fire

Before we tackle practical strategies for how to face your fears, it's necessary to dispense with a common and extremely misleading misconception about courage. Without this knowledge, crippling confusion in the heat of battle is practically inevitable. So write this down and post it wherever you will see it every day—on your bathroom mirror, refrigerator door, and in your car:

Courage is not a *feeling*.

It is a deliberate choice and the cumulative result of numerous small actions that add up to true bravery. Courage is not something one either possesses at birth or doesn't, like blue eyes or an ear for music. It's a skill that we all must consciously set out to acquire and then methodically cultivate, no matter how difficult the journey. The *Oxford English Dictionary* defines the word this way: "the ability to do something that frightens one." Courage is an *ability*, not a superpower bestowed on a blessed few. In other endeavors, we recognize that "ability" is the reward for years of hard work and determination—the ability to pole vault, paint a portrait, prepare a gourmet meal, or write a novel.

"The ability to do something that frightens one"—regardless of how one feels at the moment—is no different. For proof, consider how soldiers are honored for bravery under fire in combat. Military commanders award medals only for what men and women *do* in the midst of a terrifying battle, not for what they *feel*. The difference between courageous action and paralyzing fear can be generally summed up in a single word: *training*. That is the process of facing small fears, far away from actual battle and long before the bombardment begins. That means doing it every day under controlled conditions, to convince your mind it is possible to feel afraid and still do what's best and right in the moment.

That's the prize within reach when you make up your mind to act courageously and face your fear instead of running from it.

Reverse a Lifetime of Conditioning

Now let's open the toolbox and examine a few proven techniques for training yourself to work through your fear, not be "worked over" by it.

Exposure Therapy

The last thing most anxious people want to feel is *exposed*, so they run for the door at the very mention of this treatment. If you hang in there, however, you'll find that the purpose of this approach is to rob your fear of its power by making what frightens you a more familiar and even routine part of your life. It is the polar opposite of avoidance, which we've already seen only deepens and prolongs your struggle with anxiety.

Exposure therapy is the psychological equivalent of inoculation. We all understand that vaccines contain small amounts of the very diseases we hope to eradicate. The idea is to train your immune system to handle tiny doses so that when a full onslaught happens, it's prepared for the worst. In the same way, your mind can be taught courage and resilience through controlled exposure to frightening circumstances. A key word here is *controlled*. Typically, exposure therapy takes place under the guidance of a trained and experienced mental health professional. The expert's job is to provide a safe environment and lots of reassurance every step of the way.

Let's say you are afraid of dogs to the point that you never walk anywhere in your neighborhood for fear of passing someone on a stroll with their dog. A visit to the park is out of the question. Your fear of feeling afraid in the presence of a dog has robbed you of enjoying the outdoors and the pleasure of an affectionate animal's attention.

In the course of exposure therapy, you might begin by sitting in your counselor's office and simply imagining a dog. You would carefully notice what your fear feels like, and instead of running from it, you'd allow it to be what it is, knowing there is no actual dog present to harm you in any way. Research and experience have shown that, before long, your fear response, while just thinking of a dog, begins to decrease and become more manageable. Psychologists call this effect "extinction."[3]

Next, under your therapist's supervision, you might sit in the same room with a leashed dog, at a distance. You would follow the same process of consciously feeling the fear and noticing its effect on your mind and body. When that step has run its course and your fear has lessened, you would move gradually closer, eventually touching the dog. Next might come a stroll through a park, knowing that dogs are present.

By sticking with this program over the course of several weeks or months, you train your brain that it's possible to feel afraid but not be overwhelmed. Soon, even the fearful feeling subsides, and you will have regained the ability to enjoy everything that life has to offer you.

Present-Moment Awareness

A person suffering from severe anxiety spends most of his or her time either remembering some frightening event that's long gone or imagining ones yet to come. In other words, their minds habitually gravitate to the past and the future but rarely give any thought to what is happening right here, right now. And there are tangible reasons why that's a real shame. A brain imaging study conducted by researchers at the University of Colorado and the Icahn School of Medicine in 2018 confirmed what therapists and mystics have known for a long time: the brain responds the same to an event, regardless of whether it is actually happening or only imagined.

In the experiment, sixty-eight healthy people were trained to associate a sound with an electric shock that was unpleasant but not painful. From there, they were divided into three groups. The first continued to hear the sound, the second was asked to simply imagine the sound, and the third heard pleasing bird or rain sounds, but none of them continued to receive the shock. Using functional magnetic resonance imaging (fMRI), the scientists were able to see how the participants' brains responded in each case. The study reports that in the two groups that heard and imagined the original sound, the response was remarkably similar. That is, both experienced the same fear of an anticipated shock.[4]

Here's the point: if you habitually spend time imagining frightening or traumatic events in the past or future, your body responds exactly as if it's really happening. But because it's not real, there is no natural closure to your heightened state of alarm, exposing your body to harmful stress hormones over long periods of time. As we have seen already, the consequences of that include a whole host of physical ailments, not to mention the tragedy of your lost enjoyment of life.

Deliberately centering your awareness in the present moment—and letting your focus on what is real right now distract your mind from the past and future fantasies for a moment—is a great way to silence your fears and find rest. It works because the mind is also incapable of holding two thoughts at the same time, and you get to choose which has the floor.

Try this: sit in a relatively quiet place where you can be undisturbed for a few moments. Close your eyes and purposely relax your body. Breathe evenly and deeply, paying attention to how that feels. Cool air in, warm air out. Feel the rising and falling of your chest and belly. Focus your mind on those sensations. When competing thoughts arise—and they will—gently set them aside and return to awareness of your breathing. Now shift attention to how your feet feel against the floor or the soft pressure of the chair on your legs and back. Listen to the sound of birds outside the window or the wind in the trees.

At some point when you are relaxed and enjoying the pleasure of simply being, expand your mental focus to include everything in the room. Ask yourself, *Is there anything present, here and now, that is frightening? Threatening? If I open my eyes, what would I see to remind me of past trauma or future disaster? Is there any evidence that those things are real?*

Almost without exception, the answer will be that anxiety has no actual reason to exist here and now. Eventually, as the study above discovered, the fearfulness goes "extinct" when robbed of its connection to reality. Do this exercise anytime you feel your body and mind tensing up with anxiety, and you'll quickly learn what a healing refuge the present moment can be.

The "Kid with a Thousand Questions" Game

Have you ever been around a child who just keeps asking questions? It's hard to think about anything else! And that's the point of this "game." The key to this technique is to have as much fun as you can being as annoying to yourself as possible. Humor, after all, is great medicine. It might go something like this (out loud if you are alone!):

"I'm terrified of elevators."
  Why?
  "Because they might fall."
  How many elevators fell yesterday in your town?
  "None."
  Then why?
  "Because the elevator might get stuck and I'd die of panic and lack of oxygen."
  Don't elevators have air holes?
  "Yes."
  Then why? Oh, you might be stinky from your morning workout, or something like that? Or somebody else might be stinky, and then what?
  "I might have to talk to somebody."
  Don't you speak English?

You get the idea. If we each had an actual annoying younger cousin who followed us around pointing out our contradictions, inconsistencies, and absurdities, we might find it harder to take our fears as seriously! Play that role for yourself from time to time and see what happens.

Know Your Enemy

Elevators are not your enemy. Or spiders or public speaking or financial calamity. As President Roosevelt rightly said, it is fear. Sometime in your past you associated those things with pain and trauma, like the study participants did with sound and shock. You learned to expect an unpleasant fearful response when your particular trigger appeared. The good news—the *very* good news—is that it's possible to *un*learn that now.

To do that, stop running away and face your fear head-on. As another Roosevelt—Eleanor—once said, "You gain strength, courage, and confidence by every experience in which you really stop to look fear in the face. You are able to say to yourself, 'I lived through this horror. I can take the next thing that comes along.'"

Your Personal Reset Plan

That you've come this far in this book is proof that you are tired of living with crippling anxiety. You are ready to take back your future from the paralysis of fear. Congratulations! Here are five strategies to get you started:

1. **Name your fears.** Chances are, you've gotten very good at avoiding the things that make you afraid. Even thinking of them can trigger a fear response, so you've learned to not do that, either. It's the adult equivalent of a child lying frozen in a dark bedroom, too terrified to turn on the light and dispel his or her fear. This strategy only serves to deepen your anxiety and prolong your recovery. Reverse that by writing down the things that have paralyzed you—all of them—honestly and clearly.

2. **Cross-examine your fears.** Now take that list and question each item as if it were a witness in court. Suppose you put on the stand

your intense phobia of driving through tunnels because you're afraid of being buried underground in a collapse. Your job in this exercise is to make the fear provide proof that it's both reasonable and proportionate to the risk. "Precisely how many times in the past month has a tunnel collapsed somewhere in the country killing everyone inside? In the past year? Decade?" Write these probing questions beside each fear on your list. Don't let them off easy.

3. **Visualize a victory.** Pick an item on your list of fears and ask yourself, *How would life be different without this?* For example, if you weren't horrified at the idea of contracting a food-borne illness, imagine how it would feel to enjoy a pleasant evening with friends in that trendy new restaurant in your neighborhood. Go deep with this exercise, picturing your freedom in vivid detail. Write and finish the sentences "This would feel really good because . . ." and "Without this fear I would enjoy . . ."

4. **Gather allies.** Nothing has greater potential to shrink a fear down to manageable size than to say it out loud to someone you trust. Locked in your limitless imagination, each possible threat can grow to monstrous proportions, like a blockbuster horror film with dark special effects and an epic soundtrack. Not so much when you put it into words over coffee. Use the list you've made and find someone to share it with.

5. **Inoculate yourself with courage.** As you read in this chapter, courage is an action. Every step you take toward your fear with the aim of facing it is an act of courage, no matter how small it seems. Pick a fear you named in your list and ask yourself, *What can I do today to take back my power from this enemy?*

CHAPTER 18

Sanity through Simplicity

Decrease and release to find peace.

Say the phrase "Simplify your life," and many people will imagine a stern-faced Henry David Thoreau sitting alone in the cabin he built beside Walden Pond. They equate simplicity with dreary austerity. For all of his exuberance, Thoreau himself sometimes painted with words that most people would find bleak, such as these: "Most of the luxuries and many of the so-called comforts of life are not only not indispensable, but positive hindrances to the elevation of mankind."[1]

We like our luxuries and our comforts, we think. *No thanks!*

But to dismiss the idea of simplicity so easily would be to greatly misunderstand Thoreau's message. More to the point, you would waste an opportunity to progress in your quest to escape from rampaging fear and anxiety. To see why, listen to his real purpose:

> Simplicity, simplicity, simplicity! I say, let your affairs be as two or three, and not a hundred or a thousand; instead of a million count half a dozen, and keep your accounts on your thumb nail. In the

midst of this chopping sea of civilized life, such are the clouds and storms and quicksands and thousand-and-one items to be allowed for.[2]

He's talking about finding freedom from clouds, storms, quicksand, and the millions of distractions we all face on the "chopping sea of civilized life." Does that description sound familiar? Does greater peace in the midst of it all sound pretty good? I suspect your answer—like mine—is a heartfelt *yes!*

There's More to Clutter than Stuff

The first step is to realize that simplicity as a way of life is not, well, *simple*. It is not just about holding a yard sale and getting rid of your surplus junk. That's a part of the program, for sure, and a big part at that. Numerous studies have consistently shown a link between material clutter in the home or workplace and depression or anxiety. Researchers have recognized that a cluttered, chaotic environment and mental illness often form a destructive feedback loop, each worsening the other.

But decluttering your physical surroundings is not the end of the story.

When I met Martin, he'd been living in a tent for nearly a year. He was a software engineer who had once worked for a rising-star tech company in Silicon Valley. At that time, he'd had a six-figure income and a nice home filled with every convenience in a trendy neighborhood. His future was virtually guaranteed. He was also, as he put it, "slowly choking to death." He felt strangled by endless pressure at work and by hours spent sitting in traffic that felt to him like "a river of toxic sludge oozing through the streets."

Though he lived alone, Martin's home had begun to resemble that of a "crazy cat woman," he said. He had no cats, but every counter was cluttered with tech magazines and manuals and dozens of gadgets he'd bought online, many of them still unopened. Unwashed laundry and dirty dishes littered every room of the house. He was well-known at work for having an office with a "filing system" that only he understood.

"Finally, I snapped," he admitted. "In one flash of insight, I saw myself as a whale covered in barnacles, and I was sinking."

So Martin quit his job, sold or gave away everything he owned, and moved "off the grid." As far off as he could. He bought a tiny tent and pitched it deep in the coastal forest north of San Francisco. He trimmed his possessions to only those things that were absolutely essential for survival.

"I was looking for peace," he recalled. "I needed a reset button I could press on modern life."

For a minute, it worked. He could breathe again. He enjoyed doing things with his hands and feeling closer to nature. He loved leaving the pressures of work—the endless deadlines and demands—far behind.

And then, that minute passed.

"I suddenly found myself sitting by the fire at night reliving every lousy moment I'd ever experienced. All my broken relationships followed me there like ghosts, along with all the same fears I'd had before, plus some new ones. Now I worried about forest fires or being discovered by a ranger or eaten by a bear. What if I had a medical emergency? On and on."

In his haste to simplify his life, Martin had forgotten the ancient saying "Wherever you go, there you are." He also failed to understand that clutter comes in many forms, most of it impervious to yard sales or bonfires. It takes an entirely different kind of broom to clean out our mental and emotional attics. Fortunately, Martin came to realize this and eventually found help.

Here's the point of sharing his story: you can too!

The Many Faces of Simplicity

Let's take a closer look at the various other areas of your life you may need to declutter to gain the upper hand on anxiety.

Simplify Your Mind

One of the wonderful things that sets human beings apart from the rest of the creatures on earth is our need to *know*. Our thirst to understand how things work and why things are as they are is responsible for every breakthrough in science, medicine, art, economics, politics, and technology in history. At our core, we are problem solvers, and our ability to gather knowledge and put it to beneficial use is our one great advantage. In today's mechanized and computerized world, it is no exaggeration to say our survival depends upon this trait.

In one respect, however, it is also a disadvantage. The "need to know" about such a wide range of topics—so we might succeed in life or at least stay a step ahead of failure—has become a mental burden we were not meant to carry. This adds to our stress and anxiety. Our distant ancestors had to know about things in their immediate environment, things they could comprehend with their senses and meet head-on with tools they made themselves. Today, we are dependent upon technologies that few of us understand and that are as far removed from daily experience as it's possible to be—satellites in space, quantum computers, or the mysterious workings of the stock market.

Before we finish our morning coffee, we keep track of wars simmering on distant continents, the traffic outlook on the route to work, fashion trends in Europe, weather reports from around the world, and our kids' schedule of after-school activities. We focus on planning the family reunion next summer, viewing the latest polls in the presidential election that's months away, shopping for deals on airline tickets, researching what could be responsible for the noise the car has started to make—*ad infinitum*. Most of what occupies our minds is utterly beyond our control and will have no effect at all on the day ahead, one way or another. The anxious fight-or-flight impulse we are wired to experience has nowhere to go but inward.

Writing for *Psychology Today*, psychotherapist Linda Esposito agrees:

> The problem is exacerbated by mental hoarding. Or when every
> third negative thought, bad memory, and personal slight fills
> the memory bank, collecting interest. Accumulating unhealthy
> thoughts takes a toll. Your mind is a mental battlefield,
> your days wasted with one psychological arm wrestle after
> another.[3]

Here's the secret I want you to grasp: none of that is inevitable. You have the power to *choose* what occupies your mind and to displace the clutter with thoughts that inspire confidence and faith, not fear. Give yourself permission to *not* know everything for a change, and you'll be astonished to learn how good that feels.

Simplify Your Emotions

In an earlier chapter, I described what I call the three toxic emotions: anger, guilt, and fear. It often surprises people seeking help at The Center that their emotional life plays a large role in healing from depression, anxiety, and addiction. But by now, that link should be clear to you. It *matters* what occupies your thoughts, and nothing dominates your mind as powerfully as your feelings.

When the apostle Paul wrote, "Three things will last forever—faith, hope, and love—and the greatest of these is love,"[4] he was offering a clear alternative to being enslaved by toxic emotions. These might include things such as unforgiveness for offenses you've suffered at the hands of others or regret over the things you've done to harm someone. Both are often followed by the fear that you'll never find your way to peace and freedom.

Once again, the good news is, you are not simply stuck in the emotional traps life has laid in your path. You can choose what to feel and how you'll respond to emotional challenges. Actively—even aggressively—pursue faith, hope, and love as your chosen way of being. This is not about denying your wounds or your mistakes. It's about taming the pain of them so you can move forward and repair what's broken, healing your life for good.

One of the clearest road maps ever drawn for how to get there is contained in Reinhold Niebuhr's Serenity Prayer:

> *God, grant me the serenity to accept the things I cannot change,*
> *Courage to change the things I can,*
> *And wisdom to know the difference.*

In these few words, we have permission to let go of what is beyond our control or was never ours to carry in the first place. It's a call to action to bravely do what we can and the acknowledgment that we need help in sorting out how to succeed.

Simplify Your Relationships

In recent decades, our society has shifted powerfully toward greater and greater inclusiveness. We have rightly seen that systematic discrimination of those who are different from us is unacceptable in a free and democratic nation.

But an unintended consequence of this is that it's perhaps harder now to be "discriminating" when sensing that people are not good for you in some way and to know when to "exclude" them from your life, or at least limit your exposure to them. Let's be clear: toxic people exist, and you are under no obligation to indulge them.

Here's a simple litmus test for determining which relationships are worth nurturing and which you can let go of: How do you feel after being around a person for any period of time? Empowered, encouraged, and enriched? Or depleted, degraded, and depressed? On your journey from anxiety to freedom, you need all the help you can get. People who function like emotional deadweight around your feet are not your friends, no matter how conditioned you are to think of them that way.

It's not easy to make changes to relationships that have been part of your life for a long time. That's true for others as well, and once you start setting and holding boundaries with people, you may find they wander off on their own. Or they may surprise you and give you what you need. Either way, you win.

Simplify Your Goals

Wisdom is often found in unexpected places. That was certainly true when the beloved *Peanuts* character Linus uttered these fateful words (with the help of legendary cartoonist Charles Schulz): "There's no heavier burden than a great potential."

That is truer today than when it was first penned. And that's because the exponential advance of the digital information age has granted us more access to opportunity than ever. The perennial American message "You can become anything you choose" has never been louder or more convincing. But it can have the unintended effect of delivering another message as well: "If you haven't 'succeeded' (as defined by popular culture), it's your own fault."

The truth is, for many people, just getting by is a constant battle. It's hard enough to pay the rent on time and put food on the table, no matter how many online educational opportunities exist. The painfully obvious difference between their lives and any common notion of "success" becomes a heavy burden of guilt they bear. But this sad condition isn't reserved for low-income people. Even those who have a rewarding career and the trappings of material prosperity can easily feel a sense of failure at not having gone further, faster.

By now you know the way past this pernicious source of stress and anxiety: exercise your power to choose for yourself what goals you invest in, and let go of the ones that don't add a buoyant sense of value to your life. Make your gift of potential serve you, not the other way around.

Simplify Your Time

If you follow the above advice and simplify other areas of your life, you are guaranteed to also reap a reward in reclaimed time. You'll spend fewer hours caught in a fog of cluttered thoughts and emotions. You'll give less precious time to people who take and never give back.

Still, the problem of cluttered time deserves attention all its own. Of all the sources of stress and anxiety in modern life, the feeling that there is too much to do and not nearly enough time to do it tops the list. Deadlines, due dates, and appointment books can feel like a pack of snarling wolves at your heels, from dawn to dusk.

Much of that is nonnegotiable—grocery shopping, parent-teacher conferences, medical appointments, and professional obligations. But if we're honest, we'll agree it's the optional things that consume the most time: television, social media, web surfing, wandering the mall, or bingeing YouTube videos. In proper proportion, there's nothing wrong with any of these. While you're in a simplifying mood, however, take a hard look at where your time goes. Freeing up a couple of hours a day can go a long way toward silencing the hounds and lowering your blood pressure.

Eyes on the Prize

These days, lots of people dream of getting out of the "fast lane" and living life more deliberately, more simply. Some succeed in finding that breathing room and some don't. For people who struggle to overcome anxiety, however, that goal is no longer optional. Simplicity is powerful medicine and should be a key part of your healing plan.

It seems only right for Thoreau to have the final word with this parting bit of encouragement: "If one advances confidently in the direction of his [or her] dreams, and endeavors to live the life which he has imagined, he will meet with a success unexpected in common hours."[5]

Your Personal Reset Plan

Too much clutter is a condition nearly all Americans share to one degree or another. But if you struggle with persistent anxiety, the need to do something about it is more urgent than most—and the reward even more valuable. Here are five ways to do that:

1. **Have less.** Go through your entire house on the lookout for things you possess that have no purpose and add no value to your life. We all accumulate such stuff over time, but runaway mental disorders feed on excessive clutter, raising the stakes for someone hoping to heal from anxiety. Commit to getting rid of at least ten items in every room, just for starters.

2. **Do less.** Next, look at your calendar. Clutter comes in many forms—including excessive busyness. Are any of your obligations there simply to distract you and fill time or to fulfill someone else's idea of what you "should" be doing? If so, consider making a new commitment to yourself and eliminate at least one optional activity a day.

3. **Eat less.** For many people, overeating is the self-medication method of choice. Guilt or regret over that, in turn, becomes yet another source of anxiety. But eating less and choosing lighter, healthier foods can be very beneficial even if that doesn't describe you. Periodic fasting is a great way to cleanse the body and clear the mind. For one week, make a commitment to purposely eat less or nothing at all during certain mealtimes. As you do, keep a journal of how you feel after those meals compared to your normal routine.

4. **Connect less online.** There is a growing body of research into the effects of internet connection—particularly social media—on mental health. Studies consistently suggest a significant link between too

much time spent online and elevated depression and anxiety. For at least twenty-four hours, put down your device and take a break. If you need help with that, numerous apps exist to assist you in sticking with your resolve to unplug. Write in your journal about the experience.

5. **Know less.** Here's a new twist on the old saying "No news is good news." Just as fasting from food for a day can reset your body's equilibrium, so abstaining from the news for a period of time will clear your thoughts and calm your worry over things beyond your control. Start with three days and notice how good *not* knowing can feel.

Back to a Better Future

Believe it! Your best life is still to come.

Now that we've reached the end of this book, it's time for me to reveal the secret agenda I have followed from page 1. Every story, every research fact, every tip and suggestion has had a single purpose: I'm organizing a *jailbreak.*

I've never done time in prison, but I know firsthand that uncontrolled anxiety feels very much as if it's made of concrete walls and iron bars. I've lived with barbed wire coiled around my mind. I know how it feels when my own thoughts snarl and snap like vicious guard dogs. The punishment of prison for actual inmates is the loss of freedom to live as they please and the reduction of their world to the size of a tiny cell. Anyone who has been backed by fear into a smaller and smaller life will instantly recognize the comparison.

In fact, it's not uncommon for prisoners serving a lengthy sentence to cut all ties with their former lives—with all the people and memories and, most of all, everything they've ever dreamed of having, doing, or being. It's too painful to consider those things, so they do their best to simply stop.

People suffering the crippling effects of anxiety often make a similar choice. They feel they've been given a life sentence and have no right to hope for better.

If that describes you or someone you love, then I've got startling news: it's high time to bust out of there. In previous chapters you have gathered the tools you need to be free once more. It's time for you to decide. Are you with me?

Don't Wait for Parole—Start Digging

Truth is, having the tools you need and *using* them are two different things. Others can show you the hidden passageways to freedom, but no one can walk through them for you. In other words, in this jailbreak, the pivotal role is yours. Here is your job.

Believe in a Better World outside the Walls

You've read this several times now in these pages, and here it is again, because its importance can't be overstated: *faith in possibility is the foundation upon which everything else is built.* The first reason for this is a matter of simple logic. No one ever invests effort and resources into a project they think is impossible. That's true of anything—repairing a car, learning a new language, or starting a business.

For many people, especially those conditioned by fear and anxiety to avoid uncomfortable risk, just about everything seems impossible. Some days that includes getting out of bed in the morning. So the idea that the day ahead might include full-fledged escape from the prison of anxiety seems about as likely as sprouting wings and flying.

Which is where the paradoxical power of belief comes into play. It is a genuine chicken-or-egg conundrum. Which comes first? A miracle? Or your faith that miracles are possible and that you can receive one for the asking? If you are a skeptic—as modern secular culture often conditions us to be—then your answer might be "Neither. Miracles don't exist, and faith is for the gullible." If that describes you, then perhaps this part of the conversation about how to heal your anxiety for good is not for you.

But if you are ready to think something new, then here's the point: belief is the key that opens the door to tremendous possibility. Again and again, Jesus told people who sought healing, "Your faith has made you well." That idea has been echoed countless times by poets, mystics, and teachers throughout history. J. M. Barrie, writer of *Peter Pan*, wrote, "The reason birds can fly and we can't is simply that they have perfect faith, for to have faith is to have wings."[1]

Before you dismiss that as impossible magical thinking, consider that an American flag stands on the moon because thousands of people conspired to convert faith into wings. You can do the same!

Think of Nothing Else

Once you've chosen to truly believe that you can be free from anxiety and that a happy, healthy life is possible outside the walls of fear, then visualize it with all you've got. Tenaciously. Ferociously. Faith is not a feeling that comes and goes on its own like the tide; it's an active choice. It is a *discipline*. If you were on the inside of an actual prison and had decided to mount an escape, it would be all too easy to notice only the apparent reasons for inevitable failure: walls, towers, guards, dogs, bars, locks. In other words, to focus on *what is* rather than *what can be*. To avoid that trap, employ one of the most powerful tools in your kit: your imagination.

Here's how it works. When you see a wall, imagine what it looks like from the other side. Picture only open gates and unmanned towers. See yourself as you'd like to be, free from anxiety and enjoying a happy, healthy life. Do that in as much detail and with as much feeling as possible. Then refuse to dwell on any other competing scenario.

Recruit Accomplices

According to information provided by the American Psychological Association, numerous studies continue to suggest that social isolation not only robs you of help others have to give, but it also has serious physical and mental consequences in itself, including an elevated risk of anxiety and depression.[2]

There's no getting around it. Achieving lasting freedom from anxiety takes a team effort. You'll need professional caregivers to help you choose the best tools available and show you how to make the most of them.

You'll need friends and family who understand your goals and help you stay the course when things get tough. Having an extended community on your side—such as you'll find in places of worship, support groups, and workshops—greatly increases your chances of success.

How about a mentor, life coach, personal trainer, music teacher, mountain-climbing guide, scuba instructor, or dance-class partner? Seek them out, and sign them on to your team. Enlist the support of people who can help distract you from your fears and encourage you to face them through new adventures.

Others may even include fellow jailbreakers, people like you who are sick and tired of being beat up by bullying guards (fears). The support you can give each other is priceless. In fact, the biggest contribution they make to your escape might be giving you someone besides yourself to think about for a change. Teamwork is good medicine, in both directions.

You get the message. If you really want out of here, don't go it alone.

Make a Plan

If you've ever watched a jailbreak movie, you know that no one ever succeeded by rushing the fences in an impulsive blaze of glory. To make it to the other side, you need a map based on a detailed understanding of how the prison is laid out and how its systems work. On the path to mental well-being, that means you have to study your mind and tease out its secrets in order to outwit its defenses. The stakes are high—the future you hope to build as a free person—and your commitment to doing everything you possibly can to succeed must be even higher.

When Angie came to me for help, all she knew was that she was terrified of social situations, which she defined as everything from waiting at a bus stop with others to attending her sister's wedding only because her mother threatened to disown her if she didn't go. I asked her to be more specific.

"I don't know!" she barked in frustration. That was an understandable response from someone who had spent so many years behind mental bars. "It just happens."

I convinced Angie it was time to make a map. She reluctantly agreed to start carrying a small notebook to write down the time, place, and circumstances of every onset of stress around others. The object was to zero in on precisely what made her uncomfortable and when in the process she typically became aware of those triggers. After about a week, she clearly saw that her threshold into discomfort was eye contact. She didn't like the intimacy of being seen. Suddenly her broad fear of "social contact" became much more precise—and therefore more manageable. Knowing her own mind in detail revealed a number of promising but previously hidden passageways out of the prison of her fear.

Sensing the possibility of escape, Angie started taking the effort even more seriously and discovered it mattered how much sleep she'd had the night before, what she'd eaten that day, and whether she was also anxious about something else at the time. These are the kinds of gems you discover about yourself when you decide to be free and make a plan for how to get there.

Expect Setbacks and Stay Calm

Turning back to the example of all the prison escape movies you've watched, the innocent hero of the story has made up his or her mind to be free, recruited accomplices, and made a detailed, foolproof plan. Then what happens? Unforeseen "disaster" strikes. The perfect plan has to be adapted on the fly or they'll never make it over the wall. In the movies, we call that a dramatic twist or a plot point, part of what makes the story entertaining. In real life, unexpected complications can seem highly threatening.

Just when things were starting to look up, your boss calls you into her office and announces you're being transferred to another location. Road construction along your route to work forces you into a detour over a terrifyingly long and elevated bridge you would normally avoid at any cost. A minor food poisoning outbreak at your kid's elementary school inflames your fear of contagious diseases. These things happen. But if you're prepared, they don't have to mean you retreat into your cell and tear up your plan.

The advice to "expect the unexpected" can seem like a hopeless oxymoron. But look closer and you'll see the liberating potential in the idea. If you accept from the outset that unforeseen challenges will arise, then you rob your anxiety of the element of surprise—the spark that ignites panic. As you plan your jailbreak, ask yourself, *What can go wrong?* Keep a list of everything that comes to mind.

Never Give Up

Early Spanish explorers sometimes burned the ships that had carried their party across the Atlantic. Though I'd never recommend anything that dramatic in your life, there is something to be learned from the mindset that commits completely to what lies ahead while taking retreat off the table for good. When some part of your plan doesn't work, don't let that send you back into your cell of old patterns of defeat. Immediately begin drawing up a new strategy. Lower your shoulder and get back in there.

I'll say it again: The stakes are high. Your determination must be higher.

Free at Last

It isn't possible to overstate the prize that waits as a reward for all this effort. You never deserved to be locked away behind the walls of anxiety and fear. Like everyone else on earth, you were born to be happy, healthy, and free.

Throughout this book you've explored the many interwoven causes and effects of uncontrolled anxiety. Some of those contributing factors you unwittingly chose for yourself—like diet, substance use, unbalanced use of technology, and so on. Others came to you as a biological inheritance, an unwanted challenge to overcome. In every case, however, you now know there are tools available to help you break your chains and finally possess what you've been looking for: freedom from fear.

You can do this. Your positive future awaits!

Self-Assessment Tools

Feeling Anxious? A Yes-or-No Assessment

Circle the answer that applies to you:

1. Do you ever feel fearful without really knowing why?

   YES / NO

2. Do you worry about a hundred little things throughout the day?

   YES / NO

3. Do certain situations cause your heart to race and your palms to sweat?

   YES / NO

4. Do you sometimes feel like you're suffocating, as if you can't get enough air?

   YES / NO

5. Do you suddenly feel light-headed, preoccupied, or on edge?

   YES / NO

6. Do you wake up in the morning tired and irritable?

   YES / NO

7. Do you have trouble falling asleep or staying asleep?

   YES / NO

8. Does your fear sometimes become so overwhelming that you're afraid you're going to die?

   YES / NO

9. Do you avoid certain people, places, and situations because of how fearful they make you feel?

   YES / NO

10. Do you find yourself thinking about all the things that could go wrong?

   YES / NO

If you answered yes to more than two of these ten questions, you likely experience anxiety to the degree that it should be addressed through the strategies described in this book and with the help of a mental health professional.

Assess Your Level of Anxiety

Many people wonder if their level of anxiety is normal and expected or if it represents a problem (or a severe problem).

This self-assessment tool will help you evaluate generalized anxiety disorder based on common symptoms experienced over a month's time. Your responses to the statements below will indicate where you might be on a scale from mild to severe anxiety and whether you should pursue treatment.

Score your responses to the following circumstances and emotions you have experienced over the PAST MONTH.	Not at all	Several days	More than half of the days	Nearly every day
1. I have felt nervous, anxious, or tense.	0	2	4	6
2. I can't stop or control my worrying.	0	1	2	3
3. I have worried a lot about several things.	0	1	2	3
4. I have had difficulty relaxing or winding down.	0	1	2	3
5. I have felt so jittery and restless that I have had trouble calming down or sitting still.	0	1	2	3
6. I easily become annoyed or irritable.	0	1	2	3
7. I feel afraid, as if something awful might happen.	0	1	2	3
8. I have trouble falling asleep or staying asleep because my mind races or I can't 'shut off' my brain.	0	1	2	3
Add up your results for each column:		1	2	21
Total score (add column totals together):	24			

Assess the severity of your anxiety:

- 1 to 8 = You are likely experiencing mild anxiety.
- 9 to 18 = You are likely experiencing moderate anxiety.
- 15 to 21 = You are likely experiencing moderately severe anxiety.
- 20 to 27 = You are likely experiencing severe anxiety.
- If your score is 20 or higher, or if you feel that anxiety is affecting your daily life, call your doctor.

Self-Care Checklist

Many people in our hurried, harried culture do not take care of themselves physically, emotionally, and spiritually—which, of course, contributes to anxiety.

Read through the list below and evaluate how effectively you take care of yourself. Put a check mark by each exercise that applies to you.

Do you . . .

- set aside ample time (at least eight hours) throughout the week for rest and relaxation?
- allow yourself to make mistakes and accept your shortcomings?
- ask for help when you need it?
- spend time with friends at least twice a week?
- exercise three times a week?
- pursue activities that will nurture your spiritual life (prayer, inspirational reading, church services, etc.)?
- intentionally practice gratitude, pausing each day to be thankful for a specific blessing in your life?
- write out your thoughts and feelings in a journal a few times each week?
- allow for "play time" once a week (pursuing a hobby, engaging in a sport, playing games, etc.)?
- eat nutritious meals most of the time?
- use your financial resources wisely, living within your means?
- identify a dream and work toward achieving it?
- share openly and honestly with trusted people in your life?
- say no to requests and opportunities when they would burden your schedule or add stress to your life?
- forgive others and let go of grudges?
- give others your full attention when interacting with them?
- recognize when you try to live up to others' expectations and allow yourself the freedom not to?
- give love to others and receive it graciously?
- celebrate accomplishments both big and small?
- seek help from others when you need it?

If you checked ten or more of these activities, you are doing well at self-care. Any less than ten and you should look for more ways to take better care of yourself, starting with the items above that you did not check off.

Assess Your Level of Optimism and Hope

Throughout this book, we've discussed the power of optimism, hope, and joy in relieving anxiety. Optimism is the default setting that looks for the good in every situation. Hope is the belief that the good really does exist. And joy celebrates the existence of what is good.

There is good all around you, and when you intentionally look for it, you'll take a step toward managing your anxiety. Begin the process by filling in the following blanks:

The Good about Me and Who I Am

The Good in My Life Right Now

The Good in My Life in the Past

The Good in My Life I Anticipate in the Future

_____

_____

_____

_____

_____

_____

Why I Choose Hope over Fear

_____

_____

_____

_____

_____

_____

Why I Choose to Live in the Moment Today

_____

_____

_____

_____

_____

_____

Assess How Anxiety Is Affecting Your Physical Health

Earlier in this book, we looked at the link between emotional health and physical health—specifically, how anxiety can compromise your physical well-being. With this in mind, take an inventory of how you're feeling physically.

Then, using this inventory, work in conjunction with your primary care physician to address any ailments and conditions. What's more, as you apply the whole-person strategies presented in this book, it's likely that you will experience improved physical wellness.

Your Heart

1. Do you find yourself worrying about your heart rate and stopping whatever you're doing to check it?
2. Is your increased heart rate one of the first signs you have of an anxiety episode?
3. What is your current resting heart rate?
4. What is your current resting blood pressure?
5. Have you ever thought you had a heart arrhythmia? If so, what did you do about it?
6. Are you concerned about the health of your heart?

Your Lungs

1. Do you ever have problems breathing or feel like you're not getting enough air? If so, how often does this happen?
2. Does this occur as a response to feeling anxious? If so, how often does this happen?
3. Are you able to regulate your breathing, or do you begin to hyperventilate?
4. During an anxiety episode, do you ever feel like you're suffocating? If so, how often does this happen?
5. How often do your hands and feet feel tingly during an anxiety episode?
6. How often do you feel light-headed during an anxiety episode?

Your Stomach

1. Do you experience high levels of gastrointestinal distress?
2. Do you often feel nauseous when anxious?
3. Do you ever experience abdominal pain when feeling anxious?
4. Have you been diagnosed with irritable bowel syndrome?
5. Have you ever been treated for an ulcer?
6. Do you regularly experience acid reflux?

Your Muscles

1. Where in your body do you feel the most tension?
2. Does your tension go away with a hot bath or a massage, or is it continual?
3. Do you experience a high degree of pain in your muscles and joints?
4. Do you grind your teeth at night?
5. Do you have TMJ or clench your jaw frequently?
6. Do you tighten your fists, shoulders, or back, perhaps not even realizing it initially?

Your Immune System

1. Do you often feel like you're fighting off the onset of illness?
2. Do you feel like you're in a constant state of fatigue?
3. When have you noticed feeling better?
4. How long does that last?
5. Do you have difficulty healing from illnesses and infections?
6. Is there a particular recurring illness or infection that just never seems to go away completely?

Your Weight

1. Has your weight increased or decreased beyond normal fluctuations?
2. Have your eating habits changed as a result of your anxiety?
3. Have you been diagnosed with high blood pressure?

4. Have you been told you're at risk for cardiovascular problems because of your weight?
5. Do you find it difficult to maintain or lose weight?
6. Have you ever had a medical test to determine your level of cortisol?

Your Head

1. Do you get tension headaches? If so, how often?
2. Is taking an analgesic (aspirin, acetaminophen, ibuprofen) effective for your headaches?
3. Do you suffer from migraines? If so, how long do they last?
4. What works best to ease your migraines' effects?
5. Have you noticed a correlation between the onset of anxiety and the onset of either a tension headache or a migraine?
6. Do you ever feel "brain fog" or dizziness during an anxiety episode?

Unmasking Myths & Misconceptions

"Roberta, you're not only anxious about life, but you're also anxious that you're not doing anxiety the right way."

The observation came from Roberta's friend and neighbor as they rounded the corner during one of their morning walks through their housing development.

Roberta shook her head. "I don't think that's what I'm saying."

Her friend pushed back. "Really? You just said you feel ridiculous even talking about feeling anxious because you can always think of someone whose life is much worse than yours. As if your feelings and struggles don't count."

Roberta pondered the words. "Sometimes I do think I should be able to just get over it on my own."

Roberta's sentiments are not uncommon among those who struggle with anxiety. Yet nagging self-talk that "I can get over this on my own" or "I feel bad for feeling this way, since my life could be worse" are misconceptions that need to be addressed.

Everyday Anxiety versus an Anxiety Disorder

Perhaps this is a good time to revisit the difference between everyday anxiety and an anxiety disorder. Roberta's thoughts that she can get through this without professional help and her perspective that many people have worse problems than her are not necessarily unhealthy responses to *everyday* anxiety.

To put it simply, *everyone* experiences everyday anxiety, which is a normal, proportionate response to the stressors we face in our daily lives. In fact, everyday anxiety can be beneficial, since it motivates us to take action to solve the problem creating stress in our lives, which then eliminates the anxiety. For example, anxiety over finances can be addressed by getting a second job, seeking a raise, or learning better money-management skills. Anxiety about passing a school midterm can be addressed by enlisting the help of a tutor, asking the teacher for guidance, or developing more efficient study habits.

It's even possible to reduce everyday anxiety by embracing a more positive outlook, such as Roberta's thought that her problems are not the worst thing that could happen to her.

But an anxiety disorder is not a proportionate response to a circumstance or problem. The hallmarks of anxiety disorders are prolonged, excessive, and obsessive thoughts leading to physical symptoms. When an anxiety disorder is present, telling yourself that "I can get over this on my own" or "I just need to adjust my perspective" does not adequately address the seriousness of the problem.

Busting Ten Myths about Anxiety Disorders

Here are ten of the most common misconceptions about anxiety disorders and the truth about these myths:

1. "Anxiety Disorders Aren't a Big Deal— Not like a 'Serious' Condition."

The danger with this myth is that it can result in individuals and families letting an anxiety disorder go untreated.

The truth is that people with untreated anxiety disorders are at a higher risk of depression, substance abuse, illness, and even suicide, so anxiety disorders *are* a big deal and need to be addressed. The good news is anxiety disorders are among the most treatable of all mental issues.

2. "I Can Get Over This on My Own."

While more than forty million adults in America struggle with an anxiety disorder, less than one-third seek treatment—and misconceptions like this contribute to that statistic.[1]

People who hold on to this myth are at greater risk of mismanaging their anxiety, self-medicating to cope, and living with prolonged anxiety that might have been successfully managed with the help of professionals.

There are, indeed, things you can do on your own to reduce anxiety, and connecting with professionals and others to learn what these techniques include is a good way to begin to appropriate them.

3. "Anxiety Disorders Are a Sign of a Character Defect or Weakness."

This misconception could not be further from the truth. As we examined in chapter 2, the reality is that anxiety disorders can be caused by relationships, environmental stress, brain chemistry, and ingested substances like alcohol, drugs, and even caffeine. Genetics is a factor as well. Anxiety can run in families, and having a close relative who struggles with anxiety increases your risk of struggling with it as well.

Exposure to traumatic events as a child or adult can contribute to the development of an anxiety disorder. Even health issues such as heart disease, diabetes, asthma, hyperthyroidism, and chronic pain can play a role.

Understanding the root causes of anxiety disorders can help eliminate shame linked to the misguided belief that anxiety is a sign of personal failure or weakness. And just as anxiety is not a sign of weakness, neither is obtaining help.

4. "I Need Medication to Improve."

We addressed this important topic in chapter 7. Again, I am not adamantly opposed to anti-anxiety medications and understand that millions of people take them, often finding them helpful. My concern rests on the fact that many individuals view medication as the *only* viable solution to their anxiety and therefore don't pursue other treatment options. For many, taking prescription meds becomes a lifelong practice, which can have harmful effects over time. While sometimes helpful in the short term, medication can lead a person to overlook or ignore the root causes of anxiety that should be addressed for true healing to occur.

What's more, there are many ways to treat anxiety that do not involve drugs. For example, several types of psychotherapy have proven helpful, including cognitive behavioral therapy (CBT) and acceptance and commitment therapy (ACT).

Done one-on-one or in a group setting, CBT addresses how we think, act, and react with the goal of reducing unpleasant emotions, thoughts, and behaviors (as we saw in chapter 12). Unlike CBT, ACT doesn't focus on reducing unpleasant emotions, thoughts, and behaviors but instead focuses on reducing the need to control these things. In other words, instead of focusing on ways to feel less anxious, ACT focuses on accepting anxious feelings while at the same time committing to act positively in spite of those feelings.

At The Center, a primary treatment approach is dialectical behavioral therapy (DBT), which helps distressed individuals to identify and modify negative, harmful thinking patterns as a means to create positive, helpful behavioral changes. The term *dialectical* derives from the concept that bringing together two opposites in therapy—acceptance and change—brings better results than either one alone. DBT focuses on acceptance of a person's experience while developing new skills to manage painful emotions and make healthy choices. This therapy technique focuses on four key aspects:

- *mindfulness*, which helps people to accept what is and to be present in the current moment
- *distress tolerance*, focusing on an individual's understanding and acceptance of negative emotions rather than avoiding them
- *emotional regulation*, providing strategies to manage and modify strong emotions that cause difficulties or troubles in a person's life
- *interpersonal effectiveness*, equipping people with techniques for interacting with others in a way that maintains self-respect, healthy boundaries, and beneficial communication

Although one-on-one or group therapy is often most effective in creating lasting change, many individual activities can lead to helpful insights and progress. Creative writing, for example, has been shown to reduce anxiety. In their book *Expressive Writing: Words That Heal*, coauthors James Pennebaker, PhD, and John Evans, EdD, explain: "Across multiple studies, people who engage in expressive writing report feeling happier and less negative than they felt before writing. Similarly, reports of depressive symptoms, rumination, and general anxiety tend to drop in the weeks and months after writing about emotional upheavals."[2]

According to Pennebaker and Evans, how you write about traumatic events matters. Using cause-and-effect words like *because, realize,* and *understand* helps you place the traumatic event in the context of your larger life story and to acknowledge growth that came from that event. And as you help your brain make sense of your experience, anxiety is often reduced.

There is another category of interventions that can make a big difference. Complementary therapy and activities are things you can do—alone or in conjunction with counseling—that improve overall well-being. In other words, learning how to manage stress, face your fears, improve the health of your body and your brain, and heal from past traumas are just a few of the actions you can take that can change how you experience anxiety struggles and transform the quality of your life.

Rest assured that if you struggle with anxiety, you are not destined to spend the rest of your life on drugs. There are alternatives.

5. "To Cope with My Anxiety, I Need to Avoid All Stressful Situations."

This approach not only doesn't work, it can actually *increase* feelings of anxiety. Avoiding stress in life is an unrealistic expectation that simply can't be met. Even if you tried to shield yourself from the outside world, staying sequestered in your home all the time (which I wouldn't recommend), you'll still experience stress. You might worry about the people you know beyond your front door, or that a tree might fall on your roof, or that your health is deteriorating. On and on it goes. The fact is, the world we live in is stressful, and we simply can't avoid it. But we can manage our stress in a healthy, productive way.

Another point about this myth: envisioning yourself as too fragile to deal with any stress is a debilitating and demoralizing way to live. Avoidance may be a common way to deal with anxiety (or rather *not* deal with it), but it keeps you stuck in the same miserable place. You don't want to be stuck, and you don't need to be.

Pursuing impossible solutions isn't the answer, especially when there are so many treatments and solutions available to you that work and can provide genuine relief to the anxious feelings that are impacting your life on a daily basis.

6. "This Is My Lot in Life, and I'll Always Be This Way. It's My New Normal."

This myth is a self-fulfilling prophecy for many. If you believe anxiety is your burden to bear in life and always will be, you won't take the necessary steps to overcome it. This kind of thinking saddens me deeply, because living with anxiety year after year is certainly *not* your lot in life, and you don't need to always be this way. There is so much more fulfillment and freedom for you to enjoy every day.

Believing that we are destined to live mired in our struggles decries the resilience of the human spirit, not to mention the ingenuity of the human brain in coming up with solutions every day that improve our quality of life on every front.

Embracing hope and striving for improvement and even transformation are characteristics of a mentally healthy person. Resist the urge to give up and embrace fatalistic perspectives.

There are too many ways of treating anxiety disorders and too many stories of success for you to resign yourself to an anxiety-riddled future without hope of reprieve. Actually, the fact that you picked up this book and have read this far tells me that you have *not* given up or bought into the lie that anxiety is your destiny.

7. "I Can Fake It Till I Make It."

Another way to state this myth is "If I just act happy and appear like nothing's wrong, then everything will be okay sooner or later. If I just muddle through, if I just suffer through it long enough, then my anxiety will eventually go away."

But denial is rarely the answer to any problem. With anxiety, millions of people tragically suffer for decades or even a lifetime, never fully experiencing the joy available to them. This often happens because they believe they can "fake it" rather than address their anxiety in a meaningful and intentional way.

Many of the myths and misconceptions in this list are based on denial, including the beliefs that "I can make it on my own" and "anxiety isn't a serious problem." The path to wholeness lies in embracing the truth, and "faking" anything is a far cry from embracing that truth.

8. "I Just Need to Practice the Power of Positive Thinking and Replace My Anxiety with Happy Thoughts."

Closely related to myth number 7 is this little gem. I'll be the first to admit that positive thoughts *are* powerful, and I've written at length about healthy self-talk in this book and elsewhere. In fact, studies continue to document the power of our thoughts and our beliefs to shape our experiences and choices.

But there is a dangerous assumption that can underlie this seemingly innocuous belief: If happy thoughts are the only answer, what do you do if happy thoughts *don't* replace your anxiety? If you hang your hat on the power of positive thinking and it doesn't work, what then? Do you experience feelings of shame or failure? What happens to your anxiety levels then?

Without ignoring the power of our thoughts, let me remind you that anxiety disorders have many causes, some of which are based on physiology, genetics, and the chemistry of our brains.

And because of that, our tool kit of solutions must include more than "happy thoughts." We must be willing to consider—and embrace—a comprehensive arsenal of proven interventions. The bottom line: positive thinking and healthy self-talk are key components of achieving well-being.

9. "I Just Need More Faith in God, More Earnest Prayers, and More Time Reading the Bible."

As a person of deep faith, I embrace all that a relationship with our Creator and a vibrant prayer life can entail. Spiritual practices are an essential part of my daily life, and I believe God is the Great Physician who ultimately brings healing. Is God capable of healing your anxiety once and for all? Of course he is! Is prayer an effective practice for achieving peace and well-being? You bet!

At the same time, this is a misconception because it assumes a single-mindedness that refuses to acknowledge all of the resources God has laid before you. Like other topics we've addressed here, this one surely has validity but can become out of balance if seen as the *only* way to address anxiety. God provides many healthy resources and helpful remedies to guide us through our difficulties and live the full life he intended.

We don't apply this methodology when we are suffering from heart disease or a broken arm, do we? We make an appointment to see our doctor or take a trip to the ER. We follow a treatment plan advised by a medical expert. So why do we persist in applying this myth to mental health issues such as anxiety and depression? These conditions, too, are often rooted in physical problems, including imbalances in brain chemistry, metabolism, sleep patterns, thyroid function, and gut biome.

Faith and prayer are powerful allies in your pursuit of wellness in your body, mind, and spirit. I encourage even my most devout clients to expand their faith in God by recognizing that he may choose to heal their emotions and transform their world using means other than faith and prayer.

10. "Anxiety Is Always Bad and Should Be Banished If Possible."

To think that we can go through life with all of its challenges, joys, and losses and never experience anxiety is ludicrous. As mentioned earlier, anxiety can never be completely avoided and can, in fact, be beneficial.

In addition to motivating us to solve problems, anxiety can serve as a warning sign, alerting us to legitimate danger or encouraging us to avoid high-risk behaviors. Anxiety also increases our heart rate, adrenaline, and blood flow to the brain, preparing us to survive in intense situations that require a fight-or-flight response.

The key to living the healthy, fulfilling life that you've always longed for begins by recognizing that anxiety and nervousness are unavoidable and understanding where everyday, "beneficial" anxiety ends and disproportionate, debilitating anxiety begins.

Think back to Roberta, who I told you about at the beginning of this appendix. For her, healing began when she learned how to identify—and correct—her long-held misconceptions about the anxiety she had battled most of her life. I want the same for you. As you begin to release the inaccurate beliefs that have been holding you back, I believe you will be astounded at the level of healing and wholeness within your grasp.

Replacing Myths with Truth

The next time you find your self-talk gravitating to one of the anxiety myths covered in this appendix, be intentional about disrupting that thought and replacing it with an accurate statement about anxiety and anxiety disorders:

Myth: "Anxiety disorders aren't a big deal—not like a 'serious' condition."
Truth: "Anxiety is a real condition with real causes. The good news is that anxiety is highly treatable, and help is available."

Myth: "I can get over this on my own."
Truth: "I don't need to get over this on my own. There are professionals and resources available to help me acquire the tools to reduce and manage the feelings of anxiety that have been dominating my life."

Myth: "Anxiety disorders are a sign of a character defect or weakness."
Truth: "Anxiety disorders can be caused by events, relationships, environmental stress, brain chemistry, ingested substances, genetics, trauma, and health conditions."

Myth: "I need medication in order to improve."
Truth: "Medications are one of many ways to treat anxiety. There are many things I can do to address anxiety that do not involve taking drugs. I have choices."

Myth: "To cope with my anxiety, I need to avoid all stressful situations."
Truth: "Stress is a normal part of life, and there are many ways I can learn to cope with anxiety so I can experience a full and satisfying life."

Myth: "This is my lot in life, and I'll always be this way. It's my new normal."
Truth: "I will not resign myself to fatalistic thinking. Anxiety is highly treatable, and I am confident there are interventions that will help me embrace a better quality of life."

Myth: "I can fake it till I make it."
Truth: "I don't need to fake anything. The truth is that I struggle with anxiety; another truth is that help is available. I don't have to do this on my own."

Myth: "I just need to practice the power of positive thinking and replace my anxiety with happy thoughts."
Truth: "Embracing positive thoughts such as gratitude is an important tool I can use to combat anxiety, but it is not my only tool. When positive thoughts don't help, there's no reason to beat myself up. There are a lot of things I can do to address anxiety."

Myth: "I just need more faith in God, more earnest prayers, and more time reading the Bible."
Truth: "Faith and spiritual practices like prayer and Bible reading are powerful allies in my pursuit of wellness. At the same time, God has given me a vast array of resources to treat and alleviate anxiety, and I am free to embrace these solutions too."

Myth: "Anxiety is always bad and should be banished if possible."
Truth: "I don't need to be afraid of all anxiety. In fact, some level of anxiety is unavoidable and even beneficial. I'm learning how to differentiate between everyday anxiety and debilitating anxiety and to get help as needed."

Innovative & Intriguing Treatment Options

In the preceding pages we've examined many proven approaches to address anxiety. Among other things, we've talked about ditching denial, unmasking myths, making peace with your path, bolstering your filters, rewiring your brain, and improving your diet.

At the same time, there are other strategies—some of which are emerging and others that have already helped many people.

Transdiagnostic Behavior Therapy (TBT)

Initially developed for use with military veterans, this treatment has been effective in reducing anxiety (as well as depression and PTSD) among this population. TBT treatment consists of twelve to eighteen individual therapy sessions, each about an hour in length. Sessions incorporate and address education, cognitive therapy, sleep hygiene, anger management, muscle relaxation, chronic pain, and more. Studies are ongoing, with the goal of making TBT more accessible to the public.

Biofeedback

This treatment helps people learn how to manage and respond to feelings of anxiety. Biofeedback measures physiological changes like increased heart rate, shallow breathing, muscle tension, and brain activity and helps participants to increase their awareness of these changes. Armed with this awareness, participants are then taught relaxation techniques and other ways to diffuse and manage how the body responds to anxiety.

Biofeedback sessions involve being connected to sensors that monitor physiological responses and provide immediate feedback on improvements as the participant practices various techniques to lower anxiety. These techniques include, among other things, visualization and relaxation and breathing exercises.

Acupuncture

Growing research supports the effectiveness of acupuncture in relieving anxiety. Experts are still discovering exactly why it works, although one study concluded that acupuncture slows the production of stress hormones.[1] And a 2015 study documented reduced anxiety in people who had failed to experience relief from other treatments, including psychotherapy and medication.[2]

Acupuncture is a technique in which very thin needles are inserted through the skin to stimulate strategic points on the body. According to traditional Chinese medicine, where acupuncture originated, there are as many as two thousand acupuncture points on the body which can be stimulated to balance the flow of energy throughout the body. Western medicine more typically sees acupuncture as a way to strategically stimulate nerves and muscles, which increases blood flow and stimulates the body to produce endorphins and opioids, which are natural painkillers.

Acupuncture has been used to relieve dental pain, headaches, neck and back pain, knee pain, morning sickness, and high and low blood pressure. Increasingly, it is being used to relieve symptoms of anxiety as well.

Aromatherapy

The idea that oils from plants can be inhaled or applied to the skin with benefits to our emotional or physical health is not new. And while research is limited, studies do point to relief, and more research is underway.

Anxiety is common among patients experiencing end-stage renal disease, and one study involving forty-six patients going through hemodialysis treatments showed that inhaling the scent of rose water noticeably reduced anxiety.[3]

Aromatherapy uses fragrant essential oils derived from plants. When inhaled or applied to the skin, these oils can have a positive effect on physical, emotional, or mental well-being. Some of the more common reasons people turn to aromatherapy include managing pain, reducing stress, relieving symptoms of anxiety or depression, improving concentration and clarity, relieving muscle soreness, and improving respiratory health.

Essential oils that seem to have the most potential for alleviating anxiety include the following:

- *valerian*: often used to promote sleep, can have a mild sedative effect on the body
- *jasmine:* believed to calm the nervous system, inducing drowsiness
- *rose:* has shown benefits for people with anxiety
- *bergamot:* has a refreshing citrus scent and has been shown to improve mood and reduce anxiety
- *lavender:* can improve sleep in general and also decrease anxiety and stress, possibly by impacting the limbic system
- *ylang ylang:* has been shown to lower blood pressure, pulse, stress, anxiety, and cortisol levels when combined with lavender and bergamot[4]

Aromatherapy may seem like a simple intervention, and it is. When using essential oils topically, never apply full-strength oils directly to your skin. Instead, add a few drops to an ounce of almond, olive, or coconut oil. If you prefer to inhale the oils, pass an open bottle beneath your nose or put a few drops in an electric diffuser or a bowl of steaming hot water.

Animal Therapy

We've heard for years that owning a pet—particularly a dog or a cat—comes with many health benefits. In one survey of two thousand pet owners, for example, more than seven out of ten participants reported experiencing mental health improvements as a result of owning a pet.[5]

Another study concluded that employees who brought their dogs to work scored significantly higher in job satisfaction and also showed a decline in stress throughout the day (as opposed to their canine-free coworkers, who actually showed an increase in stress by the end of the day).[6]

Why do pets improve our mental and physical health?

For starters, researchers who conducted a review of sixty-nine studies on human-animal interactions surmised that an increase in oxytocin might be behind the reduced stress and improved mood experienced by many pet owners.[7]

In addition, pets provide cuddling, company, and in the case of dogs needing to be walked, exercise and sunlight.

Herbal Teas

The simple act of holding and sipping a cup of hot tea is relaxing. Add into the equation the medicinal value of many herbs, and it's little wonder that people turn to tea to say goodbye to stress.

Did you know, for example, that peppermint includes menthol, which acts as a natural muscle relaxant?

Or that preliminary studies show passionflower extract to be promising in reducing generalized anxiety disorder—without the side effects of some medications?[8]

Blended teas available on the market that combine passionflower with other herbs include Traditional Medicinals' Cup of Calm and Yogi's Honey Lavender Stress Relief.

Weighted Blankets

Weighted blankets are exactly what the name suggests. Weighing between five and thirty pounds, weighted blankets are filled with tiny glass beads or plastic pellets. Imagine the weight of the lead vest worn during dental X-rays.

The science behind weighted blankets has to do with deep pressure stimulation. In one study, after using a weighted blanket, a third of participants showed a 33 percent decrease in measurable anxiety symptoms, while 63 percent reported decreased feelings of anxiety.[9] Weighted blankets have also proved helpful to people with autism and ADHD.

How heavy a blanket should you try? Look for a blanket that weighs in at around 10 percent of your body weight.

Relief through Relaxation

Relax is, admittedly, a loaded word.

Few people in our frenzied modern society have a clue what it really means, much less how to do it. You can see it on the faces of nearly everyone walking down a crowded city sidewalk, sitting in traffic, or trudging through the grocery store after a hectic workday. Even when doing supposedly "relaxing" things, like walking their dog or pushing a child on a swing at the park, people seem hounded by nervous tension. Telling them to simply relax is a good way to make them cry—or start a fight.

If that's true for average people, then what must those who struggle to manage intense anxiety feel? They tend to hear the word *relax* from others—or themselves in the middle of the night—more often than most, in a variety of contexts:

- *The well-meaning suggestion:* "You should learn to relax more."
- *The sharp-edged question:* "Why can't you just relax?"
- *The frustrated command:* "Just relax, for heaven's sake!"

You might as well tell them they should learn to be taller or have better eyesight. That's because someone suffering from an anxiety disorder frequently has only one available response to comments like these: "I *can't* just relax! That's the whole problem!" The very thought of relaxation pushes them into yet another downward spiral of guilt, fear, and anxiety.

I want to propose two ideas that will lead to a way out of that cycle. First, it's true: you really *should* learn to relax more if you want to tame your anxiety and enjoy a healthier, fuller life. And second: yes, you can! Perhaps you haven't yet, but you most certainly can.

A Word of Warning

Throughout this book, I have emphasized that overcoming anxiety is indeed possible and that doing so will require intentional, purposeful effort on your part. It does no good to offer easy answers and simplistic solutions.

The same is true when it comes to learning to relax. Choosing to employ the time-honored tools and techniques of healing relaxation requires real determination. You'll need the willingness to let go of some cherished habits and replace them with new ones. Most of the suggestions that follow are quite enjoyable and take less time than watching a YouTube video. All are useless, however, until you decide to apply them. That's not meant to be discouraging or a cause for more guilt. Far from it! My purpose is to empower you to make use of the single most important healing resource at your disposal—*choice*. It's the ability to deliberately fight for your own health and well-being.

Relaxation as a healing practice perfectly illustrates why, at The Center, we advocate a whole-person approach rather than expecting talk therapy or pharmaceuticals alone to do all the heavy lifting. Counseling and medications exist to help you achieve equilibrium when your disorder has spun too far out of control so you can take the reins again and make the healthy choices only you can make. Think of it this way: if you elect to eat nothing but jalapeño pizza three meals a day, can you really expect antacids to offer you lasting relief from indigestion? Choosing to make relaxation a part of your healing practice is the equivalent of changing the menu and eating more wholesome foods. The hardest part is confronting the habits that keep you stuck.

Another fact we must acknowledge is that, in many respects, our modern culture is like a cafeteria that serves little else but jalapeño pizza. That is, there is not much in the course of typical daily life that leads us to relax, slow down, take a break, breathe deeply, and enjoy the moment. Quite the opposite. News sources encourage us to worry about everything under the sun. Social media stokes our fear of being left behind. Work is often an endless chain of obligation and stress. And we are driven by clever marketers to run ourselves ragged chasing nonstop entertainment and ever more stuff.

But though the cards may be stacked against us, we're far from out of the game. According to researchers at Mayo Clinic, "Relaxation techniques are a great way to help with stress management. Relaxation isn't only about peace of mind or enjoying a hobby. Relaxation is a process that decreases the effects of stress on your mind and body. Relaxation techniques can help you cope with everyday stress and with stress related to various health problems, such as heart disease and pain."[1]

Mayo Clinic experts go on to list the benefits of practicing relaxation techniques:

- slower heart rate
- lower blood pressure
- slower breathing rate
- improved digestion
- regulation of blood sugar levels
- diminished activity of stress hormones
- increased blood flow to major muscles
- reduced muscle tension and chronic pain
- improved concentration and mood
- better sleep quality
- decreased fatigue
- less anger and frustration
- a boost in confidence to handle problems[2]

Sounds good, right? Here's the point: these advantages are unlikely to spontaneously sprout in your life like wildflowers in a meadow. You have to plant the seeds yourself, shelter them, and nourish them. But if you do, nothing in this whole, crazy, high-speed world can rob you of their power to change your life for good.

Setting the Stage for Success

Step one is to survey the existing landscape of your life and clear away the obstacles in your path, starting with noise and visual clutter.

Sensory overload is a kind of bottleneck that happens when your five physical senses receive more input from sounds, imagery, smells, and proximal motion than the brain can process at one time. Although anyone can experience overload from time to time, researchers have found that people already suffering from a mental disorder—like anxiety or PTSD—are especially prone to its onset. Symptoms, in fact, often overlap with those of many anxiety disorders. They include "difficulty focusing due to competing sensory input, extreme irritability, restlessness and discomfort . . . [and] stress, fear, or anxiety about your surroundings."[3]

All of these effects are the very antithesis of "relaxing." It makes sense, then, if you've decided to make purposeful relaxation a part of your healing plan, to first take a hard look at your surroundings and your habits for ways you may be working against yourself. Some sources of sensory input are difficult to manage, like noisy neighborhood kids or train whistles from nearby tracks. But many distracting noises and images are directly within your power to limit.

Imagine you are planning a romantic dinner at home. Perhaps it's your anniversary. Or, if you are single, you've invited someone special, maybe a person you hope could be the *one*. Close your eyes and picture the perfect setting. Soft, pleasing light. Soothing music. Clean rooms free of clutter and distraction. The television is dark, cell phones silenced. The goal is to create the perfect environment for focusing on nothing but each other.

Now picture the opposite scene. How romantic could the evening be if a muted television in every room flashes images of mayhem in the world while the stereo provides a soundtrack of hard-driving techno? Or if your date has trouble finding a place to sit because every surface is occupied by piles of clutter? If the kitchen sink is a foot deep in dirty dishes? How special or loved would either of you feel if incoming text messages had priority over intimate conversation?

Sadly, some variation of scenario number two is all too common and far more disruptive than most people realize. That's true not just on special occasions like I've described but also in daily life. If your surroundings are a swirl of jarring noise, chaos, and clutter, then—like people seeking romantic connection—you have some choices to make and work to do before you can realistically expect to "relax." With that done, you'll be ready to do the following.

Calm Your Body

As we've seen, anxiety doesn't exist only in your head. It produces measurable effects in the body as well. One of those is chronic muscle tension, which can lead to all sorts of related conditions, such as headaches, joint pain, insomnia, and respiratory difficulties.

The fight-or-flight state of alert we all enter when threatened is a normal and healthy response. It keeps us alive in crisis situations by preparing us to deal with danger. Then, when the coast is clear, we stand down and our mental and physical equilibrium returns. People with an anxiety disorder, however, generally live with a hyperactive fear response all the time. Their brains never sound the all clear, so they remain watchful, alert, and tense.

As a result, many people grow to view the problem as a one-way street: anxiety makes them tense—period. They are often surprised to hear that the reverse is true as well: like the proverbial snake eating its own tail, physical discomfort due to uneased tension has a way of reinforcing the feelings of anxiety that caused it in the first place. The good news is, bodily tension is not inevitable but can be managed with a variety of easy-to-learn techniques, and doing so can be a powerful tool in your quest to reclaim your life from crippling anxiety.

One method of relieving bodily tension is progressive muscle relaxation (PMR). PMR involves purposely tensing various muscles in your body so you can then release and relax them. The idea is to train yourself to recognize when you've become tense and then to relax automatically.

A typical sequence starts by tensing the muscles in your toes and feet for four to ten seconds, then consciously letting that tension go for ten to twenty seconds. From there, move up through various muscle groups, repeating the process until you reach the neck and head.

PMR was introduced by American physician Edmund Jacobson in the early twentieth century and is still widely used today. Many variations and guided exercises are available online.

Relax Your Mind

It should be clear by now that the body and mind do not have distinctly separate roles to play in presenting symptoms of an anxiety disorder. They are intertwined and reinforce each other, whether positively or negatively. For that reason, dividing relaxation techniques under the headings "mind" and "body" is somewhat arbitrary. Individual methods often contain elements of both mental and physical exercise.

Nevertheless, here are techniques specifically aimed at calming your mind, even when not supported by a physical component like yoga.

Meditation

Once again, conflicting definitions and interpretations of this practice abound. For many people, the word conjures images of sitting painfully for hours without moving, sometimes in distant and drafty temples. We see that portrayal often enough in movies, and indeed, for some, meditation is just that. Thankfully, that's not the only way to meditate. In fact, just a little research reveals that there is no "right" or "wrong" way. It is a remarkably flexible and adaptable technique for calming the mind that's available to anyone, anytime. You can meditate while sitting, standing, walking, running, doing dishes, or knitting a sweater.

The core objective is simple: to place your full attention on your breathing—or some other physical sensation—and allow that attention to displace other thoughts. That works because it's not possible to think two things at once. Some say the goal is to empty the mind of other thoughts and focus only on the breath or the rhythm of walking or the sensation of warm, soapy water in the sink. Others claim that emptying the mind is too much to expect and that the aim is to observe your thoughts without picking them up and running with them, as you normally are prone to do. Just notice your thoughts, without judging them, and then gently draw your attention back to breathing.

Whatever meditation path you choose, there is real value in the technique. By focusing attention on some physical sensation, you are asking your mind to entertain only what is happening right now, in the present moment. Competing, anxious thoughts nearly always concern past or future conditions that are nowhere to be seen in the now.

In *Finding Nowhere: How to Be Happier and Healthier by Living Fully in the Present Moment*, the authors write,

Many of the most persistent problems we face have *no tangible reality* in the present. They have roots reaching back into earliest childhood or forward to the end of our lives. People get stuck in the painful past or the fearful future, not realizing that those experiences (or potential experiences) are not occurring in the present. Usually, what happened in the past to inflict painful wounds stopped happening long ago. Future circumstances, which can cause crippling fear, are only possibilities and not foregone conclusions. Distress and dysfunction only exist in this moment as thoughts, feelings, and beliefs *about* distant events.[4]

Anxiety, by definition, is a heightened state of alert that's focused on past and future challenges and threats. Meditation offers a powerful way to leave those thoughts behind, even if only for a moment. Most people who stick with it, however, report that it becomes easier and easier to calm their mind for longer and longer.

There are far too many different techniques and practical meditation tips to discuss in detail in this appendix. With a little searching, you can find the one that's right for you.

Visualization

This is a more proactive technique that begins with a powerful question: What do you *want*? If you are struggling with anxiety, then the answer seems obvious. You want to heal and get your life back. But visualization asks you to get more specific than that and to picture what your life would be like if you got your wish.

For example, you might say, "I want to feel safe enough to go to lunch with my coworkers." Then, employing some of what you learned in meditation or yoga, you would sit quietly and picture—in as much detail as you can muster—what that outcome would look like. Delicious food on the table, everyone laughing and enjoying themselves, yourself included. Go crazy filling in the colors and textures. See the sunlight on the table, the flowers in a vase. Hear the music in the distance. *Be there* in your imagination, fully present and free to enjoy it. Most importantly, imagine how that would *feel* to you.

Pretty good, I'll wager. And *relaxing*.

The value of this exercise is to replace fearful thoughts with awakened hope and possibility. What you can see, you can achieve. It also flips the script on your inner dialogue, asking you to focus on what you *do* want rather than what you *don't* want. Many people with an anxiety disorder have stopped daring to hope for more than simply getting through the day. Visualization opens the door again on a brighter future.

Born to Be Free

Human beings were never meant to live in a constant state of fear or alert. We all share the same birthright—health and happiness. And we all have obstacles to overcome on that path, some higher than others. If anxiety is your obstacle, rest assured: it *is* surmountable! You can be happy, healthy, and relaxed again. What's missing, at least in part, may be your belief in that possibility and your determination to fight for it.

Start filling in those blanks today. Take a deep breath, choose the relaxation techniques that make sense to you, and give them your very best effort.

The Roots of Anxiety: Childhood Troubles & Traumas

Negative patterns of anxiety are established in childhood, based upon life circumstances, experiences, and perceptions. What's more, these patterns can be exacerbated by physical realities and predispositions. By delving into the origins of anxiety, you'll be better equipped to address your own struggles and safeguard the children in your life from crippling anxiety throughout their growing-up years and eventually adulthood.

Anxiety and worry are often rooted in a lack of security. Children learn to feel secure in their surroundings, family, routines, and personal abilities. This sense of security provides a stable, strong foundation on which to venture forth into life. When this doesn't happen, young people develop a foundation of insecurity, ill-suited for adulthood and its challenges, risks, and dilemmas.

A child with a sense of *security* looks out across the gulf to adulthood and sees a broadly supported expanse with plenty of room to move and solid railings to hold. There's no need to focus on the abyss below because there is no fear of falling. Instead, the child has a wide-open view of the wonders that await. A child with a sense of *insecurity* looks across the gulf to adulthood and sees a gap-filled, narrow track hemmed in on all sides by frayed, untrustworthy ropes. Forget looking up and out; there's an absolute need to focus on the abyss below because each fearful step forward contains the potential for falling. What starts out in childhood translates into adulthood.

There are a variety of situations and conditions that lead to this kind of insecurity growing up, including these:

- *Death of a parent.* When a parent dies, a protective shield is ripped from the child. Even within a family with a surviving parent or other supportive adults, children experience psychological shock when a parent dies.
- *Abandonment or rejection by a parent.* When a parent discards a child through abandonment, a child assumes all is not right with him or her. When a parent intentionally chooses to reject a child, a child learns to feel inferior and flawed.
- *Divorce.* Overwhelmingly divorce not only sunders the relationship of the spouses but also rips apart the world of the children.
- *Frequent relocation.* Often parents view a move as a positive change due to a new house or a new job. Children, however, have different priorities, and the things they cherish—such as a friend, teacher, school, or activity—can be sacrificed in a decision to relocate.
- *Learning disabilities.* Imagine what it would be like to go to school every day, apprehensive that you won't be able to meet expectations.
- *Difficulties in school.* Children often worry about their work in school, but they also worry about social interactions. A child who is bullied, unsuccessful, or simply unnoticed learns to distrust what could happen tomorrow.
- *Family alcoholism or drug abuse.* When alcohol or drug abuse is present in the home, it becomes a home of calm and crisis. There are lulls between violent storms, whose appearance is not so much a matter of if but when.
- *Emotional abuse.* If a child is told over and over that they are not good enough, they'll believe it and be fearful of venturing out much as an adult.
- *Physical and sexual abuse.* The devastation of physical and sexual abuse is so vast that it permeates all aspects of a child's life. This includes the concept of secrecy and holding on to the family truths in secret.

- *Perfectionism in the family.* This is one of the most pervasive ways a child is taught to worry. No one can be perfect all the time, so every task, every expectation has a built-in guarantee of failure.
- *A fearful or insecure parent or significant adult.* Some parents communicate hostility and negativity that damage the self-esteem of their children. Other parents can be more passively damaging through a pattern of constant doubt, fear, worry, and anxiety.

Is it any wonder that children who grow up in these circumstances would develop an anxious outlook on life? Is it any wonder they come to experience anxiety as a "normal" way to live? Consistent worry can become a pattern that eats away at the foundation of life. But as we've explored throughout this book, even the most seemingly entrenched patterns of anxiety can indeed be overcome, leading to a life of inner peace and contentment.

Recommended Resources

Books on Nutrition & Anxiety

21 Days to Eating Better: A Proven Plan for Beginning New Habits by Gregory L. Jantz (Zondervan, 1998)

The Anti-Anxiety Cookbook: Calming Plant-Based Recipes to Combat Chronic Anxiety by Jennifer Browne (Skyhorse, 2019)

The Anti-Anxiety Diet: A Whole-Body Program to Stop Racing Thoughts, Banish Worry, and Live Panic-Free by Ali Miller (Ulysses Press, 2018)

The Body God Designed: How to Love the Body You've Got While You Get the Body You Want by Gregory L. Jantz with Ann McMurray (Siloam, 2007)

Breakthrough Depression Solution: Mastering Your Mood with Nutrition, Diet, and Supplementation by James Greenblatt (Sunrise River Press, 2016)

Happy Gut: The Cleansing Program to Help You Lose Weight, Gain Energy, and Eliminate Pain by Vincent Pedre (William Morrow Paperbacks, 2017)

The Microbiome Diet: The Scientifically Proven Way to Restore Your Gut Health and Achieve Permanent Weight Loss by Raphael Kellman (Da Capo Lifelong Books, 2014)

The Microbiome Solution: A Radical New Way to Heal Your Body from the Inside Out by Robynne Chutkan (Avery, 2016)

The UltraMind Solution: The Simple Way to Defeat Depression, Overcome Anxiety, and Sharpen Your Mind by Mark Hyman (Scribner, 2010)

Books on Emotional Health & Anxiety

Controlling Your Anger before It Controls You: A Guide for Women by Gregory L. Jantz with Ann McMurray (Revell, 2013)

Finding Nowhere: How to Be Happier and Healthier by Living Fully in the Present Moment by Alan Wartes and Keith Wall (Amazon Services, 2019)

Happy for the Rest of Your Life: Four Steps to Contentment, Hope, and Joy—and the Three Keys to Staying There by Gregory L. Jantz with Ann McMurray (Siloam, 2009)

Healing the Scars of Childhood Abuse: Moving beyond the Past into a Healthy Future by Gregory L. Jantz with Ann McMurray (Revell, 2017)

How to De-Stress Your Life by Gregory L. Jantz (Revell, 2008)

The Mindful Way through Anxiety: Break Free from Chronic Worry and Reclaim Your Life by Susan M. Orsillo and Lizabeth Roemer (Guilford Press, 2011)

Books on Addiction & Anxiety

Don't Call It Love: Breaking the Cycle of Relationship Dependency by Gregory L. Jantz and Tim Clinton with Ann McMurray (Revell, 2015)

Food Junkies: The Truth about Food Addiction by Vera Tarman (Dundurn Press, 2014)

Healing the Scars of Addiction: Reclaiming Your Life and Moving into a Healthy Future by Gregory L. Jantz with Ann McMurray (Revell, 2018)

Books on Children/Adolescents & Anxiety

Anxiety Relief for Kids: On-the-Spot Strategies to Help Your Child Overcome Worry, Panic, and Avoidance by Bridget Flynn Walker (New Harbinger Publications, 2017)

The Conscious Parent's Guide to Childhood Anxiety: A Mindful Approach for Helping Your Child Become Calm, Resilient, and Secure by Sherianna Boyle (Adams Media, 2016)

Helping Your Anxious Teen: Positive Parenting Strategies to Help Your Teen Beat Anxiety, Stress, and Worry by Sheila Achar Josephs (New Harbinger Publications, 2017)

Stress and Your Child: The Hidden Reason Why Your Child May Be Moody, Resentful, or Insecure by Archibald D. Hart (Thomas Nelson, 2005)

Under Pressure: Confronting the Epidemic of Stress and Anxiety in Girls by Lisa Damour (Ballantine, 2020)

Understanding Teenage Anxiety: A Parent's Guide to Improving Your Teen's Mental Health by Jennifer Browne and Cody Buchanan (Skyhorse, 2019)

Books on Brain Function & Anxiety

Anxious: Using the Brain to Understand and Treat Fear and Anxiety by Joseph LeDoux (Penguin Books, 2016)

Heal Your Drained Brain: Naturally Relieve Anxiety, Combat Insomnia, and Balance Your Brain in Just 14 Days by Mike Dow (Hay House, 2018)

Rewire Your Anxious Brain: How to Use the Neuroscience of Fear to End Anxiety, Panic, and Worry by Catherine M. Pittman and Elizabeth M. Karle (New Harbinger Publications, 2015)

Tame Your Anxiety: Rewiring Your Brain for Happiness by Loretta Graziano Breuning (Rowman & Littlefield, 2019)

Books on Exercise & Anxiety

8 Keys to Mental Health through Exercise by Christina Hibbert (W. W. Norton, 2016)
Exercise for Mood and Anxiety: Proven Strategies for Overcoming Depression and Enhancing Well-Being by Michael Otto and Jasper Smits (Oxford University Press, 2011)
Spark: The Revolutionary New Science of Exercise and the Brain by John J. Ratey and Eric Hagerman (Little, Brown, 2008)

Books on Spirituality & Anxiety

The Anxiety Cure: You Can Find Emotional Tranquility and Wholeness by Archibald Hart (Thomas Nelson, 2001)
Anxious for Nothing: Finding Calm in a Chaotic World by Max Lucado (Thomas Nelson, 2019)
The Inner Voice of Love: A Journey through Anguish to Freedom by Henri Nouwen (Image, 1999)
Unafraid: Living with Courage and Hope in Uncertain Times by Adam Hamilton (Convergent, 2018)

Books on Technology & Anxiety

#Hooked: The Pitfalls of Media, Technology, and Social Networking by Gregory L. Jantz with Ann McMurray (Siloam, 2012)
12 Ways Your Phone Is Changing You by Tony Reinke (Crossway, 2017)
Alone Together: Why We Expect More from Technology and Less from Each Other by Sherry Turckle (Basic Books, 2017)
iDisorder: Understanding Our Obsession with Technology and Overcoming Its Hold on Us by Larry Rosen (St. Martin's Griffin, 2013)
Irresistible: The Rise of Addictive Technology and the Business of Keeping Us Hooked by Adam Alter (Penguin, 2018)
Rewired: Understanding the iGeneration and the Way They Learn by Larry D. Rosen (St. Martin's Griffin, 2010)

Organizations Offering Help for Anxiety & Mental Health

American Psychological Association: www.apa.org. The largest association of psychologists in the world, the APA offers access to the latest information on depression and related topics like ADHD, eating disorders, and suicide.

Anxiety and Depression Association of America: www.adaa.org. This organization provides detailed facts about various conditions, including anxiety and its symptoms.

Brain and Behavior Research Foundation: www.bbrfoundation.org. This site provides information about depression, anxiety, and other related conditions. The foundation provides support for research into depression and related conditions.

Mental Health America: www.mentalhealthamerica.net. This is one of the foremost nonprofit organizations in the mental health field providing up-to-date news and information.

National Alliance on Mental Illness: www.nami.org. This organization provides education and support pertaining to a wide variety of mental health conditions.

National Institute of Mental Health: www.nimh.nih.gov. As the country's largest organization focusing on mental health, NIMH publishes detailed information on the latest findings related to depression, anxiety, ADHD, OCD, and other mental health conditions.

Notes

CHAPTER 1: LIVING IN THE AGE OF ANXIETY

1. "Facts and Statistics," Anxiety and Depression Association of America, accessed June 19, 2020, https://adaa.org/about-adaa/press-room/facts-statistics.
2. Graham C. L. Davey, "Is There an Anxiety Epidemic?" *Why We Worry* (blog), *Psychology Today*, November 6, 2018, https://www.psychologytoday.com/us/blog/why-we-worry/201811/is-there-anxiety-epidemic.

CHAPTER 2: CAUSES & CATALYSTS

1. "Anxiety Disorders: Overview," Mayo Clinic, May 4, 2018, https://www.mayoclinic.org/diseases-conditions/anxiety/symptoms-causes/syc-20350961.
2. Tanja Jovanovic, "What Is Anxiety?," Anxiety.org, accessed September 27, 2020, https://www.anxiety.org/what-is-anxiety.
3. Jovanovic, "What Is Anxiety?"
4. Jovanovic, "What Is Anxiety?"
5. Harvard Medical School, "What Causes Depression? Onset of Depression More Complex than a Brain Chemical Imbalance," Harvard Health Publishing, June 24, 2019, https://www.health.harvard.edu/mind-and-mood/what-causes-depression.
6. "After the Trauma: How to Manage Anxiety and Stress," Anxiety and Depression Association of America, accessed June 23, 2020, https://adaa.org/about-adaa/press-room/press-releases/after-trauma-how-manage-anxiety-and-stress.
7. Faith Brynie, "How Anxiety and Depression Begin in a Child's Brain," *Brain Sense* (blog), *Psychology Today*, November 4, 2013, https://www.psychologytoday.com/us/blog/brain-sense/201311/how-anxiety-and-depression-begin-in-childs-brain.
8. Robin Marantz Henig, "Understanding the Anxious Mind," *New York Times Magazine*, September 29, 2009, https://www.nytimes.com/2009/10/04/magazine/04anxiety-t.html.
9. Marantz Henig, "Understanding the Anxious Mind."

10. Joshua P. Smith and Sarah W. Book, "Anxiety and Substance Use Disorders: A Review," *Psychiatry Times* 25, no. 10 (October 2008): 19–23, https://www.ncbi.nlm.nih.gov/pmc/articles/PMC2904966.

CHAPTER 3: THE THREE-HEADED MONSTER
1. Matthew 11:28-30.
2. Portions of this section are adapted and condensed from Guy Winch, "10 Crucial Differences between Worry and Anxiety," *The Squeaky Wheel* (blog), *Psychology Today*, March 14, 2016, https://www.psychologytoday.com/us/blog/the-squeaky-wheel/201603/10-crucial-differences-between-worry-and-anxiety.
3. Portions of this section are adapted and condensed from Luana Marques, "Do I Have Anxiety or Worry: What's the Difference?" *Harvard Health Blog*, Harvard Health Publishing, July 23, 2018, https://www.health.harvard.edu/blog/do-i-have-anxiety-or-worry-whats-the-difference-2018072314303.
4. "What Is Stress?," American Institute of Stress, accessed July 1, 2020, https://www.stress.org/what-is-stress.
5. Adapted and condensed from Harry Mills, Natalie Reiss, and Mark Dombeck, "Types of Stressors (Eustress vs. Distress)," Cascade Mental Health Care, accessed September 28, 2020, https://www.cascadementalhealth.org/poc/view_doc.php?type=doc&id=15644&cn=117.

CHAPTER 4: WHAT IS YOUR ANXIETY TYPE?
1. Stephanie Pappas, "Brain Scans Show Distinctive Patterns in People with Generalized Anxiety Disorder in Stanford Study," Stanford Medicine, December 7, 2009, https://med.stanford.edu/news/all-news/2009/12/brain-scans-show-distinctive-patterns-in-people-with-generalized-anxiety-disorder-in-stanford-study.html.
2. "Post-Traumatic Stress Disorder," National Institute of Mental Health, last revised May 2019, https://www.nimh.nih.gov/health/topics/post-traumatic-stress-disorder-ptsd/index.shtml.
3. Janine D. Flory and Rachel Yehuda, "Comorbidity between Post-Traumatic Stress Disorder and Major Depressive Disorder," *Dialogues in Clinical Neuroscience* 17, no. 2 (June 2015): 141–50.
4. "Facts and Statistics," Anxiety and Depression Association of America, accessed September 29, 2020, https://adaa.org/about-adaa/press-room/facts-statistics.
5. "About OCD," International OCD Foundation, accessed September 29, 2020, https://iocdf.org/about-ocd/.
6. "Obsessive-Compulsive Disorder," National Institute of Mental Health, accessed September 29, 2020, https://www.nimh.nih.gov/health/topics/obsessive-compulsive-disorder-ocd/index.shtml.

CHAPTER 5: HOW ANXIETY AFFECTS YOUR LIFE
1. "Facts and Statistics," Anxiety and Depression Association of America, accessed September 29, 2020, https://adaa.org/about-adaa/press-room/facts-statistics.
2. "Facts and Statistics."
3. Harvard Medical School, "Anxiety and Physical Illness," Harvard Health Publishing, May 9, 2018, https://www.health.harvard.edu/staying%20healthy/anxiety_and_physical_illness.

4. "Mental Health in the Workplace," World Health Organization, May 2019, https://www.who.int/mental_health/in_the_workplace/en/.

CHAPTER 6: THIS IS YOUR BRAIN ON ANXIETY

1. University of British Columbia, "Patients with Mood, Anxiety Disorders Share Abnormalities in Brain's Control Circuit," Neuroscience News, October 30, 2019, https://neurosciencenews.com/mood-disorder-brain-networks-15150/.

2. Francis S. Lee, B. J. Casey, and Conor Liston, "Social Anxiety Susceptibility Is Traced to a Specific Brain Circuit and Genetic Variation," Brain and Behavior Research Foundation, May 23, 2019, https://www.bbrfoundation.org/content/social-anxiety-susceptibility-traced-specific-brain-circuit-and-genetic-variation.

3. Michael Miller, "Staying Sharp: 5 Ways to Boost Your Brain Power," Six Seconds, December 17, 2018, https://www.6seconds.org/2018/12/17/neurogene-what-5-research-backed-ways-to-grow-vital-new-brain-cells/. See the original research source: Timothy J. Schoenfeld et al., "Stress and Loss of Adult Neurogenesis Differentially Reduce Hippocampal Volume," Biological Psychiatry 82, no. 12 (December 15, 2017): 914–23, https://www.biologicalpsychiatryjournal.com/article/S0006-3223(17)31585-8/abstract.

4. Harvard Medical School, "Generalized Anxiety Disorder," Harvard Health Publishing, May 17, 2019, https://www.health.harvard.edu/mind-and-mood/generalized-anxiety-disorder.

5. "Causes: Post-Traumatic Stress Disorder," National Health Service, last updated September 27, 2018, https://www.nhs.uk/conditions/post-traumatic-stress-disorder-ptsd/causes/.

6. The information on adrenaline, norepinephrine, and cortisol is adapted from Sarah Klein, "Adrenaline, Cortisol, Norepinephrine: The Three Major Stress Hormones, Explained," HuffPost, April 19, 2013, https://www.huffpost.com/entry/adrenaline-cortisol-stress-hormones_n_3112800.

7. William C. Shiel Jr., "Medical Definition of Neuroplasticity," MedicineNet, accessed October 1, 2020, https://www.medicinenet.com/script/main/art.asp?articlekey=40362.

8. Psalm 139:14.

CHAPTER 7: IF YOU WANT TO CHILL, SHOULD YOU TAKE A PILL?

1. "Achievements in Public Health, 1900–1999: Control of Infectious Diseases," Morbidity and Mortality Weekly Report (MMWR) 48, no. 29 (July 30, 1999): 621–29, Centers for Disease Control and Prevention, https://www.cdc.gov/mmwr/preview/mmwrhtml/mm4829a1.htm.

2. "National Center for Health Statistics: Therapeutic Drug Use," Centers for Disease Control and Prevention, last updated April 13, 2020, https://www.cdc.gov/nchs/fastats/drug-use-therapeutic.htm.

3. Matej Mikulic, "Total Drug Prescriptions Dispensed in the U.S. 2009–2018," Statista, November 8, 2019, https://www.statista.com/statistics/238702/us-total-medical-prescriptions-issued/; Matej Mikulic, "Prescription Drug Expenditure in the

U.S. 1960–2020," Statista, June 12, 2020, https://www.statista.com/statistics/184914
/prescription-drug-expenditures-in-the-us-since-1960/.

4. Teresa Carr, "Too Many Meds? America's Love Affair with Prescription Medication,"
Consumer Reports, August 3, 2017, https://www.consumerreports.org/prescription
-drugs/too-many-meds-americas-love-affair-with-prescription-medication/.

5. Jackson Bentley, "What You Need to Know about Anxiety Medication: Pros
and Cons," Resources to Recover, May 22, 2018, https://www.rtor.org/2018/05/22
/anxiety-medication-pros-and-cons/.

6. "Drug Addiction (Substance Use Disorder)," Mayo Clinic, October 26, 2017,
https://www.mayoclinic.org/diseases-conditions/drug-addiction/symptoms-causes
/syc-20365112.

7. Tim Newman, "Do Antidepressants Work Better than Placebo?" Medical News
Today, July 18, 2019, https://www.medicalnewstoday.com/articles/325767.php.

8. Stephanie Stahl, "Marijuana Not Helpful in Treating Mental Health Problems,
Research Says," CBS Philly, November 7, 2019, https://philadelphia.cbslocal.com/2019
/11/07/marijuana-not-helpful-in-treating-mental-health-problems-research-says/.

9. Jayne O'Donnell, Trevor Hughes, and Stephanie Innes, "Is Marijuana Linked to
Psychosis, Schizophrenia? It's Contentious, but Doctors, Feds Say Yes," *USA Today*,
January 31, 2020, https://www.usatoday.com/story/news/nation/2019/12/15/weed
-psychosis-high-thc-cause-suicide-schizophrenia/4168315002/.

10. Jamie Ducharme, "There's 'Scarce Evidence' to Suggest Cannabis Improves Mental
Health Symptoms, a New Research Review Says," *Time*, October 28, 2019, https://
time.com/5710682/cannabis-marijuana-mental-health/.

11. American Society of Addiction Medicine, "Public Policy Statement on Marijuana,
Cannabinoids and Legalization," September 21, 2015, https://www.asam.org/advocacy
/find-a-policy-statement/view-policy-statement/public-policy-statements/2015/09/22
/public-policy-statement-on-marijuana-cannabinoids-and-legalization.

12. Nora D. Volkow et al., "Adverse Health Effects of Marijuana Use," *New England
Journal of Medicine* 370, no. 23 (June 5, 2014): 2219–27, https://www.ncbi.nlm.nih
.gov/pmc/articles/PMC4827335/; Amresh Shrivastava, Megan Johnston, and Ming
Tsuang, "Cannabis Use and Cognitive Dysfunction," *Indian Journal of Psychiatry*
53, no. 3 (2011): 187–91, http://www.indianjpsychiatry.org/article.asp?issn=0019
-5545;year=2011;volume=53;issue=3;spage=187;epage=191;aulast=Shrivastava.

13. American Society of Addiction Medicine, "Marijuana, Cannabinoids and
Legalization."

CHAPTER 8: INVENTORY YOUR INNER WORLD

1. Sarah Bloch-Elkouby, "What to Do to Fight the Isolation You Feel When You're in
Distress," Anxiety and Depression Association of America, accessed October 2, 2020,
https://adaa.org/learn-from-us/from-the-experts/blog-posts/consumer/what-do-fight
-isolation-you-feel-when-youre.

2. "Understand the Facts: Substance Use Disorders," Anxiety and Depression Association
of America, accessed October 2, 2020, https://adaa.org/understanding-anxiety
/related-illnesses/substance-abuse.

CHAPTER 9: PUT DOWN THE SHOVEL

1. Manfred E. Beutel et al., "Procrastination, Distress and Life Satisfaction across the Age Range—A German Representative Community Study," *PLoS One* 11, no. 2 e0148054 (February 12, 2016), https://www.ncbi.nlm.nih.gov/pmc/articles/PMC4752450/.

2. These findings are chronicled in Jeanne E. Arnold et al., *Life at Home in the Twenty-First Century* (Los Angeles: The Cotsen Institute of Archaeology Press, 2012). See also Jack Feuer, "The Clutter Culture," *UCLA Magazine*, July 1, 2012, http://magazine.ucla.edu/features/the-clutter-culture/.

3. Susan Krauss Whitbourne, "5 Reasons to Clear the Clutter out of Your Life," *Fulfillment at Any Age* (blog), *Psychology Today*, May 13, 2017, https://www.psychologytoday.com/us/blog/fulfillment-any-age/201705/5-reasons-clear-the-clutter-out-your-life.

4. James E. Cutting and Kacie L. Armstrong, "Facial Expression, Size, and Clutter: Inferences from Movie Structure to Emotion Judgments and Back," *Attention, Perception and Psychophysics* 78, no. 3 (2016): 891–901, https://www.ncbi.nlm.nih.gov/pubmed/26728045.

5. James Cutting, at Susan Kelley, "Here's Looking at You, Kid: Filmmakers Know How We Read Emotions," *Cornell Chronicle*, January 25, 2016, https://news.cornell.edu/stories/2016/01/heres-looking-you-kid-filmmakers-know-how-we-read-emotions.

6. Lisa Kaplan Gordon, "The Link between Clutter and Depression," HouseLogic, accessed October 3, 2020, https://www.houselogic.com/organize-maintain/cleaning-decluttering/clutter-depression/.

7. Uma Naidoo, "Gut Feelings: How Food Affects Your Mood," *Harvard Health Blog*, Harvard Health Publishing, March 27, 2019, https://www.health.harvard.edu/blog/gut-feelings-how-food-affects-your-mood-2018120715548.

8. Sarah Wilson, *The Anti-Anxiety Diet: A Two-Week Sugar Detox That Tackles Anxiety* (New York: HarperCollins, 2018), https://books.google.com/books?id=mpI_DwAAQBAJ&printsec=frontcover#v=onepage&q=fire&f=false.

9. Mahmood Bakhtiyari et al., "Anxiety as a Consequence of Modern Dietary Pattern in Adults in Tehran—Iran," *Eating Behaviors* 14, no. 2 (April 2013): 107–12, https://www.sciencedirect.com/science/article/pii/S147101531200147X.

10. Ananya Mandal, "Sugar Cravings Worsened by Lack of Sleep," News Medical, January 11, 2018, https://www.news-medical.net/news/20180111/Sugar-cravings-worsened-by-lack-of-sleep.aspx.

11. Rick Nauert, "Dehydration Influences Mood, Cognition," PsychCentral, August 8, 2018, https://psychcentral.com/news/2012/02/20/dehydration-influences-mood-cognition/35037.html; Denise Mann, "Even Mild Dehydration May Cause Emotional, Physical Problems," WebMD, January 20, 2012, https://www.webmd.com/women/news/20120120/even-mild-dehydration-may-cause-emotional-physical-problems#1.

12. Guy Winch, *Emotional First Aid: Healing Rejection, Guilt, Failure, and Other Everyday Hurts* (New York: Hudson Street Press, 2013), 141.

13. "Gratitude Is Good Medicine," UC Davis Health, November 25, 2015, https://health.ucdavis.edu/medicalcenter/features/2015-2016/11/20151125_gratitude.html.

14. "Gratitude Is Good Medicine."

CHAPTER 10: MAKE PEACE WITH YOUR PAST

1. Marwa Azab, "Inside the Thinking Maze of Anxious Minds," *Neuroscience in Everyday Life* (blog), *Psychology Today*, April 13, 2018, https://www.psychologytoday.com/us/blog/neuroscience-in-everyday-life/201804/inside-the-thinking-maze-anxious-minds.
2. Anne Trafton, "How Expectation Influences Perception," MIT News, July 15, 2019, http://news.mit.edu/2019/how-expectation-influences-perception-0715.
3. Arielle Schwartz, "How Does EMDR Therapy Work? Dr. Arielle Schwartz," October 10, 2017, https://drarielleschwartz.com/how-does-emdr-therapy-work-dr-arielle-schwartz/#.XbvdcehKiUk.
4. Francine Shapiro, "The Role of Eye Movement Desensitization and Reprocessing (EMDR) Therapy in Medicine: Addressing the Psychological and Physical Symptoms Stemming from Adverse Life Experiences," *Permanente Journal* 18, no. 1 (Winter 2014): 71–77, https://www.ncbi.nlm.nih.gov/pmc/articles/PMC3951033/.
5. For more information, see James W. Pennebaker and John F. Evans's book *Expressive Writing: Words That Heal* (Enumclaw, WA: Idyll Arbor, 2014).

CHAPTER 11: PRACTICE MIND OVER MOOD

1. Shelley Kind and Stefan G. Hofmann, "Facts about the Effects of Mindfulness," Anxiety.org, February 10, 2016, https://www.anxiety.org/can-mindfulness-help-reduce-anxiety.
2. Yvo M. C. Meevissen, Madelon L. Peters, and Hugo J. E. M. Alberts, "Become More Optimistic by Imagining a Best Possible Self: Effects of a Two Week Intervention," *Journal of Behavior Therapy and Experimental Psychiatry* 42, no. 3 (September 2011): 371–78, https://www.sciencedirect.com/science/article/pii/S0005791611000358.

CHAPTER 12: MANAGE YOUR EMOTIONS TO ALLEVIATE ANXIETY

1. Vara Saripalli and Kathleen Davis, "How Does Cognitive Behavioral Therapy Work?" Medical News Today, September 25, 2018, https://www.medicalnewstoday.com/articles/296579.php.
2. "Cognitive Behavioral Therapy," Mayo Clinic, March 16, 2019, https://www.mayoclinic.org/tests-procedures/cognitive-behavioral-therapy/about/pac-20384610.
3. "Cognitive Behavioral Therapy."
4. Robert J. DeRubeis, Greg J. Siegle, and Steven D. Hollon, "Cognitive Therapy versus Medication for Depression: Treatment Outcomes and Neural Mechanisms," *Nature Reviews Neuroscience* 9, no. 10 (2008): 788–96, https://www.ncbi.nlm.nih.gov/pmc/articles/PMC2748674/.

CHAPTER 13: BOLSTER YOUR BODY

1. Anthony Coniaris, "Healing of Soul and Body," Saint George Greek Orthodox Church, accessed October 3, 2020, http://stgeorgegoc.org/pastors-corner/fr-ricks-sermons/healing-of-soul-and-body.
2. Coniaris, "Healing of Soul and Body."
3. Scott Gottlieb, "Men Should Eat Nine Servings of Fruit and Vegetables a Day," *BMJ* 326, no. 7397 (2003): 1003, https://www.ncbi.nlm.nih.gov/pmc/articles

/PMC1169355/; Elaine Magee, "Take the Fruit and Vegetable Challenge," WebMD, accessed October 3, 2020, https://www.webmd.com/food-recipes/features/take-the -fruit-and-vegetable-challenge#1.

4. "Exercise for Stress and Anxiety," Anxiety and Depression Association of America, accessed October 3, 2020, https://adaa.org/living-with-anxiety/managing-anxiety /exercise-stress-and-anxiety.

5. "Exercise for Stress and Anxiety."

6. "Physical Activity Guidelines for Americans," US Department of Health and Human Services, last reviewed February 1, 2019, https://www.hhs.gov/fitness/be-active /physical-activity-guidelines-for-americans/index.html.

7. John J. Ratey, "Can Exercise Help Treat Anxiety?" *Harvard Health Blog*, Harvard Health Publishing, October 24, 2019, https://www.health.harvard.edu/blog/can -exercise-help-treat-anxiety-2019102418096.

8. Kathleen Smith, "Anxiety and Sleep," Psycom, March 31, 2020, https://www.psycom .net/anxiety-and-sleep/.

9. Smith, "Anxiety and Sleep."

10. *BMJ*, "Anxiety Might Be Alleviated by Regulating Gut Bacteria," ScienceDaily, May 20, 2019, https://www.sciencedaily.com/releases/2019/05/190520190110.htm.

11. "Antibiotic Use in Outpatient Settings, 2017," Centers for Disease Control and Prevention, August 8, 2019, https://www.cdc.gov/antibiotic-use/stewardship-report /outpatient.html.

CHAPTER 14: FORTIFY YOUR FILTERS

1. "Cyber Bullying Statistics," Bullying Statistics, http://www.bullyingstatistics.org /content/cyber-bullying-statistics.html; Maeve Duggan, "Part 1: Experiencing Online Harassment," Pew Research Center, October 22, 2014, https://www.pewresearch.org /internet/2014/10/22/part-1-experiencing-online-harassment/.

2. Anna Vannucci, Kaitlin M. Flannery, and Christine McCauley Ohannessian, "Social Media Use and Anxiety in Emerging Adults," *Journal of Affective Disorders* 207, no. 1 (January 2017): 163–66, https://www.ncbi.nlm.nih.gov/pubmed/27723539.

CHAPTER 15: REWIRE & RESET YOUR BRAIN

1. Valerie Balandra, "Can a Neurotransmitter Imbalance Be Causing Your Mood Problems?" Integrative Psychiatry, September 6, 2012, https://www.integrativepsychiatry .net/can_a_neurotransmitter_imbalance_be_causing_your_mood_problems.html.

2. "Neurotransmitters," Integrative Psychiatry, accessed October 4, 2020, https://www .integrativepsychiatry.net/neurotransmitter.html.

3. Alan Carter and Jennifer Berry, "Top 10 Evidence Based Supplements for Anxiety," Medical News Today, July 22, 2019, https://www.medicalnewstoday.com/articles /325823.php.

4. Joseph Mercola, "Could a Hug a Day Keep Infection Away?" Mercola, February 7, 2015, https://articles.mercola.com/sites/articles/archive/2015/02/07/benefits-hugging .aspx.

5. Mercola, "Could a Hug a Day Keep Infection Away?"

6. "Fish Oil," Mayo Clinic, October 24, 2017, https://www.mayoclinic.org/drugs
   -supplements-fish-oil/art-20364810.
7. Michael Wotman et al., "The Efficacy of Lavender Aromatherapy in Reducing
   Preoperative Anxiety in Ambulatory Surgery Patients Undergoing Procedures in
   General Otolaryngology," *Laryngoscope Investigative Otolaryngology* 2, no. 6 (2017):
   437–41, https://www.ncbi.nlm.nih.gov/pmc/articles/PMC5743169/.

CHAPTER 16: FIND STRENGTH IN SOUL CARE
1. Carl Sagan, *The Demon-Haunted World: Science as a Candle in the Dark* (New York:
   Ballantine Books, 1996), 29.
2. Psalm 103:8-9, 11-13, NLT.
3. Luke 11:9-10, NLT.
4. Alex Korb, "The Grateful Brain," *PreFrontal Nudity* (blog), *Psychology Today*,
   November 20, 2012, https://www.psychologytoday.com/us/blog/prefrontal-nudity
   /201211/the-grateful-brain.
5. Jenny Santi, "The Secret to Happiness Is Helping Others," *Time*, August 4, 2017,
   https://time.com/4070299/secret-to-happiness/.
6. Matthew 6:33, NLT.

CHAPTER 17: BECOME BOLD & BRAVE
1. Susan Biali Haas, "Help for Anxiety: Facing Your Fears Will Heal Your Brain,"
   Prescriptions for Life (blog), *Psychology Today*, August 27, 2018, https://www
   .psychologytoday.com/us/blog/prescriptions-life/201808/help-anxiety-facing
   -your-fears-will-heal-your-brain.
2. Paul W. Frankland and Sheena A. Josselyn, "Facing Your Fears," *Science* 360, no. 6394
   (June 15, 2018): 1186–87, https://science.sciencemag.org/content/360/6394/1186.
3. Marianne Cumella Reddan, Tor Dessart Wager, and Daniela Schiller, "Attenuating
   Neural Threat Expression with Imagination," *Neuron* 100, no. 4 (November 21,
   2018): 994–1005, https://doi.org/10.1016/j.neuron.2018.10.047.
4. Reddan, Wager, and Schiller, "Attenuating Neural Threat Expression with Imagination."

CHAPTER 18: SANITY THROUGH SIMPLICITY
1. Henry David Thoreau, *Walden* (New York: Longmans, Green, 1910), 12.
2. Thoreau, *Walden*, 77.
3. Linda Esposito, "Minimalism: When Living with Less Means More Mental Health,"
   From Anxiety to Zen (blog), *Psychology Today*, December 22, 2016, https://www
   .psychologytoday.com/us/blog/anxiety-zen/201612/minimalism-when-living-less
   -means-more-mental-health.
4. 1 Corinthians 13:13, NLT.
5. Thoreau, *Walden*, xi.

EPILOGUE: BACK TO A BETTER FUTURE
1. J. M. Barrie, *The Little White Bird* (Leipzig, Germany: Bernhard Tauchnitz, 1903), 138.
2. Amy Novotney, "The Risks of Social Isolation," *Monitor on Psychology* 50, no. 5
   (May 2019): 32, https://www.apa.org/monitor/2019/05/ce-corner-isolation.

APPENDIX 2: UNMASKING MYTHS & MISCONCEPTIONS

1. "Understanding the Facts of Anxiety Disorders and Depression Is the First Step," Anxiety and Depression Association of America, accessed September 22, 2020, https://adaa.org/understanding-anxiety.
2. James W. Pennebaker and John Frank Evans, *Expressive Writing: Words That Heal* (Enumclaw, WA: Idyll Arbor, 2014), 11.

APPENDIX 3: INNOVATIVE AND INTRIGUING TREATMENT OPTIONS

1. Ladan Eshkevari, Eva Permaul, and Susan E. Mulroney, "Acupuncture Blocks Cold Stress-Induced Increases in the Hypothalamus-Pituitary-Adrenal Axis in the Rat," *Journal of Endocrinology* 217, no. 1 (March 15, 2013): 95–104, https://www.ncbi .nlm.nih.gov/pubmed/23386059.
2. Nick Errington-Evans, "Randomised Controlled Trial on the Use of Acupuncture in Adults with Chronic, Non-Responding Anxiety Symptoms," *Acupuncture in Medicine* 33, no. 2 (April 1, 2015): 98–102, https://journals.sagepub.com/doi/10.1136 /acupmed-2014-010524.
3. Farzaneh Barati et al., "The Effect of Aromatherapy on Anxiety in Patients," *Nephro-Urology Monthly* 8, no. 5 (September 2016): https://www.ncbi.nlm.nih.gov /pmc/articles/PMC5111093/.
4. Jin Hee Hwang, "The Effects of the Inhalation Method Using Essential Oils on Blood Pressure and Stress Responses of Clients with Essential Hypertension," *Journal of Korean Academy of Nursing* 36, no. 7 (December 2006): 1123–34, https://www.jkan.or .kr/DOIx.php?id=10.4040/jkan.2006.36.7.1123.
5. "Survey: Pet Owners and the Human-Animal Bond," Human Animal Bond Research Institute, accessed September 24, 2020, https://habri.org/2016-pet-owners-survey.
6. Randolph T. Barker et al., "Preliminary Investigation of Employee's Dog Presence on Stress and Organizational Perceptions," *International Journal of Workplace Health Management* 5, no. 1 (March 23, 2012): 15–30, https://www.emerald.com/insight /content/doi/10.1108/17538351211215366/full/html.
7. Andrea Beetz et al., "Psychosocial and Psychophysiological Effects of Human-Animal Interactions: The Possible Role of Oxytocin," *Frontiers in Psychology* 3 (July 3, 2012): 1–15, https://habricentral.org/resources/1227.
8. Shahin Akhondzadeh, "Passionflower in the Treatment of Generalized Anxiety: A Pilot Double-Blind Randomized Controlled Trial with Oxazepam," *Journal of Clinical Pharmacy and Therapeutics* 26, no. 5 (October 2001): 363–67, https://www.researchgate .net/publication/227531401_Passionflower_in_the_treatment_of_generalized_anxiety _A_pilot_double-blind_randomized_controlled_trial_with_oxazepam.
9. Brian Mullen et al., "Exploring the Safety and Therapeutic Effects of Deep Pressure Stimulation Using a Weighted Blanket," *Occupational Therapy in Mental Health* 24, no. 1 (March 2008): 65–89, https://www.researchgate.net/publication/233228002 _Exploring_the_Safety_and_Therapeutic_Effects_of_Deep_Pressure_Stimulation _Using_a_Weighted_Blanket.

APPENDIX 4: RELIEF THROUGH RELAXATION

1. "Relaxation Techniques: Try These Steps to Reduce Stress," Mayo Clinic, April 18, 2020, https://www.mayoclinic.org/healthy-lifestyle/stress-management/in-depth /relaxation-technique/art-20045368.

2. "Relaxation Techniques."

3. Kathryn Watson, "What Is Sensory Overload?" Healthline, September 27, 2018, https://www.healthline.com/health/sensory-overload.

4. Alan Wartes and Keith Wall, *Finding Nowhere: How to Be Happier and Healthier by Living Fully in the Present Moment* (Seattle, WA: Amazon Services, 2019), xiv.

About the Authors

Mental health expert **Dr. Gregory Jantz** pioneered whole-person, holistic care. Now recognized as one of the leaders in holistic treatment, Dr. Jantz continues to identify more effective, cutting-edge forms of treatment for people struggling with eating disorders, depression, anxiety, and trauma. He is the founder of The Center: A Place of Hope, which was voted one of the top 10 facilities in the United States for the treatment of depression.

Dr. Jantz is a bestselling author of more than 37 books. He is a go-to media source for a range of behavioral-based afflictions, including drug and alcohol addictions. Dr. Jantz has appeared on CNN, FOX, ABC, and CBS and has been interviewed for the *New York Post*, Associated Press, *Forbes*, *Family Circle*, and *Woman's Day*. He is also a regular contributor to the *Thrive Global* and *Psychology Today* blogs. Visit www.aplaceofhope.com and www.drgregoryjantz.com.

Keith Wall, a twenty-five-year publishing veteran, is an award-winning author, magazine editor, radio scriptwriter, and online columnist. He currently writes full time in collaboration with several bestselling authors. Keith lives in a mountaintop cabin near Manitou Springs, Colorado.

Discover the tools to help you *overcome anxiety* so you can create a new, more *peace-filled life.*

Let Dr. Jantz, one of the foremost leaders in holistic health, guide you through the steps of discovering the mental, emotional, physical, and spiritual roots of anxiety to help you reclaim peace and joy for your future.